AF598935

Reggae My Life Is

COPELAND FORBES

IRAWMA
International Reggae & World Music Awards

Reggae My Life Is

COPELAND FORBES

Downsound Book Publishing Limited
22 Belmont Road, Kingston 5, Jamaica

A catalogue record of this book is available
from the National Library of Jamaica

ISBN
Paperback: 978-976-655-040-0
eBook: 978-976-655-041-7

Cover and book design by Maria Papaefstathiou
Photo editing by Nikos Glykeas

Printed in Greece

For my beloved mother
LILLIAN FORBES
whose hard work and support
have been the foundation
of all that I have achieved.

CONTENTS

FOREWORD
By Rob Kenner

"Woke up this morning with a funny, funny feeling," Peter Tosh sang at the top of "Reggaemylitis" a track from his fifth solo album, *Wanted Dread & Alive*. As a founding member of The Wailers ,who became a solo superstar, Tosh witnessed, first-hand, the viral spread of Jamaican music throughout the world while the Stepping Razor unicycled his way all around planet earth with his trusty M-16-shaped guitar at the ready, and sometimes a cutlass on his waist (just in case). By his side for most of those travels—from rocking stadiums with the Rolling Stones to visiting a bush doctor in Benin—was his cook, personal assistant, road manager, business partner, booking agent, advisor, and all-around impresario, Copeland Forbes.

Tosh's catchy song was a kind of musical diagnosis, detailing the contagious, outrageous, incurable, yet desirable condition that afflicted the artiste himself, his bredren Copeland, and so many other diehard devotees of Jamaican music, whether 'ayaad' or abroad. "Reggaemylitis" permeated the entire human structure, from the bones to the blood, from the toes up to the brain, transforming ordinary people into full-blown musical addicts. How else to explain the phenomenal impact of this indigenous musical genre from a relatively small Caribbean island upon global pop culture? How to account for all the arenas filled with Brazilian or Japanese reggae fans singing song after song, word for word, in perfect Jamaican patois—a language to which they had no prior exposure except through Jah music? How to explicate the multiple spinoff subgenres, from hip hop to trip hop to jungle to dubstep to EDM to reggaeton and Afrobeats to (heaven help us) "Tropical House" derived from or directly inspired by the sounds of the Kingston ghetto? As Copeland Forbes has observed, "When you have a situation where everybody wants to sing like you, look like you, walk like you, talk like you, dress like you, then you must be something special".

Of course, reggae is more than a musical form. It's a culture—or better yet a "livity" (Rasta slang for a way of life) with the power to set one's soul on fire. Nobody knows this better than Copeland Forbes. It is only fitting, then, that he should title this no-holds-barred memoir *Reggae My Life Is*—a play on words, inspired by the aforementioned Tosh tune—for his devotion to the worldwide development of Jamaican music is unparalleled. Awarded the Order of Distinction by the Jamaican Government in 2017 for his outstanding contributions as a cultural stalwart, Forbes has spent most of his seventy-plus years hastening the progress of this music, working tirelessly to uplift a galaxy of Jamaican stars ranging from classic roots rockers to the dappa dons of dancehall. He "overstands" reggae profoundly because he is cut from the same cloth as the artistes who created it.

When Bob Marley sang "No Woman No Cry", reminiscing about the days, "when we used to sit in a government yard in Trench Town," Forbes knew exactly what the Tuff Gong meant because he and his eleven brothers and sisters grew up in a Trench Town tenement, too. "My siblings and I were poor, but poverty never owned us," Forbes writes. "We carried ourselves with dignity and decorum and were never given to self-pity."

Forbes attended the same school as future reggae icons Bunny Wailer and Marcia Griffiths. The lessons he learned as a youth growing up in Trench Town would serve him well throughout his progression from boy scout—who attended to such visiting dignitaries as Princess Margaret of England and His Imperial Majesty Emperor Haile Selassie I of Ethiopia—to being a member of the musical ensemble the Harmonicats—who almost auditioned for the legendary producer Duke Reid but turned away from Treasure Isle at the last moment because he felt "gun shy". Forbes went on to join a dance group known as the Coasters who performed with the popular Mighty Vikings band at night clubs and fetes all over Jamaica during the 1960s.

He credits his scouting career for opening doors to international travel. But, by the time young Copeland Forbes relocated to New York City his style was more *Superfly* than boy scout. He drove a "pimped out" Lincoln Continental and dressed in platform shoes, bell bottoms, and a Fedora hat. He managed to land a gig dancing for Johnny Nash, the American soul singer who was then billed as the "King of Reggae" and was soon flown to LA to dance on the nationally televised programme *Soul Train*. He auditioned for a part in the 1971 Hollywood classic *The French Connection*, playing a lookout in a memorable scene alongside Roy Scheider and Gene Hackman, portraying undercover cops disguised as Santa Claus. "We won five Oscars from that movie," Copeland remarks casually, but such accomplishments elevated his personal brand and prepared him to rise to meet a destiny that had not yet been revealed to him.

The well-connected journalist, G. Fitz Bartley, became a mentor to young Forbes, introducing him to Bob Marley in 1973 during the **Catch a Fire** tour. That fateful meeting at New York's famous Hotel Chelsea marked the beginning of a new chapter in the Copeland Forbes story, the proverbial "first day of the rest of your life".

Recognizing something in the young man, Bob Marley gave him an opportunity with which he ran—and never looked back.

"That's when my sojourn in the business started," Forbes recalls. "From then on it was a nonstop journey, going from one group to the other and all the important things that happened throughout in reggae music. I was just honoured to be present for most of the stuff that happened." After serving for almost fifty years as manager and/or tour manager and/or booking agent for a who's who of legendary figures, from Dennis Brown to Gregory Isaacs to Black Uhuru to Freddie McGregor, Forbes often jokes that it's easier to ask which artistes he has *not* worked with. By his own estimation, "I've had the privilege to work with over 98 per cent of the artistes in about ten different capacities". There's no point in quibbling over the calculations at this point. With the publication of his memoirs, Copeland Forbes can add one more line to his resume: reggae historian.

From Bob Marley's One Love Peace Concert to Jimmy Cliff's gut-wrenching performance in the South African township of Soweto during the heights of the apartheid regime, Forbes has witnessed more than most. But it's the behind-the-scenes machinations of Jamaican music's improbable rise to being a global cultural force that makes *Reggae My Life Is* such an indispensable resource.

The genesis of the book you hold in your hands can be traced to Forbes' 40th anniversary tour, which included the talents of Shocking Vibes dancehall duo Tanto Metro and Devonte. Their manager, Clyde McKenzie, encouraged Forbes to gather his endless array of colourful anecdotes into a memoir for the benefit of posterity. It wasn't the first time someone had suggested that he write an autobiography, but Forbes felt as if, "One book couldn't hold it, cause I had to talk a lot of things. Cause there has been a lot of action. And at the same time," he adds with a laugh, "Every artiste get concerned now because they say I know everything about them."

As a fellow traveller on the reggae music path, Clyde McKenzie, recognized the value of Forbes' story. "There were factors which attracted the audience ," he says. "And there were also issues which caused us not to have optimized on the outcomes. Some of the problems we experienced at the time could be addressed today with technology—the guys missed shows on the road because they didn't have cell phones and GPS," he added. But, it's harder to explain away missed opportunities like the time a famous Jamaican singer didn't show up for a sold-out show at Carnegie Hall in New York because he was having too much fun driving around London in a Rolls-Royce, or the time a rising reggae star ghosted Good Morning America because his manager thought he should be paid to perform on national television.

"One of the things Copeland has tried to do is to create a kind of cautionary tale," McKenzie explains. "To say, 'Here are some of the pitfalls. These are some of the things that we encountered along the way. Let's not go down that road again'. There are some very funny stories in here, but we tried to make sure that we didn't give the appearance that we were dishing on anybody. But the fact is that there are historical gems in this book, and there are times when you show the human side of the artiste—the mistakes they might have made—and you put it in a way that suggests these were great, talented people who sometimes fell through the cracks because of improper guidance."

It's often been said that the Lord moves in mysterious ways. The same could be said for some of Forbes' clients—who sometimes went to extraordinary lengths to avoid turning up at paid gigs or to disentangle themselves from contractual obligations. He's also seen the determination and resilience with which Jamaican artistes spread their music to the world like the time the Mighty Diamonds and U Roy performed at a British punk rock festival and were pelted with eggs and tomatoes, or the time a legendary R&B act were so thoroughly frustrated by Bob Marley & The Wailers that they ditched their opening act on tour and left them stranded on the road.

Few are better qualified to speak on all of the triumphs, the travails and the missed opportunities along the way than Copeland Forbes. "I decided I would take some time and put this book together," says Forbes. "It took me years because I've been traveling on the road. You know I still do tours here, there, and everywhere. But I put down some stories about how to harness the thing, and how to deal with it professionally."

This long-awaited book arrives not a moment too soon, coming at a time when the dominance of Jamaican musical expression continues to reach new heights even as fewer and fewer Jamaican artists and music industry professionals benefit from the music's success. For it to be distributed by a newly established, Jamaican-based company Downsound Book Publishing is a victory in and of itself. More than being brutally honest and immensely entertaining, this book is a beacon by which to navigate towards a brighter, more prosperous future as Jamaican creators reap the rewards of their oversized impact on world culture, bringing it all back home to the beautiful island in the sun where that culture was created.

Rob Kenner is a veteran music journalist, a founding editor of VIBE magazine, the publisher of Boomshots media, and the author of the *New York Times* bestseller *The Marathon Don't Stop The Life and Times of Nipsey Hussle* (Atria Books).

ACKNOWLEDGEMENTS

After so many years of wanting to tell my story I am now able to say *Reggae My Life Is* has become a reality. I cannot begin to tell how elated I am to have finally realized my goal of publishing my own reflections on a life in music. I would like to begin by thanking the many persons who have assisted me, at the various stages of my life, in my effort to make a contribution to the business of music.

There are many people who have played integral roles in my personal and professional development. I would first, and foremost, want to acknowledge my mother, Lillian Forbes, whose hard work and support have been the foundation of all that I have achieved. Many thanks to my biological father George Forbes who left us suddenly for Zion in 1973. Sleep peacefully in Heaven Georgie Porgie.

I would like to express my gratitude to renowned Jamaican educator Mrs Edith Dalton James, my former teacher and headmistress at Chetolah Park Primary School, who was a second mother to me.

I also wish to thank the man who was the guiding light and the father figure in my life .The man whose shoes I have tried to fill, Mr Robert Cecil Blackman (Sir B), my scout master.

I must thank my wife Juanita Reid Forbes who has been tireless in her contribution to my life and this book. Juanita, the many hours you have spent working on this book, sometimes without sleep at nights, were not in vain.

I would like to thank my siblings: Sylvia Hillary-Wilson, Merlene (Claudette) Davis, Fay Forbes-Wallace, Alfred Forbes, Patrick Forbes, Veronica Forbes, Sonia Forbes-Grant, Denton Forbes, Paul Forbes, Beresford Forbes and Junior Forbes. Your brotherly and sisterly love and support have been sources of comfort and inspiration.

I want to thank my children: Colin, Shernett, Kevin and Christopher. Colin, you have played an important role in my business as well. All my nieces, nephews, cousins, uncles, aunts, in-laws and outlaws, too numerous to mention individually, many thanks to you all for the great encouragement.

The idea of writing this book was hatched some two decades ago when I paid a visit to Clyde McKenzie's office to book some of the acts, he was representing, for the celebration of my fortieth anniversary in the music business. I started relating some of my encounters in the music industry and both Clyde and Howard 'Big Mac' McIntosh suggested that I should write a book.

I must single out Clyde McKenzie for special commendation. He and I spent so many hours exchanging ideas and documents, especially over the 16 months leading up to the completion of the manuscript. I would also like to thank his wife Maxine and his children Daneilla and Trimane who were instrumental in the collation of the manuscript.

I would like to thank Danielle Harrison for her patience in the coordination of the transcription and printing of the various iterations of the manuscript.

I want to thank Joseph Bogdanovich for his entrepreneurial insight in recognizing the value of my recollections. I am, indeed, honoured to know that *Reggae My Life Is* will be the first book to bear the DownSound Books imprint.

I wish to thank Maxine McDonnough for her invaluable assistance in the editing and preparation of the manuscript, Maria Papaefstathiou for her outstanding design and Nikos Glykeas for his impressive photo editing.

Thanks to the following promoters and players in the music fraternity.

Synergy Production Jamaica Limited, Reggae Sunsplash team: Ronnie Burke, Tony Johnson, Don Green, Charles Campbell, Ed Barclay, John Wakeling, Junior Lincoln, Robert Lee, Junior Taylor, Richard Lowe, Tommy Cowan, all their spouses and the rest of the Sunsplash teamsters.

Summerfest Productions/Reggae Sumfest team: Johnny Gourzong, Walt Crooks, Robert Russell, Walter Elmore, Sydney Reid, Joe Bogdanovich and the present team.

Klaus Maack and the Summerjam team, Gina and the Rototom Reggae Sunsplash staff.

Danielle "Dee" Pater & The Reggae Geel Crew, Moss Jacobs and Nederlander Group. Barbara Barbino (Bob Marley Festivals USA), Rob Hallett – Robomagic (UK), Bill Graham Presents

Fabrizio Lagana – Mr Roots and Culture (Italy), Bagga John and all British promoters

Richard Branson – Virgin CEO, Christopher Blackwell, Denise Mills, Suzette Newman, Trevor Wyatt (Island Records), Garance Production, Michael "Eppy" Epstein, Ardie "Cuban" Wallace, Tony Carr, Habte Selassie, Clinton Lindsay, Jamusa (Denver Silvera), Doctor Dread (Gary Himelfarb), Elise Kelly, Herbie Miller, Warren Smith, John T Hodgson, Lady C (Winsome Charlton), Ron Muschette, Richie Burgess, Michael Barnett (Kool FM), Mikey Thompson, Rosamond Brown, Fae Ellington, Maxine Stowe, Barbara Blake-Hanna, Lee Jaffe, Barrington "Barry G" Gordon, Patrick Lafayette,

Stokey Love, Karl Mullings, Colin "Ileydread" Levy, Owen Brown, Desmond Elliot, David " Squeeze" Annakie, Winston Chin Quee, Byron Lee and Lee Enterprise, Neville Lee and Sonics Sound Massive, and Lindsay Oliver Donald.

Thanks to all the record companies that were associated with my journey.

In particular, thanks to the indies: VP Records; Ras Records; Shanachie Records; Island/Mango; Jet Star, Heartbeat Records and Greensleeves

Thanks to some key booking agents and promoters.

Peter Schwartz- The Agency Group Ltd./WMA, George Michailow, Paul Lamonica and Jody Wenig (La Wenig), George Crooks-Jammins Production, Groovin Team-Ras Clem, Anthony Turner, Chris Roberts, Ken Williams – Reggae Global Jamaica 24/7, Dave Betteridge, John Huie – FBI/Creative Artists, Denise Jones (Jones and Jones), Oliver Millwood, Eddie Brown, Wilf Walker, Jerome Hamilton and Headline Entertainment Staff, Sharon Burke and Solid Agency Posse, Jamaican Dave Inc (Dave Russell), Eddie Edwards (Grace Jamaica Jerk Fest), Bobby & Peter Poppat, Earl Harris, Isaiah Laing, Heavy D and The Supreme Promotion staff, Raymond Paris.

I wish to thank the following persons with whom I have worked throughout the years and for whom I have the highest regard.

Olivia "Babsy" Grange, Danny Sims, Julian Jingles, Val Hackett, Pat Meschino, Stan Evan Smith, M Peggy Quatro (*Reggae Report*), Andrea Davis & The IRD Staff, Winford Williams and the On-Stage TV Crew, Kaati and The *Reggae Festival Guide* team, Herman Hall and the *Everybody's Magazine* staff, Kevin Jackson, Lenny Salmon, Roy Sweetland, Clifton "Specialist" Dillon, Steve James, Tesah Carnes, Julian Schmidt and the staff at Reggaeville, Robert Bryan and the Grizzly Crew, Candida Becerra Mosquera (Cuba), Chris Chin, Miss Pat, Randy Chin, Clive Chin, Joel Chin, Richard Lue and the VP staff, Donovan Germain and Penthouse staff, Patrick Roberts and the Shocking Vibes staff, Enid Harrow, Leyla Turkkan, Richie Williams, Castro Brown, Mike Pantaleoni, Gussie Clarke and the Anchor crew, Mikey Bennett and the Grafton crew. Roy Francis and the Mixing Lab posse, King Jammy, George Phang, Bunny "Striker" Lee, Ras Mubarak (Ghana), Peter Simon, Gbenga X- Adebija (Nigeria), Amy Wachtel, Chester McCalla, Tony Cobb, Beverly "Sista Irie" Shaw, Deon Mattis, Tony Laing, Supt Gladston Wright, Ewan Simpson, Denise "Isis" Miller, Marcia "Isha" Elliott, David Rodigan, Louie Burke, Alphanso Walker, Silvero and Alphanso Castro, Sasha Lawla, Mervis Walsh, Michael Savage, Lois Grant, Daddy Ernie, Charlie Comer, Lister Hewan-Lowe, Andell Forgie, Earl Chin, Nancy Jonap, Dr Everold

Haffizulla (my personal doctor), Dera Tompkins, Jeff Barnes and Winston Barnes, Don King, Rev. Al Sharpton, Teresa Delpozo, Anthony Miller, Clinton "Clinny" Haughton, Tullah Carter, Chris Kimsey, Patrick Blackwood, Carl "Hu Hu" Jackson, Tanya Grant and family, Louise Fraser Bennett, Eddie and Paul Sims, Neville Garrick, Joe Armone, Steve Armone, Bunny Francis, Packy Malley, Bert Padell, T. Boots Harris, DJ Bones (Duhane Howard), G T Taylor, Kshema Francis, Bob Clark, Big A Andrea Williams (Ka'Bu' Ma'at Kheru), Robert "Chuckles" Stewart, Martin Lewis, Ketch Kelly, Danny Williams and family (UK), Gregory "Flash" Gordon, Brande Lindsay & Staff at Global Access Entertainment Worldwide Inc. John Swaby, Brigga, Dennis Thompson, Pete Juliana, David Rowe, Karl Pitterson, Steven Stewart, Brandon Naylor, Rabbi, Errol Brown, Soljie Hamilton, Pants, Christopher Daley, Dwight "Coolie" Bancey, Jaco Thelwell, Delroy Thompson, Zola Burse, Philip "Fattis" Burrell and family, Errol Minto and family, Paolo Novaro, Casper Quinn, Claudette Kemp, Marco Tuffgong, Lukkee Chong, Jahcoustic Joe, Tammy Huff Beveridge, John Dubois, Paulette Bierderman, Timo Klingsman, Angela Thame, Geoffrey Chung, Clive Hunt, Jim Parker (my friend for life), Carl Mullings, Balfour Henry, Teddy Laidley, Ryan Bailey, Howard Campbell, Leroy "Dreamy" Riley, Alfred "Duwi" Reid, Yasmine Peru, Maureen Sheridan, Worrell King, Trevor "Leggo Beast" Douglas, Russell Gerlach, Richard Johnson, Brian Bonitto, Janet Davidson and family, Gregory Isaacs Foundation, (June Isaacs, Colin Leslie, Yvonne Chang-Oliver, Junior Sinclair, Lancelot Cowan, Leonard Francis), Peter Tosh Foundation (Niambe McIntosh, Akayda McIntosh, Melody Melody Cunningham, Brian Latture), Kingsley Cooper and the Pulse Staff, Steve Creighton, Ephraim Martin and his wife Justice Shelvin, Marie Hall and IRAWMA staff.

Reggae historians: Roger Steffens, John Masouri, Dr Sonjah Stanley Niaah, Dr Dennis Howard, Professor Donna P Hope, Professor Carolyn Cooper, Dr Michael Barnett, Professor Clinton Hutton.

Lloyd Stanbury: Special thanks for guiding me through the intricacies of so many legal matters.

Rob Kenner: Special thanks to you Rob Kenner for writing the Foreword for this book. Your wit and eloquence are magnificent.

G Fitz-Bartley: Thanks to the late G. Fitz Bartley who was my guiding light when I started out in the entertainment business. He was instrumental in kickstarting my music career, introducing me to some major players in the US music fraternity – Soul Train TV, Apollo Theatre, Lloyd Price, Turntable, Joe Blues Showtime – and many international promoters and media personnel. He was a heavyweight, large and in charge.

Don Taylor: Don Taylor was one of the most experienced artiste managers in the reggae music fraternity, having started from the rank of a valet and personal assistant for the likes of Chuck Jackson, Little Anthony and The Imperials, Franky Lymon and The Teenagers, Marvin Gay and Bob Marley and the Wailers. Many thanks to Don for sharing his musical prowess with me, even though we had our differences

Thanks to all the promoters and contributors in South America, Africa, Japan and Australia.

Rafael Lima Costa, Henrique Pesqueira, Israel Mizrach, Pinto Atamaraty, Alexandre Santos

Alessandro Caribe, Javier Da Rocha (Argentina), Pedro Luna (Peru), Winston "TShaka" Mayanja (Uganda), Victor (Kilamanjaro) (Ghana), Peter Noble and his Bluesfest team (Australia), Minoru Hatanaka, Sonny Ochiai – Tachyon Co. Ltd/Reggae Japansplash Team

Artists and bands with whom I have worked in my over fifty years as booking agent, road manager/artist manager/tour organizer and manager:

Mighty Diamonds, Junior Reid, Dennis Brown, Mutabaruka, Realistic Band, Freddie McGregor, The Techniques, Sugar Minott, Culture, Errol Dunkley, Boris Gardner, Big Youth, Shinehead, Everton Blender, Tony Rebel, We the People Band, The Coasters (Errol T Quinty-Leonard, "Tighten Up" Mundy, Theophilus Evans, Naggo Morris), Browne Bunch, Frankie Paul, Queen Ifrica, Carlene Davis, Girlztown Band, Beres Hammond, Barrington Levy, Pam Hall, Audrey Hall, Raymond Hall, Beenie Man, TOK, J.C. Lodge, Black Soil Band, 809 band, Lieutenant Stichie, Christopher Martin, Monyaka Band, Half Pint, Lady Saw (Marion Hall), Black Eagles Band, Marcia Griffiths, Inner Circle (Ian, Roger, Touter, Lancelot, Trevor, Jacob), Maxi Priest, The Caravans Band, Ziggy Marley and The Melody Makers, Zak Starky and Shhh, Bunny Wailer and Solomonic Reggaestra, Hugh Hendricks and The Buckaneers, Mighty Vikings, Sonny Bradshaw, The Revolutionaries, Bob Marley and The Wailers, Black Uhuru, Taxi Gang Band, Soul Syndicate, Chaka Demus and Pliers, Luciano, Fire house crew, John Holt, Mikey General, Jah Messenjah Band, Delroy Washington, Gregory Isaacs, Slim Smith, Sizzla Kalonji, Jah Postles Band, I-Three, Nadine Sutherland, Ikaya, Sane Band, Sly and Robbie, Gem Myers, Roots Radics Band, Aswad, Steel Pulse, Capleton, Tanto Metro and Devonte, Wailers Band, Buju Banton, Bob Andy, Tanya and Carrie Mullings, Word Sound and Power, Peter Tosh, Leroy Sibbles, Sagittarius Band, Andrew Tosh, Dre Tosh, Stepping-Stone Band, Judy Mowatt, B.B. Seaton and The Gaylads, Ken Boothe, Tarrus and Jimmy Riley, The Tamlins, Jimmy Cliff, Live Wyya Band, Rita Marley, Assassin (Agent

Sasco), Ruff Cutt Band (UK & JA), Shabba Ranks, Coco T, Bigger Morrison Band, Third World Band and Family, Satta Band, U-Roy, Culture, Fabulous 5 Band, Fela Kuti and Africa 80, The Meditations, Roots Harmonics Band, Tony Gregory, Cherry Natural, Bushman, Chalice, King Sunny Adé, Burning Spear, Denroy Morgan, Junior Kelly, Etana, Yellowman, Leroy Smart, Heptones, Toots and The Maytals, Morgan Heritage, Josey Wales, Jah Cure, Sanchez, Sugar Minott, Joanna Marie, Jah 9, Dillinger, Warrior King, Tippa Irie, Jesse Royal, Lloyd Parks, Dean Fraser, Abyssinians, Shaggy, Ini Kamoze, Brigadier Jerry, Ninjaman, Ernest Ranglin, Asham Band, Oneness Band, Wayne Jobson, Ernie Smith, Pinchers, Noddy Virtue, Dwayne Stephenson, Peter Couch, Chronixx, Native Band, Mick Jagger & Keith Richards, Betty Wright, The Jackson Family, Keith & Tex, Sonny Okosun & Family, Tinga Stewart, Chosen Few, Scotty, Israel Vibration, Tanya Stephens, Richie Spice, Banner Banner, Kabaka Pyramid, Romain Virgo, Cutty ranks, Carl Dawkins and Kotch Band

A WORD FROM THE PUBLISHER

(Photo credit - Adrian Creary)

I have been called many things, but no one had ever accused me of being a publisher prior to my association with Copeland Forbes and *Reggae My Life Is*. Let me say this is a label I happily accept.

Reggae My Life Is represents a significant contribution to the documentation of the accomplishments and missteps in Jamaican music. I believe that this book will serve as a reference point for many discussions and debates about the music of an incredible people.

Copeland Forbes is without question one of the most consequential figures in modern Jamaican music and I am happy to have been able to collaborate with him in the release of this significant cultural publication. I wish to also thank Clyde McKenzie for making this project a reality.

I am indeed proud and happy that *Reggae My Life Is* will be the first publication bearing the DownSound Book Publishing imprint which I have had the great privilege of establishing. Let me hasten to state that we will be moving vigorously to chronicle more stories about Jamaican music so that posterity can build on the achievements and learn from the mistakes of those who took the sounds of a small Caribbean nation to the world.

Joe Bogdanovich
Publisher

"I often wondered whether the authorities at the hospital had given her an employee or frequent user discount, after all she enlisted the services of this maternity facility on 12 separate occasions."

▶ Pg 27. Chapter 1

INTRODUCTION

The story of Jamaican music is an amazing one. In some instances it would seem like a work of fiction. How could a country, with fewer than three million nationals, have managed to secure such an extraordinary hold on the global popular imagination? What explains the phenomenon of Bob Marley, Ernest Ranglin, Clement Dodd? What did we do right and what mistakes did we make? What forces have collaborated to produce Shaggy, Sean Paul, Toots, Jimmy Cliff, Sly and Robbie, Grace Jones, to name but a few?

Many argue that despite its enormous influence, Jamaican music has not realized its potential, pointing to the failure of international partners to market it successfully to a worldwide audience. There are certainly kernels of truth in this analysis. There were a number of record labels which expressed an early interest in Jamaican music only to retreat from the association due to their lack of understanding of our cultural nuances. Jamaican originated labels and associated labels such as Island and VP Records have proven to be the most adept at promoting and marketing the music of this small Caribbean nation. Those major record labels with Jamaican executives have fared better at promoting our music than their counterparts that do not have our nationals within their ranks. Far more was expected from the music that has given birth to such internationally successful genres as reggaeton and hip hop than we have managed to achieve yet we have come a long way.

Having spent the major portion of my life working with some of the most amazing talents from the Jamaican soil, I remain convinced that while some of these acts have brought great recognition to our country, some have done considerable damage to the image of the nation.

This book does not, in any way, intend to embarrass or belittle any artiste, producer, promoter or their associates. The principal objective of this project is to provide current and future players with the opportunity to learn from the experiences of others.

In several instances ego, ignorance and greed have been the principal causes of our failure to realize the potential of our music. The dissolution of two of our most successful Jamaican groups can be traced directly to a combination of these factors.

Many of our artistes, producers and promoters have not taken a long-term view of the business. They have simply been about instant gratification.

I asked several knowledgeable persons in the business if they were aware of any time that Bob Marley had been paid for a show and did not appear. No one, to date, has been able to cite one instance in which Marley failed to honour his commitment to a promoter. The latter-day success stories, which include Shaggy and Sean Paul, are renowned for their punctuality and reliability.

Insufficient mainstream media access and other structural challenges have helped to retard the international growth of our music, but I strongly contend that some of these hurdles could have been surmounted had we been more strategic in the positioning of our music.

Technological developments have made the business of music far simpler to manage than it was during much of the last century. However, technology will never be a substitute for discipline and commitment. Having cell phones means that artistes are now better able to stay in constant touch with their teams but only if these entertainers will answer their calls or have someone do it for them.

Many artistes and players in the business have not taken the time to inform themselves of the intricacies of their trade. This is regrettable, given the fact that technology has provided us with so many ways to enlighten ourselves today. I am not expecting artistes to be experts in the business of music; however, they should familiarise themselves with the basics of their trade.

My hope is that, by reading *Reggae My Life Is*, players in the music business will be able to identify best practices while coming to terms with some of the worst errors others have made. If debutantes and practitioners in the music business can derive useful lessons from reading this book, then my efforts would not have been in vain.

Many are unaware of the emotions artistes such as Toots, Jimmy Cliff, Bunny Wailer, Black Uhuru and Third World evoke around the world. One would have had to be on the road with these entertainers to get a true sense of how popular they are in far flung places. We hope this book will help to provide a clearer view of the history of Jamaican music and put into context some of the events which have shaped our lives.

If I have had any measure of success over the last six decades, it has been due mainly to my undying love for what I do. Talent is important, but the right temperament is critical to the success or failure in this business. Many careers have floundered not because of an absence of talent but due to a lack of vision and self-control.

This book is designed to demonstrate the perils artistes and their management face in their travels. It is not an easy road. It is important that we give credit to the pioneering figures who, through their efforts, have made it less difficult for those who have and will come after them.

It is important to view many of the decisions made by these musical pioneers within the context of their times and circumstances. We should be careful how we use our current values and knowledge to analyze decisions which were made in the past. It is not helpful to be judgmental.

About This Book

Each chapter of this book is a story of a particular experience and is intended to stand on its own. However, there are some personalities who are mentioned across several chapters given the many facets to their careers and personalities. Admittedly, there is a significant degree of overlap in the narrative due to the many interactions among the various players in the industry. An incident might be alluded to in one chapter and expanded on in another.

While we do not attempt to sequence the chapters strictly based on their chronological order, we do try to ensure that the narrative unfolds in a logical temporal pattern.

Finally, I believe that it might be important for me to cite some of the roles I have played in the music industry so that people who might not be *au fait* with the intricacies of the business will have a better understanding of some of what is required to keep the show on the road and the artiste satisfied.

As a road manager, I was in charge of taking care of the artistes' affairs while they travelled on assignment. I ensured that all the requests made by the artistes' management, including accommodation, payment of outstanding balances and travel arrangements, were honoured. I have also worked as a tour manager which, as the name suggests, is concerned with overseeing the various legs of concerts which are part of a tour. I have played the role of artiste manager which is the equivalent of a general manager in corporate entities. In some circumstances, I have had to play multiple roles simultaneously and in others I have taken on different assignments sequentially. I have made my share of errors and, hopefully, have learnt from my mistakes and those of others.

"Mr Superfly" Copeland Forbes in the Big Apple (NYC), 1970.

CHAPTER 1

IN THE BEGINNING

At the time of my birth, my mother, Lillian Hillary Forbes, was living in an area on the outskirts of Kingston called Jones Town; 5 Pouyatt Street to be exact. It was not very far from the sprawling maternity hospital (Victoria Jubilee) where she worked as a cook and would often retreat to make additions to our family.

I often wondered whether the authorities at the hospital had given her an employee or frequent user discount, after all she enlisted the services of this maternity facility on 12 separate occasions. I was the fourth of her 12 children and was preceded by my three sisters.

My father, George Forbes, was largely absent from home. He worked with Billings, a mattress company. I am not sure if there was any link between his job and his sleeping habits. Bowler, as he was more popularly known, served as a caretaker at the Chetolah Park Primary School, where my mother also worked. My parents were married to each other, and my father sired all but one of my mother's 12 children. My father was not a significant factor in my own upbringing. He lived with a woman simply known as Miss Brown. She bore him no children. His seasonal visits to our home would usually result in my mother making another trip to the hospital, as a maternity patient.

My mother was born in Santiago de Cuba. She often held two jobs simultaneously. She was the main provider for her ever-expanding brood and would use her position at the hospital to secure a regular supply of food not just for her family but also for our neighbours, many of whom would hold vigils outside our door in the evenings until she returned home from work.

We lived in what was described as a tenement yard – a collection of rooms which were usually owned by a landlord who rented living spaces to different individuals mostly from rural backgrounds. These tenements were located behind walls or fences which were usually accessible through a numbered gate. They were the original gated communities, without the luxury associated with their modern counterparts.

In these tenements there were usually one bathroom, one toilet, and a kitchen serving all of the families living within a quadrangle. There was one central pipe in the yard with a concrete cistern which would be used by all the tenants to fetch water for washing, cooking and cleaning. There was usually no other source of the precious liquid on the compound save for the communal bathroom. Some tenants, who did not want to use the community bathroom, would fill utensils with water and take them to their respective rooms for bathing, cooking or washing dishes.

Next door to some of these tenements, one could find several well-appointed single-family homes. These upscale dwellings allowed for privacy among members of a household and belonged to civil servants or owners of small but lucrative businesses. The occupants would enjoy such comforts as indoor plumbing, individual bedrooms, dining room, living room, a study, and kitchen – all under one roof.

Although these single-family homes sometimes adjoined the tenements, their respective circumstances were worlds apart. Yet, there was considerable intermingling between the dwellers of the single-family homes and those of the tenements.

Initially, my mother rented only one room in the tenement at Pouyatt Street. This was woefully inadequate by the time I was born, and we soon ran out of space. These one-room dwellings were all-inclusive. The living, dining and sleeping areas were all in one with no pre-existing physical partitioning. Any attempt at intimacy was a risky proposition especially if there were children who were beyond infancy. In an effort to secure additional space for the family, my mother was forced to rent an adjoining room which had been vacated by another tenant

My mother was also employed as a household helper at the on-campus residence of the principal of the Chetolah Park Primary School, Mrs Edith Dalton James, a renowned educator and political figure.

I attended Chetolah Park Primary School; it was within easy walking distance of my home. Marcia Griffiths and Bunny Wailer are among its distinguished alumni. It would not be farfetched to state that the internationally popular "Electric Boogie" could trace its origins to this school as a number of the performers on that track and in the accompanying video – myself included – attended this institution.

Forbes and his son, Kevin, on a Sunday evening cruise around NYC in his pimped-up Lincoln Continental. (Copeland Forbes Archives)

It is important for me to provide context for the area in which I grew up, now pejoratively referred to as the ghetto. What prevailed in my childhood is in stark contrast to what exists today. There was great diversity in the backgrounds of the residents of my neighbourhood. Yet, there was little by way of separation. Everyone mingled freely. Decency was the only reliable guarantee of respect in our community.

My siblings and I were poor, yet we carried ourselves with dignity and decorum. We were never given to self-pity. Poverty did not define us.

The landlord at Pouyatt Street, a Mr Wong, eventually raised the rent placing it out of my mother's reach. My family was forced to move from Jones Town to the adjoining community of Trench Town. Both areas shared the Kingston 12 postal code, which later gained notoriety in the songs of Bob Marley and the Wailers. Leaving Jones Town, however, was a step down the social ladder. Trench Town was the more impoverished of the two adjoining communities.

While the bathroom at Pouyatt Street served only the tenants who lived in the yard owned by Mr Wong, the one in Trench Town was accessible to all Jamaicans. Taking a bath in Trench Town was an exercise in patience and tolerance. One had to wait in long lines, standing behind strange men and women queuing for a chance to have a bath. Calls of nature had to be answered in an outhouse, called a pit latrine, which did not have the benefits of flushing. We had no choice but to keep our heads high if we did not want to endure the odour of the ordure.

Becoming a member of the Boy Scouts is perhaps the most consequential decision I ever made. I learned a great deal from my involvement with the movement and, most importantly, my association with the scouts provided me with many opportunities for personal development. It was through the Boy Scouts that I would make my first trips abroad. It was as a boy scout that I travelled first to Trinidad in 1961 and to Greece in 1963. I would later visit Idaho in 1967 and Minnesota in 1968, all courtesy of the Boy Scouts.

My first 9 to 5 job in the United States at Full Cut, a famed diamond trading entity in New York, was also due to my scouting connections. I had needed a recommendation from a prominent figure from the area to secure the job and I was able to call on a high-ranking police officer from New Jersey whom I had met at a scouting Jamboree in Idaho a few years earlier. He was a part of the scout movement and gave me a glowing recommendation.

Reggae Legend Bunny Wailer and schoolmate Copeland Forbes each received a citation from the City of Hartford, Connecticut for their contribution to Reggae Music, globally.

Marcia Griffiths performs a tribute to Bob Marley at the Bayfront Amphitheatre in Miami, Florida, 1988.

Reggae Queen Marcia Griffiths and Copeland Forbes doing the Electric Slide while Marcia performs the hit song "Electric Boogie" on the **Reggae Sunsplash** US tour, 1990.

I attended scout meetings at the All Saints All Age School, located less than 200 metres from Chetolah Park. All Saints was a hub of activity. Its large fields were magnets for lovers of cricket and football from near and far. Members of its alumni include: former member of Parliament, Paul Buchanan; musicians Bunny Wailer (who earlier attended Chetolah Park) and Gregory Isaacs; journalist and playwright Barbara Gloudon, her sister, poet Lorna Goodison, and their brothers Bunny, Howie, Kingsley, Karl, Nigel and Keith who would go on to distinguish themselves nationally and internationally in various fields of endeavour.

The All Saints Boy Scouts troop was led by Mr Robert Cecil Blackman (Sir B), an exemplary human being, whose surname seemed to have accurately captured his melanin rich complexion. He was a disciplinarian who knew how to have his young charges abide by the rules without his having to resort to harsh measures.

Mr Blackman was quite a proficient musician. He played the organ at the Moravian Church. He taught me to play the piano and the harmonica. Sir B would also have an impact on modern Jamaican popular music through his mentorship of renowned bassist Jackie Jackson who was at the heart of the rhythm section at the Treasure Isle Studio owned by Arthur 'Duke' Reid. Jackie's mother was a tenant at Sir B's home in Vineyard Town, a swanky part of Kingston at the time.

I joined a musical quartet known as the Harmonicats which consisted of members of the All Saints Boy Scouts. We played the mouth organ, an instrument made popular by 'Big Mama' Thornton and later Stevie Wonder. The group performed at tea parties and other community events. We were well received at our various gigs. I was so impressed with the quality of the quartet that I attempted to embark on a recording career with the group. I went down to Treasure Isle Studio on Bond Street for an audition. I was, however, unable to muster the courage to enter the studio. The intimidating figure of the gunslinging owner, Duke Reid, gave me second thoughts. I suppose I was just gun shy.

Queen's Scout Copeland Forbes

Mr Blackman was not only willing to share his vast knowledge but also his incredible connections. He held a senior position with what was then the Royal Mail Postal Service. He used his vast network of contacts to secure employment for members of the scout troop. He taught me to cook, a skill which served me well when I often had to prepare my own meals while traveling around the world.

Sir B had impeccable taste in clothing. His footwear was exquisitely crafted and would call considerable attention to his feet. One day I had a special scouting assignment and, unfortunately, had damaged the only pair of dress shoes I owned. Mr Blackman provided me with one of his expensive pairs of shoes. His feet were at least two sizes larger than mine and while I had always wanted to walk in his shoes, my time seemed to have come too soon. I, however, stepped up to the occasion. I was going to fill his shoes even if they needed a bit of stuffing. I was able to secure the temporary enlargement of my feet by padding the toes of my borrowed shoes with newspaper. I was worried that things might get twisted. However, I was able to stand up to my peers.

Scouting also gave me the opportunity to mingle with royalty at home. I was selected for ceremonial duties on the visits of Princess Margaret in 1962 and Emperor Haile Selassie in 1966. In both instances I had the privilege of being the official door opener for their vehicles on various legs of their journeys. I also had the honour of being named Mayor of the Day for the Parish of Kingston in 1965, because of my affiliation with the Boy Scouts.

I became part of a group performing under the name The Coasters which would snatch the coveted first prize in the national dance contest staged by the Jamaica Cultural Development Commission in 1970. We subsequently began getting gigs to perform at various nightclubs in the corporate area. We were affiliated with the popular show band the Mighty Vikings which provided live entertainment at such famed venues as the Sombrero Club, and Flamingo Hotel in Kingston. We performed regularly at the Dingho Club on Windward Road.

Top bass man Jackie Jackson. (Brian Levy Photo)

We were not only required as dancers to be light on our feet but also to be quick on them. Scarcity of funds demanded ingenuity in the preparation of our costumes. One of our tricks was to spray paint our shoes to match our suits. One night we had not engaged in our spray-painting rituals. We had, mistakenly, thought we had shoes to match our suits for the occasion. We only realized that we needed a paint job shortly before we were due to perform. We were saved by a hardware store which was still open at the time of our performance. Our shoes did not dry in time for our performance, and we were splashing the wet paint all over as soon as we walked onto the stage. Some patrons thought that the paint splashing was supposed to add colour to our performance and was a part of our act. We did nothing to dispel that notion.

Journalists, Julian 'Jingles' Reynolds, Tony 'the Cat behind the Glass' Cobb and the inimitable G. Fitz Bartley, were fixtures at our performances. My relationship with these scribes would prove useful when I migrated to the United States .Bartley would prove particularly helpful in my efforts to establish myself on the entertainment scene in New York.

One of my earliest acquisitions (as a resident of New York) was a Lincoln Continental. It was a pimped-up ride. I drew my fashion inspiration from the movie *Superfly*. My attire would include platform shoes, the obligatory trench coat (during the winter) and bell bottom pants which were usually topped by the mandatory fedora. This image was created to attract a certain type of feminine attention.

I lived with my sisters, Fay and Sylvia, on the Upper West Side of Manhattan near the Audubon Theatre where Malcolm X had been assassinated. We had many friends who would visit regularly, including Lascelles Perkins and G. Fitz Bartley. The latter had become a most influential figure as a writer for the *Philadelphia Enquirer*. Bartley

Mayor for a Day, Copeland Forbes, inspecting the Guard of Honour at the Kingston Fire Brigade Headquarters, 1965.

prided himself as a powerbroker on the New York entertainment scene. He seemed to know everyone who mattered. They valued his judgement. He took great pleasure in making things happen. He was what Malcolm Gladwell would call a 'connector'. I benefited greatly from his ability to pull people together.

While walking past the 20th Century Fox building in Manhattan, my friends and I saw a billboard inviting people to audition for a bit part in a movie. My three friends and I decided that we should try out for the movie. We entered the building and filled out the necessary paperwork but were not very optimistic about the prospects. Interestingly, all four of us had been associated with the very popular Teenage Dance Party (TADP) and Where It's At in Jamaica where we had honed our performance – particularly dancing – skills.

Queen's Scout Copeland Forbes was the official car door opener for HRH Princess Margaret who represented HRH Queen Elizabeth at Jamaica's first independence celebration in 1962. Forbes was on duty at the opening of Parliament at Gordon House in Kingston, 6 August 1962.

Weeks after the audition, I received a call from the people at 20th Century Fox telling me that I had been selected for a role in the movie. It was a bit part but I was elated. The film – *The French Connection* – would become a box office success winning five Oscars.

My appearance in the movie was a boost to my resume. Bartley was able to highlight this accomplishment in his conversations with Earl Harris who was looking for Jamaican artistes to perform on his showcase at the Apollo Theatre. My sister Fay and I had been members of a dance group and Harris selected us to be a part of his extravaganza on the strength of Bartley's recommendation.

Soon, Johnny Nash was in town. He had been dubbed the "King of Reggae". He had done some songs –from Jamaican songwriters including Bob Marley and Ernie Smith– that had scored big internationally. Nash was due to appear on Soul Train, the hugely popular television variety show which Don Cornelius hosted. Nash needed Jamaican dancers to complement his performance. Bartley arranged to have Johnny and his management, along with CBS executive Logan Westbrook, come over to the Apollo to see my dance group perform. They came, they saw, and we conquered. Bartley scored once more.

Fitz and I had a lot of fun together, even when the joke was on me. I remember him suggesting that we go to the Jackson 5 Concert at Madison Square Garden (MSG) as he was able to secure all access passes. There was one snag, it required a bit of impersonation. One of Bartley's colleagues at the *Philadelphia Enquirer* was unable to attend the show. He promised to give Fitz his tickets. However, to secure the tickets someone had to represent himself as Dick Green from the *Philadelphia Enquirer*. Fitz chose me to go in and represent myself as the reporter. I did as I was instructed. Thankfully, there was no need for any form of identification. However, Joe Jackson (father of Michael) was standing near the ticket booth. When he heard me identify myself as Dick Green, he started screaming at me. He believed that I was the reporter from the *Philadelphia Enquirer*, whom he had never seen before but with whom he had a beef. I was not in a position to tell Joe that I was not the man he thought I was. I had to absorb his abuse. I was sweating profusely while beating a hasty retreat.

I managed to escape Joe and his tirade. I went back to my car. Bartley and Alan Cole (the great Jamaican football icon and one time manager of Bob Marley), whom I had driven to the Drake Hotel to pick up the tickets, were missing. It was only after leaning against my car that I heard a rapping and realized that both men were lying, flat on their stomachs, inside my car. As soon as I realized that they were in the car, I jumped in and sped off. I handed the envelope to Bartley without checking its contents. Fitz had said that there would have been four passes waiting for us. I took it for granted that there were four all access passes in the package.

We headed to Long Island to pick up my date, Charlise. She worked in the same building (Rockefeller Plaza) as I did, and I had met her through her love of diamonds. She was always coming to Full Cut to check on the precious stones. I suppose if there was one girl who believed that diamonds were a girl's best friend, it was Charlise.

When Fitz, Skill Cole and I reached Long Island, Charlise was dressed to the nines. She was stunning. She had told her friends that she was going to Madison Square Gardens to see the Jacksons and that she had an all-access pass. We, with Charlise on board, headed back to MSG. I dropped off Fitz, Skill and my date at one of

Copeland Forbes performing with The Coasters at the State Theatre, Kingston, 1970. (Copeland Forbes Archives)

Copeland heading to the Apollo Theatre, New York, for a special guest appearance at the James Brown Revue, 1972. (Copeland Forbes Archives)

the backstage entrances at MSG and went to park the vehicle. When I returned, I saw my date standing by herself. I asked her for Fitz and Skill, she said that they had already gone inside. She handed me the tickets that they had left with her. I confidently proceeded to enter the venue with my date in tow. I noticed that the usher had taken us to an elevator, and we were going high above the venue. I protested saying that we had all access privileges. The usher politely informed me that my ticket was not reflecting my purported status. We were provided with binoculars to view the event. We were socially distanced from the stage.

Copeland performs at the Rainbow Gardens Club in Rice Lake, Wisconsin in 1968. (Copeland Forbes Archives)

Shocked by the sudden drop in our status, my date immediately lost her ability to speak. She briefly regained her voice for a few seconds, just enough to point out Fitz and Skill mingling backstage with the bigwigs, noting drily, "I just saw your friends backstage". She once again lapsed into silence. I left Fitz and Skill at the Garden. I didn't want them to accompany me to drop her home as that would have been like rubbing salt in her wounds. When we reached her home in Long Island, she simply stepped out of the car and headed into her house without a backward glance. I was now history. Clearly, I did not have her ticket.

Despite distractions like Charlise, it didn't take long for me to decide that it was important to get the young mother of my children to New York. My ultimate aim was to get married and lead a respectable life. I began planning my wedding in earnest, sending funds down to my fiancée to cover the costs of our nuptials. I had a guest list of 1,000 persons. Unbeknownst to me, my fiancée had sent out an additional 400 invitations. We were looking at a guest list of about 1,800 people.

Before I left New York for Jamaica, I had a dream which filled me with dread. I communicated my concern to my eldest sister, Sylvia who had not been to Jamaica in five years and had secured her leave from work. She was not about to hear about any change of heart on my part and let me know this in no uncertain terms.

I journeyed to Jamaica and discovered that all the arrangements I had expected were not in place. We had not confirmed a pastor or a church. The planning for the event was in disarray. I had to draw on some of my connections in Jamaica, with whom I had regularly done business in New York, to bail me out. Derrick Harriot was a tower of strength. He provided me with funds in Jamaica which I would reimburse in New York.

When I finally got to the pastor at St Luke's Anglican Church in Cross Roads, he told me that my fiancée had come to see him but had not returned to confirm the date. He, nevertheless, said he could accommodate my bride and me on the date that my fiancée had discussed with him but that he had three other weddings for that day.

My ceremony was slated to be a grand affair. Members of my scout troop had been selected to provide a guard of honour for my bride and me at the church. Yet, my fairy tale wedding was quickly turning into a nightmare. I had brought a double-breasted suit from New York which needed to be altered. My Jamaican tailor, father of the legendary Jamaican songwriter and artiste Wilfred Jackie Edwards, seemed to have mixed up my measurements with those of a midget. When I tried

From left: Frankie Crocker, Ken Williams (WLIB), Copeland Forbes, G. Fitz Bartley, Byron Malcolm (Inner Circle's road manager) and Basil Walters (journalist) at Reggae Sunsplash, Montego Bay, 1992. (David Rodney photograph)

on the altered trousers the ankles were just below my knees. I could not pull up my trousers to my waist. The prospect of wearing knickers to my wedding was a frightening one. Luckily, I had a reasonably long jacket and was therefore able to cover my shortcomings. I was on pins and needles although I was wearing suspenders. I had to be very guarded in my steps, one slip and everything could have become undone.

When I reached the church on my wedding day, three other grooms were waiting for their brides who had all chosen the wrong day to be fashionably late. The pastor was operating on a first come first served basis. My four-year-old son, Colin, was screaming uncontrollably while a bat (large moth) hovered menacingly above the heads of the guests in the church. My mother saw this as a bad omen.

My fiancée turned up late at the church. When I asked the reason for her tardiness, she told me that she had been watching the local television dance show *Where It's At* and had lost track of the time. The pastor went through with the ceremony, much to the relief of my poor mother whose heart was about to give way.

After the formalities at the church, we headed to the venue for the reception on Duhaney Drive, located in a suburb of St Andrew. I had harboured notions of having a large wedding, but my nuptials had grown into a festival. There was more drama to unfold.

The Four Tops had performed in Kingston on the night of our wedding. No one informed me that our wedding reception would serve as their after party. A throng of

Forbes in the 20th Century Fox movie *The French Connection*, winner of five Academy Awards, 1970.

Copeland and Millie (a member of his dance group in NY) on Soul Train with Don Cornelius, 1973. (Copeland Forbes Archives)

Forbes 2006 family reunion with matriarch, Lillian Forbes, at front centre. Back row (L-R) Junior, Beresford, Sonia, Copeland, Paul, Denton, Alfred, and Patrick. Front row (L-R) Claudette, Sylvia, Veronica, and Fay. (Copeland Forbes Archives)

uninvited guests descended on the site of our festivities seeking food and refreshment. Not being able to distinguish our real guests from the interlopers, we had to feed everyone present. We quickly ran out of refreshments. We had to get a truck to go to as many bars as it could find in Kingston to buy liquor for our "guests". We managed to save face as a number of the bartenders were willing to sell us their entire stock for that night.

A year after our dramatic wedding my wife joined me in New York. However, living together was a tall order for two people who had spent a considerable period of their relationship apart. The marriage soured. We separated and eventually divorced.

CHAPTER 2
CATCH A FIRE

The Wailers embarked on the eponymous *Catch a Fire* tour in 1973 to support their debut album for Island Records, to which they had been recently signed. The tour kicked off in Britain and included Bob, Bunny and Peter who were supported by the Barrett brothers (Aston "Familyman" and Carlton "Carly" on bass and drums, respectively) along with Earl "Wire" Lindo on keyboard. Bunny Wailer quit the group at the end of the UK tour.

After playing at Paul's Mall in Boston the Wailers' **Catch a Fire** tour came to New York in the summer of 1973. It was then that G. Fitz Bartley introduced me to Bob Marley and recommended that I join the Wailers' team as a member of the road crew. I remember the only question Bob asked was, "What month you born?". I told him August and he said, "You born to be a leader man". He had no further questions. I was on the Wailers' bandwagon.

In New York, Bob and the Wailers opened for the iconic rocker Bruce Springsteen at Max Kansas City where they did 14 shows in six days. The Wailers' set included such standards as: "Bend Down Low"; "Lively up Yourself"; "Slave Driver"; "Stop That Train"; "Kinky Reggae"; "Four Hundred Years" and "Get Up, Stand Up", among others.

The Wailers then teamed up with Sly and the Family Stone (a renowned funk band) to continue their musical sojourn across the United States. Sly and the Family Stone were genuine hit makers. They had chalked up numerous Billboard chart toppers including "Everyday People" in 1969 and "Family Affair" in 1971. The Wailers

Wailers left stranded by Sly & The Family Stone outside the hotel in Las Vegas, 1973. (Chuck Krail photograph)

opened for Sly and the Family Stone at several important venues including the US Naval Academy at Annapolis in Maryland and the Santa Clara Fairground at San Jose in California. When the tour reached the Ice Palace in Las Vegas, Nevada, the headliners seemed to have had a change of heart. Sly and the Family Stone got up earlier than scheduled and commandeered the tour bus which they shared with the Wailers. They left the Wailers out in the cold.

I remember Bob calling his mother who was then living in Delaware. The news that we had been dumped soon reached California. A Jamaican, by the name of Gus Brown, and his friends drove from California to rescue us. They knew of a club in California called the Matrix. It was a hub for rock bands. Gus and his pals told the owner about the Wailers from Jamaica and asked if he would allow them to play at the venue. The owner was at first hesitant and originally decided to allow the Wailers to play for two nights. However, the Wailers ended up performing for four nights. They gave amazing performances and did some recording sessions at Capitol Records Studio which handled distribution of the Wailers' albums for Island Records in the USA.

On the road there were several fans who described reggae as "back to front music". I did not understand what they meant at the time, though I realised that it was not a slur. I would later learn that reggae stressed different beats from those in modern pop music. While pop music placed the stress on the first and the third beats reggae put the accent on the second and the fourth notes in the bar. This feature was also distinctive of ska. Legendary Jamaican producer Clement 'Sir Coxsone'

Dodd earned the Downbeat moniker due to this characteristic of the music which he was instrumental in spawning.

The Wailers' sophomore album *Burning* was launched on 19 October, while the group was on tour in the US promoting the *Catch a Fire* album which had been released five months earlier on 4 May 1973. Joe Higgs had joined the tour as a substitute for Bunny.

In November, the Wailers headed back to the UK. Peter Tosh got sick while they were in Britain. Some of the tour dates had to be cancelled due to Peter's illness. As soon as he recuperated, they completed the itinerary and returned to Jamaica.

When they got home Peter Tosh quit the group as did Wire Lindo, the keyboard player. The Barrett brothers remained with Bob. Tyrone Downie, Donald Kinsey, Al Anderson, Touter Harvey, Alvin "Seeco" Patterson and Earl "Chinna" Smith and the I-Three would become part of the Wailers' aggregation at various points. Junior Marvin joined the band in 1977.

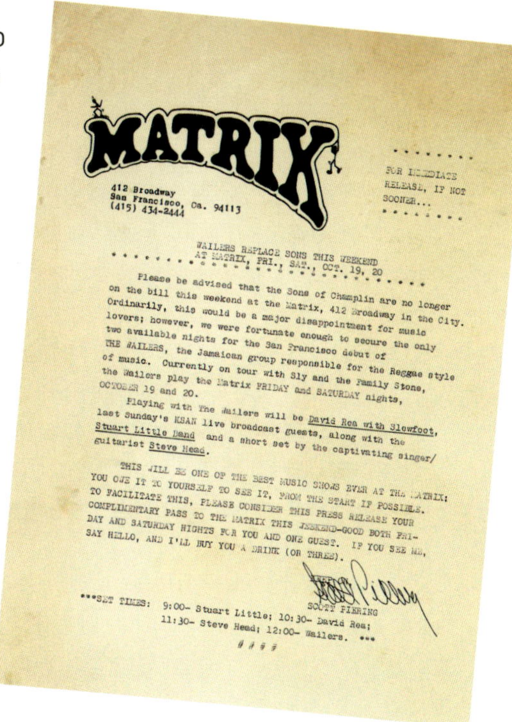

MATRIX

412 Broadway
San Francisco, Ca. 94113
(415) 434-2444

FOR IMMEDIATE RELEASE, IF NOT SOONER...

WAILERS REPLACE SONS THIS WEEKEND
AT MATRIX, FRI., SAT., OCT. 19, 20

Please be advised that the Sons of Champlin are no longer on the bill this weekend at the Matrix, 412 Broadway in the City. Ordinarily, this would be a major disappointment for music lovers; however, we were fortunate enough to secure the only two available nights for the San Francisco debut of THE WAILERS, the Jamaican group responsible for the Reggae style of music. Currently on tour with Sly and the Family Stone, the Wailers play the Matrix FRIDAY and SATURDAY nights, OCTOBER 19 and 20.

Playing with The Wailers will be David Rea with Slowfoot, last Sunday's KSAN live broadcast guests, along with the Stuart Little Band and a short set by the captivating singer/guitarist Steve Head.

THIS WILL BE ONE OF THE BEST MUSIC SHOWS EVER AT THE MATRIX; YOU OWE IT TO YOURSELF TO SEE IT, FROM THE START IF POSSIBLE. TO FACILITATE THIS, PLEASE CONSIDER THIS PRESS RELEASE YOUR COMPLIMENTARY PASS TO THE MATRIX THIS WEEKEND-GOOD BOTH FRIDAY AND SATURDAY NIGHTS FOR YOU AND ONE GUEST. IF YOU SEE ME, SAY HELLO, AND I'LL BUY YOU A DRINK (OR THREE).

SCOTT PIERING

***SET TIMES: 9:00- Stuart Little; 10:30- David Rea; 11:30- Steve Head; 12:00- Wailers. ***

# # # #

Matrix club rescue the "Wailers" after Sly & The Family Stone left them stranded in Las Vegas on the **Catch A Fire** tour, 1973.

The group was once again Bob Marley and the Wailers, as it had been known prior to its signing to Island Records. After the split, Bob, Peter, and Bunny would have three reunions in Jamaica: the first was the Marvin Gay charity show, the second was at the Jackson 5 event and the third was at the Stevie Wonder concert.

Tosh kickstarted his solo career with the release of numerous singles with Joe Gibbs and on his own Intel Diplo label. During this period Peter hooked up with Bunny on a regular basis. Bob, the Barrett brothers, along with the newly recruited members of the Wailers, and the I Three (Rita Marley, Judy Mowatt and Marcia Griffiths) recorded a new album, *Natty Dread.* It was released in 1975.The reconstituted Bob Marley and The Wailers hit the road to promote the new album. The claim that it was Chris Blackwell who named the group Bob Marley and The Wailers after Bunny and Peter had left the group in 1973 and 1974, respectively, is not entirely true. The group had called itself Bob Marley and the Wailers well before the trio signed to Island.

The Stepping Razor

Peter, in turn, started working on his first solo album *Legalize It*. The title track became a global anthem but was declared unfit for airplay in Jamaica. Columbia Records signed Peter and released the album in June 1976. Peter formed his own band Word Sound and Power with such notable musical figures as Sly Dunbar on drums, Robbie Shakespeare on bass, Tarzan and Wire Lindo on keyboards with Donald Kinsey and Al Anderson on guitars. In 1977, Tosh did another album *Equal Rights* on the CBS Records label. The title track from that album was also a hit.

In 1978, Tosh was part of the "One Love Peace Concert" held in Jamaica at the National Stadium. The event was staged by warring factions from the two major political parties (JLP and PNP). Some of the figures involved with this event included: Claudie Massop, Buckie Marshall, Tantan, Tek Life and Tony Welch. Tommy Cowan produced the event.

Mick Jagger and Keith Richards of The Rolling Stones came to the island to attend the event. Peter Tosh put on one of the most memorable performances I have ever witnessed. During his appearance onstage, Tosh addressed both Prime Minister Michael Manley and the Leader of the Opposition Edward Seaga in very stern terms using some choice Jamaican expletives to emphasize his point. Tosh was soon signed to Rolling Stones Records.

Wailers' Wail 'N Soul 'M label, 1967.

Later that year, Peter recorded *Bush Doctor*, his first album for Rolling Stones Records, at the Bearsville Studio in upstate New York. The Stones were also rehearsing for their **Some Girls** tour. I believe it was Keith Richards who said, "Why not have Peter on the tour with us?" Peter later went on tour with The Rolling Stones. He had a night off and went down to the Star Light Bowl in California where Bob was playing. Bob began performing "Get Up, Stand Up" (which he co-wrote with Tosh). Peter walked onto the stage, took the microphone and began singing with Bob. When Peter sang the lines "sick and tired of the ism schism", Bob Marley shouted, "Ladies and gentleman, Peter Tosh". The place went wild. After the performance, Bob and Peter went to the dressing room and

Wailers reunion at the Marvin Gaye show, Carib Theatre in Jamaica, 1974. (Lee Jaffe photograph)

Wailers reunion at the Marvin Gaye show at the National Stadium in Jamaica, 1974. (Lee Jaffe photograph)

gave each other high fives. I remember hearing one of them say, "Yes di Pope feel dah one ya". The sitting Pope died shortly after.

Tosh returned to Jamaica after the **Some Girls** tour and started to prepare for the release of his *Bush Doctor* album which was scheduled for the fall of 1978 and would be promoted through a European tour.

Tosh was in Half-Way-Tree waiting to meet his band members to rehearse for his European tour when a life altering incident occurred. Peter had a marijuana spliff in his hand. Suddenly, a man walked up to him and grabbed it from him. Peter forcibly took back the spliff. The man again snatched it from him. Both men started to wrestle. Two other men walked up to them and started to hit Peter. It was then that Tosh realized that he had been tussling with a plain clothes policeman. Peter was taken to the nearby police station where he endured a brutal beating. They threw him in a cell and left him to bleed. Some of the inmates, recognizing who he was, applied first aid to save his life.

Peter later told me that he had received warnings about possible reprisals against him for his blunt message to the political leaders at the Peace Concert. He said sources close to the security forces had informed him that his name was on a list of people who were being targeted by the authorities. Peter was deemed too out-spoken, and it was felt that he needed to be put in his place.

Despite his injuries, Peter went ahead with the European tour. The *Bush Doctor* album was released. The first single "Walk & Don't Look Back" – a collaboration with Mick Jagger – was getting significant airplay worldwide.

The year ended on a very high note with Peter Tosh and his Word Sound and Power band appearing on Saturday Night Live on NBC. Tosh and his special guests, Mick Jagger and R&B singer Gwen Guthrie, performed the single "Walk & Don't Look Back" on the show.

In 1979, the *Bush Doctor* was creating waves across the globe. Later in the year, Tosh released *Mystic Man*, the second album on the Rolling Stones label. Tosh did a massive tour which started in California and made its way across the USA. He then went over to Europe and played most of the major festivals on the continent including Pink Pop and the famous Montreaux Jazz Festival. Peter returned to Jamaica in July of that year and did the famous Reggae Sunsplash (held in Montego Bay) before heading back to Europe.

Peter loved fishing. I remember one night while we were at Martha's Vineyard in Massachusetts (for a two-night performance at the Hot Tin Roof in 1979) he went out on a lake not far away and came back at about 1:00 in the morning with a load of

Peter Tosh performs at the One Love Peace Concert, 1978. (Peter Simon photograph)

NEW MUSICAL EXPRESS

TOSH BRUTALISED

EX-WAILER Peter Tosh was arrested and held overnight by Jamaican police last Tuesday. In the process he sustained a broken arm and severe head wounds which later received over twenty stitches.

Despite his injuries, Tosh — now emerging as one of the leading international figures of Jamaican music — will still be visiting the UK in late October for a series of dates to coincide with the release of his new album and single on Rolling Stones Records.

THRILLS

THE FIRST SPACE GUITAR TAKES OFF

For Peter Tosh help is custom-made

MONTREAL — (CP) — Jamaican reggae star Peter Tosh has come to expect hassles with customs officials, largely because of his much publicized stand in favor of marijuana use.

But when one member of Tosh's entourage was left out in the cold early yesterday, Canadian customs came to the rescue.

The Tosh crew was travelling by bus to Montreal for his concert last night when the bus was stopped for the usual border check at Lacolle, Que., about 50 kilometres southwest of Montreal.

Copeland Forbes, Tosh's personal assistant, took advantage of the stop to use the men's room at the customs office, but by the time he returned the bus had already departed.

Then Canada Customs stepped in.

Using his CB radio, the official broadcast, "Preacher Nine to Peter Tosh's bus, Preacher Nine to Peter Tosh's bus," for about 25 minutes before the bus responded.

The customs man, who was not identified beyond his CB handle, then used his own car to drive Forbes to his companions.

"Not only were we not hassled at the border, but they bent over backward for us, and we're very grateful," a spokesman for Tosh said.

fish. He asked me to steam the fish with crackers for him. I called my mother in New York and asked her how to steam fish with crackers. She gave me the instructions. I had broad responsibilities. I had to prepare Peter's meals (which were mostly ital and vegetarian), look after his clothes, deal with all his PR assignments, and play the role of the MC for the shows. It was not easy, but I developed a rhythm.

The crew and I left Massachusetts and headed for Montreal. When we reached the border checkpoint, I decided that I wanted to use the bathroom and get myself refreshed. I was the first to get off the bus. I had wanted to be processed quickly so I could use the rest room. After I went through immigration I proceeded to the men's room where I spent a considerable amount of time. I thought that our entourage would have been subjected to a thorough search for contraband at the border (after all that was how Jamaican entertainers were treated) so I took my time in the rest room. When I went outside to check on the bus, I noticed that it was missing. I assumed that it had simply moved to another spot. The officials were a bit surprised to see me and asked if I was with the tour bus. They told me that the bus had left over a half an hour before. I had miscalculated and was left stranded.

One of the customs officers asked if the driver of the bus was a speedster. I told him no. He promised he would take me to catch the bus. He drove very fast, but the bus was out of reach for the most part of the journey. We finally caught the bus when it was about to enter Montreal. The incident was reported in the *Montreal Gazette* the following day with the headline, "For Peter Tosh Help Is Custom Made". Peter Tosh had not been on the bus. He and his publicist, Charley Comer, had flown to Canada from Martha's Vineyard.

Peter Tosh and Bob Marley sing "Get Up Stand Up" in California, 1978. (Michael Ochs Archives)

Peter Tosh and Mick Jagger perform on Saturday Nite Live, 1978. (Peter Simon Photo)

Tosh at the sound check for the One Love Peace Concert at the National Stadium, Kingston, Jamaica, 1978. (Lee Jaffe photograph)

Peter Tosh and Stones' Keith Richards backstage at Tosh's NY concert, 1979.

The climax for the year was the magnificent No Nuke concert series at Madison Square Garden. The five-day event featured artistes such as: Bonnie Raitt; Jackson Browne; John Hall; Bruce Springsteen; Crosby Still & Nash; Carly Simon; James Taylor and Peter Tosh among others.

Mick Jagger, Copeland Forbes and Sly Dunbar backstage at Saturday Nite Live, 1978. (Peter Simon photograph).

CHAPTER 3
WHEN THE RIGHT TIME COME

In 1976, the Mighty Diamonds were really hot, and I had the great honour of managing them. It was in 1976, too, that I first met Don Taylor. He was managing Burning Spear, Max Romeo and Bob Marley and The Wailers. The Mighty Diamonds and Burning Spear were scheduled to appear at an event slated for Madison Square Garden (MSG). Don and I set a meeting for 3 December at the Sheraton Hotel in Kingston, Jamaica. We wanted to discuss the possibility of using only one backing band for all our artistes performing on the show which was scheduled for January 1977 at the Felt Forum inside the MSG.

Don and I eventually agreed that Spear and Diamonds would use their own bands on the show. The Mighty Diamonds would be backed by the Revolutionaries with Sly Dunbar, Ansel Colins, Sticky Thompson, Duggie "Rad" Bryan and Lloyd Parks who would be complemented by a three-man horn section led by Lester Sterling. Burning Spear would be accompanied by the Black Disciples band with Robbie Shakespeare, "Touter" Harvey, Leroy "Horsemouth" Wallace and Earl "Chinna" Smith supported by a horn section led by Dirty Harry.

On the conclusion of our meeting at the Sheraton, Don suggested that we go up to Hope Road where Bob Marley & The Wailers were rehearsing for the upcoming Smile Jamaica concert, which was scheduled to take place on 5 December at the National Heroes Park. I declined the invitation as I had to visit my mother. Don went to the rehearsal. While I was at my mom's house, I heard that there was a shooting incident at 56 Hope Road.

Mighty Diamonds.

Don Taylor, 1976.

I rushed to the Tuff Gong Studio. Don Taylor was lying in a pool of blood on the ground. He had received five shots in his abdomen and had to be airlifted to Miami for treatment. Bob Marley was grazed on his left arm and taken to the University Hospital. Rita had suffered superficial wounds. There were no band members to be seen. I was terrified.

I was surprised to see Don a few weeks later at the show in Madison Square Garden. He had accompanied Burning Spear for the performance. He was walking with a cane to support his back. He moved with a crouch and was clearly in pain, but he would not give up. Don was a tough customer.

The Mighty Diamonds were signed to Virgin Records and they chose the UK for their first tour. We took the Revolutionaries (which included Sly Dunbar, Ansel Colins, Lloyd Parks, Tony Chin, and Lloyd "Guitsy" Willis) which had the authentic reggae sound. We were booked for the Reading Rock Festival. Punk Rock was then the rage. The head of Virgin Records, Richard Branson, wanted the group to be exposed to the rock scene. The Diamonds were not punk rockers. This created its own set of challenges.

As soon as the Diamonds started to perform, the patrons started throwing eggs and tomatoes. I tried, vainly, to prevent the missiles from hitting the musicians and their instruments. I remember a tomato splattering on Ansel Collins keyboard. He started screaming at the audience, threatening to commit murder. Suddenly, his face was dripping with the yolk of an egg smashed against his head. The artistes and the musicians wanted to leave the stage, but Sly Dunbar would have none of it. The supply of eggs and tomatoes seemed endless. The fans could have made an omelette the size of the stadium had that been their intention. Eventually, the barrage stopped. I don't know whether the fans had run out of eggs and tomatoes or out of energy. Whatever their reasons, the Diamonds kept on going reeling off hits like "Right Time", "I Need a Roof" and "Poor Marcus".

One of the perpetrators of the missile throwing was later held by a member of the British contingent travelling with us and was brought backstage. He knelt and apologised for hurling the objects on the stage.

In 1977, the Mighty Diamonds went on to record their second album for Virgin Records at the Sea Saint Recording Studios in New Orleans. The album was produced by Marshall Sehorn and Allen Toussaint who rented a car for which I was the designated driver. I was the only one in our entourage with an American driver's licence and so the vehicle was rented in my name.

We were staying at the Holiday Inn. We had a day off and I was in my room relaxing when I heard a knock on my door. It was the housekeeper. She told me that a member of the group had crashed a car by the poolside. On my way to see what had happened, I ran into Bunny heading from the scene of the accident. He was mad. He kept saying. "I told him, but he wouldn't hear". I asked him who he was referring to. "Tabby" he responded.

When I reached the pool, I saw three crashed cars. One of them was a spanking new Mustang which the owner said he had bought just three months before. Tabby, the lead singer of the group,

BLACK ECHOES

TODAY'S MUSIC WEEKLY

AUGUST 14, 1976 15p

● Weather Report — Page 11
● Herbie Hancock — Page 18
● New Spear LP reviewed — Page 14

Set to conquer Britain?

JA Reggae stars fly in

ARRIVING IN the UK this weekend, Friday 13, Reggae stars U-Roy and the Mighty Diamonds, with the Revolutionaries Channel One backing band — set for massive promotion by their record company, Virgin.

Following head-line billing at London's Lyceum Ballroom on August 18, and an appearance at the Reading Festival on August 27, U-Roy and the Mighty Diamonds fly to France where they will play a festival at Corbieres on August 28.

Returning to the UK, the artists will play Birmingham Barbarella's (30); with further dates to be confirmed by Virgin between August 19-30.

Also on the bill at the Lyceum, will be new Virgin artist Delroy Washington.

The Revolutionaries consist of: Lloyd "Officially" Parks, of Skin, Flesh and Bones on Bass; Lowell "Sly" Dunbar on drums; Ansell Collins — of Dave and Ansell Collins Double Barrell fame — keyboards; and Albert Chin on guitar.

There was initially some apprehension that the Jamaican musicians would not in fact be arriving until next week, due to superstitions regarding travelling on Friday 13, but this has since been resolved.

For the benefit of anyone who would like to greet the artists at the airport, U-Roy and the Mighty Diamonds will be arriving at Heathrow Airport at 7.30 a.m. on Friday — via Air Jamaica flight JN 001. BLACK ECHOES will be interviewing them for a full spread next week.

Above: U Roy

Left: The Mighty Diamonds

Promotional material for U-Roy and Mighty Diamonds, Reading Punk Rock Festival, 1976. *(Echoes Magazine)*

Mighty Diamonds *Planet Earth*, third Virgin Records album, 1978. (Forbes photograph, Copeland Forbes Archives)

could not drive but decided to take a spin in our rented vehicle. It was apparent that when he crashed into the first vehicle, he kept pressing the gas pedal instead of releasing it. He slammed into one vehicle which then crashed into another.

I called the recording studio to tell them what had happened. They instructed me to inform the cops that I was the one who had been driving. When the police arrived, one of them exclaimed, "Jesus Christ what the hell is this?" He then proceeded to ask for the driver. I raised my hand with much trepidation. I had no choice. If I had not claimed it, Tabby would have gone to jail.

The owner of the red Mustang was almost in tears. His wife was hysterical. The police asked me what had really happened. I didn't know where to start. I told him I was coming around the corner when I hit the red car and then the green one. "When you crashed into the first car, you did not realize that you had hit something?" he asked. I told him that after I had hit the first vehicle I panicked. He asked for my driver's licence which had been suspended in New York. I gave it to him.

While I was in England, I had left my car parked out on the road in the Bronx. I had been away for quite a while and had not been paying the outstanding parking tickets which had been accumulating. My driver's licence was suspended for the unpaid tickets. Back in those days if one's licence was suspended in New York it would have been difficult to check it in New Orleans. The system was not digitally linked then as it is today. After the police left, Marshall Sehorn called the wrecker. We then went to the car rental company for a replacement. We got a brand-new car.

We warned everyone not to touch the replacement vehicle as I was the only designated driver. I drove the vehicle back to the hotel where I noticed that there were six police cars parked outside. What was worse was that the vehicles belonged to the accident division of the police force. I became nervous. I wondered whether the police had discovered that my licence had been suspended and had come to arrest me. I quickly got the artistes out of the vehicle and sped away from the hotel. I spent the night at the home of a girl I had met in New Orleans.

I didn't go to the studio or to the hotel for two days. I was scared as hell. I called the hotel as I wanted to find out from the artistes if they had heard of anyone

Copeland Forbes, Brazilian artiste Soraia Drummond and Richard Branson at Strawberry Hills Resort, Jamaica, 2006. (Copeland Forbes Archives)

looking for me. They were afraid to pick up the phone. I had to call the recording studio and ask them to send someone over to the hotel to tell the artistes that I had been trying to reach them. I finally managed to speak to the Diamonds and asked if they knew of anyone looking for me. I found it strange that they said no. I plucked up some courage and decided to go over to the hotel. I soon realized there was a coffee shop at the hotel and that the police usually went there for their breaks. The police were not looking for me, I smelled the coffee and was relieved.

We had been in New Orleans for a week, when we got word that the Diamonds had to leave for New York to do a photo shoot for their album *Ice on Fire*. I sent the Diamonds ahead of me as I had some unfinished business in New Orleans. I would be flying solo to New York. The night before my scheduled flight to New York, I saw the number 72 in a dream. When I got to the airport, my flight number was 72. I thought it was a bit ominous but boarded, nonetheless. I took a seat at the back of the aircraft. While the plane was climbing, I heard a loud explosion. The stairs at the back of the plane had fallen open. The entrance beneath the tail of the plane had become a gaping hole threatening to suck anything which was untethered out of the aircraft. I was terrified.

I wanted to get up and go to the front. The flight attendant told me that I should remain in my seat, or I would be sucked from the plane. I held on to my seat for dear life. Suddenly, I heard a little sound and I saw the stairs coming back into the plane. I was relieved.

The pilot announced that the plane would be returning to the gate for safety reasons. When we got back to the gate, I came off the plane, went back to the hotel and stayed in New Orleans for another two days.

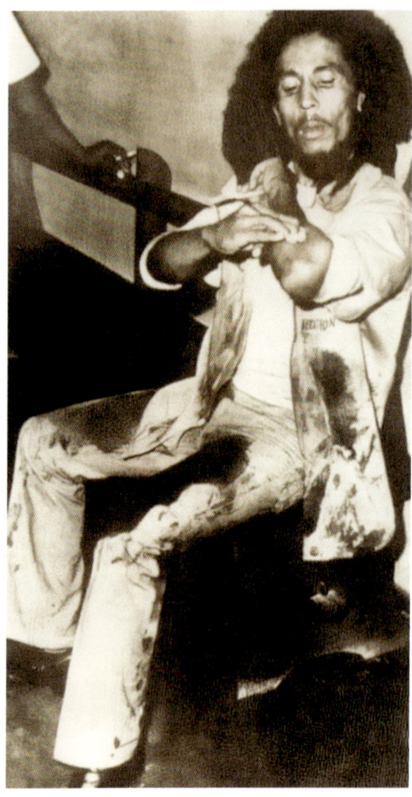

A wounded Bob Marley after he was shot at the rehearsal for the Smile Jamaica Concert in Kingston. (Clive Williams Photo)

Bob Marley performs at Smile Jamaica Concert, Kingston, 1976.

CHAPTER 4

REGGAE ON BROADWAY

In 1977, Inner Circle (featuring Jacob Miller) was the headliner for a show at the Beacon Theatre. Other acts included Culture, Meditation, Dillinger and the Monyaka Band out of New York. Everything was going smoothly. I was by the mixing board, with the world-renowned engineer, Dennis Thompson, when a shot rang out. Someone had fired a gun inside the theatre. There was a stampede as everyone rushed for the exit. The glass doors were broken. Fortunately, no one died or was seriously injured.

We were billed for another show in New York the following week. The Inner Circle was not included in the line-up but all the other artistes from the Beacon Theatre event were scheduled to perform. The promoter, Ken Williams, had a house in Brooklyn and had arranged for the artistes and musicians to stay there to cut costs.

We were all at Ken's house when Culture (Joseph Hill) and Dillinger got into a fight. Hill gave Dillinger a beating. Dillinger left and went to visit relatives in the Bushwick area of Brooklyn. When he returned to the house, he was armed with a Glock 9 millimetre handgun. Hill was in the kitchen cooking some rice and cabbage and was not aware that Dillinger had returned with a gun. Hill turned around and saw Dillinger slapping the weapon and stuttered, "Iyah me have some food". Hill seemed to have lost his appetite for a fight and made a peace offering to Dillinger. A man named Dillinger, with a gun in his hand, was not to be taken lightly especially if one had just given him a drubbing. Hill quickly shared a portion of his meal and handed it to Dillinger. The animosity immediately subsided. The food clearly lightened the mood.

Inner Circle featuring Jacob Miller, 1977. (Courtesy Circle Music Archives)

Ken Williams was persistent. He had a passion for the business. A few years later (1980 to be exact) Ken was ready to stage another show at the Beacon Theatre. Dennis Brown was the headliner. Junior Tucker, Carlene Davis and Ruddy Thomas were the supporting acts. They would be backed by Lloyd Parks and the We the People Band. It was the Labour Day weekend and Bob Marley was in town preparing for his show at the Madison Square Garden with The Commodores. He asked me to tell Lloyd Parks that he would make a surprise appearance and do two songs on the show. He wanted Lloyd to rehearse "Who the Cap Fit" and "Rat Race".

The night before the show, Dennis was still not in town. We called England and heard that he had left for the USA. On the day of the show, there was still no sign of him. The promoter went to the airport. Dennis was scheduled to come in on the last flight from London that evening. The Beacon Theatre was already packed.

The promoter called from the airport to say that the flight had come in but there was no sign of Dennis Brown. The show was scheduled to start at 8:00 pm. When it got to 9:30 pm, the manager of the theatre asked the reason for the delay. I told him we could not start the show without the headline act who was still in London. "Jesus Christ, we're sitting on a bomb!", he exclaimed. He insisted that we postpone or cancel the show.

The owner of the theatre told us not to say anything to the audience until he had alerted the police, ambulance and fire department. He recalled what had happened three years before in a similar situation. He didn't want to take any chances. He called the authorities the police, ambulance and firefighters surrounded the theatre.

The management informed us that the theatre would be available the following Friday so we could reschedule the show. We then faced the challenge of telling the

Crown Prince of Reggae Dennis Brown live. (Dreamy Riley photograph)

audience. Who would face the music? The audience was growing restless. We turned to Tommy Cowan to make the announcement. He was not billed to emcee the show but was there in his capacity as Junior Tucker's manager. Tommy had been present at the Beacon when all hell had broken loose in 1977. He had been the manager of Inner Circle when that incident occurred. Tommy said he would be addressing the audience from his dressing room and that he would need a microphone with a 100ft lead to make the announcement. He refused to go on stage.

We were adamant that he would have to make the announcement from the stage. Tommy would have none of it. We settled on G.T. Taylor who was living in New York and was part of the comedic team The Ticklers. G.T. walked out and began to address the audience. "Good evening, ladies and gents, we have a little problem here". There was an immediate uproar. The patrons began rushing towards the stage. G.T. ran for cover. This was no joke.

I told Lloyd Parks that he and his band should walk out on stage and start playing. We decided that the artistes who had been booked for the show should perform two songs after which we would make the announcement that the show was postponed until the following Friday and that the tickets for the current show would be valid for the upcoming one. Those who did not want to use the rain check would get a refund.

We decided that I would make the announcement. When I told the audience about the postponement there was obvious disapproval. However, the music seemed to have suppressed any urge for violence. Many of the patrons continued dancing after the announcement. The ambulance, the police and the fire trucks were waiting expectantly outside. They would have nothing to do. Everyone left in an orderly fashion. My plan worked.

I remember Max Romeo telling me that we were the luckiest people in the world. He was familiar with some of the types who were in the audience which included gangsters who were armed and dangerous. He warned that we might not be as

Bob Marley and Ken Williams (left) at Club Negril, New York, 1980.

Promoter Ken Williams meets Bob Marley at Essex House Hotel, 1980.

fortunate the next time so we should ensure that we honoured our commitment for the rescheduled show. The promoter had to put up all the performers for another week at a hotel in New York. Tommy seemed to have been a beneficiary of the aborted show. It was there that he met his wife, Carlene Davis.

We found Dennis the following Tuesday after calling all over London. I later realised that Dennis had wanted an airline ticket to take someone with him from London and was miffed that he did not get it. Hence his no show. I told him to come on the Wednesday, two days before the rescheduled show. He said that he wouldn't be able to make it on that day and would be in on the Thursday. We rebooked his flight. He came in on the Thursday.

What was interesting was that on the night of the postponement, Bob had been outside the venue waiting in a limousine for Dennis to arrive. Had I known then I would have told the crowd that Dennis Brown was not there, but Bob was in the house.

When Dennis arrived in New York we took him from the airport straight to WLIB where Ken Williams interviewed him on radio. Bob heard that Dennis was in town and left his hotel and went over to the radio station. Bob sat in on the interview and apologized to the listeners on Dennis' behalf. He reminded the listeners that the show was on and that it would be rocking. Bob was a huge Dennis Brown fan.

We had twice the number of patrons at the Beacon Theatre for the rescheduled show than we had the week before. We had to turn back hundreds of fans. Yet the promoter still suffered a loss. The promoter had to carry additional costs which he had not bargained for, thanks to Dennis. I cannot remember if I was ever paid for my services. Dennis was huge but he was costly. However, Ken and I have remained good friends.

CHAPTER 5
MANY RIVERS TO CROSS

y professional relationship with Jimmy Cliff began in 1980. That was also the year Don Taylor and I started our business association. Don was then Cliff's manager. Our first tour would be to South Africa.

By this time, however, Don's relationship with Bob Marley was growing sour. It was alleged that there were some financial irregularities during the **Survival** tour in 1979, and that there was an incident in 1980 involving improper accounting for a gig in Gabon. Don Taylor and Bob Marley went their separate ways in 1980.

Don sent me to Jamaica to secure visas and work permits for members of Jimmy Cliff's team for the South Africa and Brazil tours. I was instructed that while in Jamaica I should arrange rehearsals for our back-to-back tours to South Africa and Brazil. Don also told me to go to Tuff Gong Records to pick up a 24-track tape containing songs by Jimmy Cliff for his album with EMI.

I went to Tuff Gong and asked for Diane Jobson, the manager. Somebody informed me that Diane was in office but needed to know why I wanted to see her. I blurted, "Don Taylor sent me to pick up Jimmy Cliff's tapes". As soon as I uttered Don's name about a dozen 'rude boys' appeared out of nowhere and surrounded me. They wanted to know, "Whey de bwoy Don Taylor deh?" According to the men, "Taylor rob the boss an im fi dead". Luckily, I knew one of the men who was baying for Don's blood. He was a well-known enforcer, my schoolmate and a member of the All Saints' Boy Scouts Troop, Colin Oldham. They called him Lip.

Bob and Pascaline Bongo at Tuff Gong Studio in Kingston, Jamaica, 1979. (Lindsey Oliver Donald photograph)

I told them Don was in Florida. They kept saying, "De bwoy de fi dead because him rob the boss". Diane Jobson told me that she was not going to give me the tape because Don owed money for the use of the studio. Diane noted that Don had to pay the bill before she would release the tape.

Bob was sitting in another room and overheard the conversation. He came outside and asked what the problem was. I told him. He said to Diane Jobson, "Listen, give the tape to Copeland because Jimmy Cliff don't have nothing to do with the problem between me and Don. You can't hold up Jimmy's career because of this". I had, inadvertently, walked into the lion's den but came away unscathed.

I went to Jimmy's house and related the story to him. He looked at me and rolled his eyes. I called Don in Miami and unloaded on him. I was upset that he had sent me into harm's way without giving me any warning. Don didn't want to tell me exactly what had happened, but I was already up to date on what had taken place in Gabon.

I heard that the president's daughter, Pascaline Bongo, had made a deal with Don in 1979 during the **Survival** tour. She wanted Betty Wright and Bob Marley to perform in her native Gabon the following year.

Bob went to Gabon. He shone brightly. Everybody had a good time. Bob and his team had a couple of days to relax and do some sightseeing. According to my sources, Pascaline and Bob were sitting in a room talking about the shows, and she just happened to mention how costly it was to stage the event. This led to Pascaline making certain revelations regarding the accounting for the tour which made Bob suspicious of his management. Bob, reportedly, called Don Taylor and asked him some pointed questions. Don tried explaining but Bob was in no mood for a story. He wanted figures. I heard that Don had to be rescued from a dreadful beating. Don caught a plane and headed back to the USA.

Jimmy Cliff did not know about what had happened in Gabon. Don had not said a word to anyone about the incident.

Jimmy, his nephew Newton, and I were having dinner at Don's house. Chuck Jackson, and Little Anthony were also Don's guests. While we were at the dining table, Chuck said, "Hey Don, what's this I'm hearing about you and Bob Marley? That you ain't together no more?" Don blurted, "I was just tired of the Wailers thing, so I decided to quit." Jimmy sat there listening and rolling his eyes. He was processing everything. Chuck Jackson posed the question again. Don dodged.

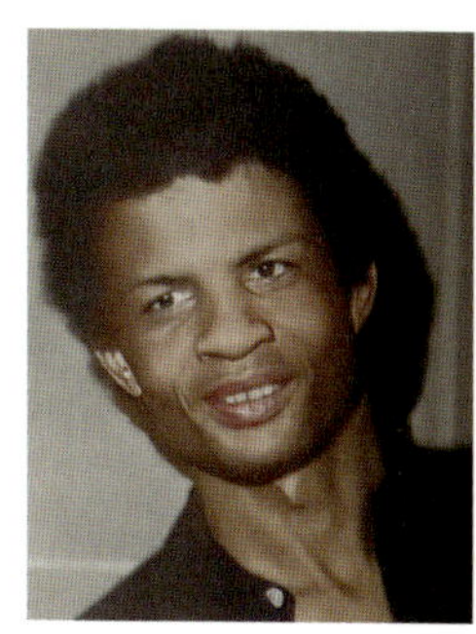

Don Taylor, 1980.

Jimmy and I went back to Jamaica to get ready for the trip to South Africa. There was no South African Embassy in Jamaica nor in Florida. I had to fly from Jamaica to Washington DC with 17 passports to get the visas for the members of Jimmy's entourage to enter South Africa. I was worried about having to travel with so many passports. I made sure to take the South African contracts with me just in case I was pulled over by the police in the United States. I later flew back to Jamaica to give the team members their passports with their South African visas.

When we were leaving Jamaica for South Africa , Earl "Chinna" Smith did not yet have a Brazilian visa in his passport. The South African visa took up the last page in his passport so there was no more available space in the book. He could not get a new passport in time for the tour. We decided that we would head to South Africa and then figure out how to get a new passport for him at one of the Jamaican consulates in the course of our travels.

When we touched down in South Africa we were elated but curious. This was the era of apartheid. Nelson Mandela was still in prison. We didn't know what to expect. A throng of reporters and media personnel greeted us at the airport. The reception was great. We were scheduled to do the first show in Soweto, the second in Durban and the final one in Cape Town.

The excitement around Johannesburg was palpable. Jimmy had re-recorded Bob Marley's "No Woman No Cry". His version had sold over a million copies in South

Africa. There were great expectations. The bus came to the hotel and picked up the entourage and we headed to Soweto. The driver of the coach was a White man, about 35 years old. He couldn't find his way to the stadium. He had never been to the Black township, although he was born in South Africa. One could tell by his body language that he was not accustomed to being around so many Black people. We saw some kids playing soccer and asked them the way to the stadium. They came on board the bus and directed us.

When we arrived at the stadium, we saw thousands of people outside the venue who could not afford the entrance fee and were trying to get in over the walls and under the barbwire. The fans went wild when they realised Jimmy Cliff and his musicians were aboard the bus. Bodies were strung across the top of the bus. The driver was nervous. I told him to take his time. When we reached the tunnel, the bus could not enter. After much effort we finally managed to get into the stadium. The fans started screaming, "Jimmy Cliff, Jimmy Cliff". Everybody was rushing towards the bus. They surrounded the bus.

When I disembarked, everyone was looking at me as if I had come from another planet. One fan said, "My brother, what are you doing in that?" I didn't understand at first what he was talking about. He was referring to the military fatigues I was wearing. We didn't know that it was illegal to wear army fatigues in South Africa. Our entire entourage was clad in army outfits. The fans were wondering what was going to happen to us. Our apparel, however, didn't seem to bother the authorities.

The security forces went on the stage and formed a ring. Their presence sparked anger among the patrons who started throwing objects at them. People took off their shoes and threw them at the security forces. There were over 60,000 people in the stadium. A DJ from a local radio station went on stage and tried to calm the crowd. He addressed the fans, "Ladies and gentlemen please stop throwing the bottles on the stage. If you don't stop, we will have to call additional security." That was a huge mistake. Bottles rained on the stage. The supply of missiles seemed inexhaustible. I implored the soldiers to leave the stage. They refused, saying they were following instructions from their headquarters.

I was speaking with the commanding officer when a large Coca-Cola bottle, which seemed specially made for the task, came flying through the air, striking the officer on the head. Blood spurted from his face. I feared the soldiers were going to retaliate by shooting into the crowd. They lifted the commanding officer off the stage. Soon all the security personnel left the platform.

I went onto the stage with my clenched fist raised, a symbol of love and unity in that region. The crowd went silent. "Ladies and gentlemen we came all the way from

Kingston, Jamaica to entertain you through the powers of reggae music, so please stop throwing the bottles so we can clean up the stage and get the show started", I intoned .There was a big roar. The missiles stopped flying. We cleaned the stage. Jimmy made his entry opening his performance with "You Can Get It If You Really Want". His performance of "No Woman no Cry" received a rapturous reception. The crowd was in a frenzy.

While Jimmy was in full flight, I saw a rope suddenly appearing from the back of the stage. A Zulu warrior (with shield and sword in hand) was rappelling down the wall. He landed in the middle of the stage. He knelt before Jimmy and hugged and then kissed his feet. Jimmy just kept on singing.

We saw Blacks, Whites and Indians holding hands in a ring and dancing together. We were told this was most unusual. The security forces were surprised by the spectacle. Jimmy performed for over two and a half hours then exited the stage. The fans would not move, they started chanting, "Jimmy! Jimmy!" He returned to the stage belting out more of his hits. When he finally left the stage after three and a half hours everybody was satisfied. The Zulu warrior who was on stage presented Jimmy with his shield and sword.

The warrior lived 15 miles from the venue, and he could not afford the entrance fee of 5 rand. The only way he was able to get into the stadium was with his rope. He told us about his remarkable life. He had cuts on his feet where dogs had bitten him as he was trying to scale the stadium walls. Fans had braved the barbed wires and dogs to get into the venue. Some punched the dogs which held onto their bleeding limbs.

The promoters had to double the security at the hotel where we were staying. A mob was waiting there to greet us. We went through the back of the hotel but were still followed into the lobby. The fans all wanted autographs from Jimmy.

We went sightseeing. Johannesburg has many historical sites. Everywhere we went we saw some of the same people. The authorities were monitoring us. The fact that we were able to bring the masses together was of concern to the elite. We had shown that our music could unite the people. I was able to confirm this six months later when I applied for a visitor's visa to go back to South Africa to see some friends, I was denied entry. Someone inside the embassy, however, told me that the authorities were nervous of our ability to unite South Africans.

We finally left Johannesburg and headed for Durban where the composition of the audience was decidedly more well-heeled. The venue was an indoor arena. Fans were seated.

In Cape Town we had the time of our lives. We visited the famed Table Mountain from where we could see Robben Island, the penitentiary in which freedom fighter Nelson Mandela was being held prisoner.

Our bass player Jimmy "Senya" Haynes went downtown Cape Town and brought back a man with a guitar to the hotel. Senya said the stranger was a fantastic guitarist.

"Senya" introduced the stranger to our guitarist Earl "Chinna" Smith. They had an incredible jam session. "Senya" kept saying that we should find a way to get the guitarist out of South Africa. The newly discovered guitarist later signed a deal with Jive Records and went to the UK where he lived for over 15 years. He currently resides in California and is none other than the great Jonathan Butler.

We left South Africa for Brazil where we were booked for five shows. Don Taylor had departed Cape Town a day before the entourage left for Brazil. He had given me 60,000 rand to take with me to Brazil. I didn't know that it was illegal to take money out of South Africa. It was the promoter who made me aware of the law. I decided to put the money in the bottom of my suitcase. We needed to pay 4,000 rand at the airport for overweight luggage. I asked the agent if we could pay the charges on our arrival in Brazil. After a lengthy discussion, I realized that I had no alternative but to tell the agent that I had funds in my suitcase, which had already been checked onto the plane. They had to go in the cargo bay of the plane and search for my suitcase. They took it back to me at the counter.

I retrieved my luggage and went into the bathroom, accompanied by our percussionist, Sydney Wolfe. The security forces manning the airport got very suspicious when they saw us going into the bathroom with the suitcase. I took out 5000 rand and put it in my pocket. I told Sydney Wolfe to put the big envelope with the balance of 55,000 rand down in his waist. I went back to the check in counter and paid for the excess weight.

As I was going through the security checkpoint, the alarm went off, indicating that I had a metallic object on my person. The security who was armed with a sub machine gun ordered me to empty my pockets. I immediately put my briefcase on the table and proceeded to follow his instruction. I pushed my hands into my pockets and I felt two giant marijuana spliffs. I almost fainted. I quickly recalled how they got there. Jimmy Cliff was going to do an interview at a radio station and didn't want to take the blunts with him. He had given them to me to keep. The promoter had told all the herb smokers not to ask anyone to get weed for them. The penalties for being found in possession of herb in South Africa was very stiff. The law in South Africa, at that time, prescribed a penalty of 15 to 20 years for possession of marijuana, especially at an airport.

Jimmy Cliff and Oneness in Johannesburg South Africa, 1980. (Copeland Forbes Archives)

I gently took my hand out of the pocket without removing the spliffs and proceeded to empty the other pockets. I found my hotel room key which I had kept as a souvenir in another pocket. The armed security pointed out that it was the key that had triggered the alarm. He instructed me to go back through the scanning machine. I did. I knew that if the alarm went off again, they would search me and find the spliffs. They would also have taken all the other members of our team off the plane and searched them. If that envelope with the 55,000 rand was found, I would be in big trouble. I paused for a while and repeated the first verses of Psalms 121, 57 and 91. Then, I went through the detector. I was overjoyed when I passed through the machine without setting off the alarms. I ran to the departure gate. As soon as I boarded the plane, the flight attendant closed the door behind me.

I took a deep breath and repeated Psalm 121, relieved that we were on our way to Argentina. When we got to the cruising altitude and the seatbelt sign was off, everyone gathered around to ask what had taken me so long to board. I related the entire incident. I told them that I had been inches away from prison. I headed to the bathroom on the plane, emptied my pocket and flushed the spliffs. I was on a high to Buenos Aires.

We still needed to get the additional pages in Chinna's passport so that he could get his Brazilian visa. Chinna and I went in search of the Jamaican Consulate in Buenos Aires. I told Jimmy Cliff and the band members that if "Chinna and I are not back in time for the flight, then you should go ahead to Rio without us".

Chinna and I found the Jamaican Consulate. The Consul General was overseas on vacation. We checked into a hotel and sent a message to the promoter in Brazil. The rest of the group went to Brazil ahead of us. The next day, the Brazilian promoter called and said he had left a message at a bank in Buenos Aires and that we should go there and ask for a particular person who would give us local currency and assist us in getting the visa. The promoter said that he had already spoken to the Brazilian Embassy in Buenos Aires and had requested that they put the visa on the currency page in Chinna's passport.

We went to the bank. I left Chinna, who was sporting dreadlocks, standing with two metal cases in his hands in front of the bank. Those going in and out of the bank looked at him in a strange manner.

We had only one day to secure the visa. We needed a medical certificate to obtain a Brazilian visa. We had to find a doctor. We paid 50,000 cruzeiros for the medical report. Chinna got his visa and wanted to go shopping for Argentinian souvenirs. He went downtown and got himself a blue and white Argentinian soccer outfit. He decided to wear it to Brazil. While we were on the plane. I noticed that the other passengers were looking at us as if something had gone wrong. One of the flight attendants asked Chinna, "Are you going to wear that to Brazil?" She added, "They will kill you". There was an intense football rivalry between both nations which sometimes became violent.

When we landed in Brazil, Chinna and I went to the back of the plane. I told him that I would disembark but that he should stay on the plane. I went and told the promoter who had come to pick us up that Chinna was on the plane decked out in an Argentinian soccer outfit and had been warned not to wear it in Brazil. The promoter and I went into one of the gift shops at the airport and bought a Flamengo shorts and jersey for Chinna. Flamengo was one of the top football clubs in Brazil. I took the outfit to Chinna so he could change his attire before disembarking. As soon as we arrived at the hotel, Chinna said he needed a smoke. The promoter granted his wish.

We had five shows in Brazil – Rio, Bel Horizonte, Salvador, Recife and Sao Paolo. Brazilian star Gilberto Gil, who had recorded a Portuguese version of "No Woman No Cry", and who later became a government minister, was also on the tour. Jimmy Cliff's hit song, "Wonderful World, Beautiful People" which he had written on a previous sojourn to Brazil was very popular in the country. Having Jimmy and Gilberto on the same tour was extraordinary. In addition to his guarantee, Jimmy was entitled to a 70/30 split for attendance in excess of 20,000 patrons.

In 1981, Jimmy toured Europe and the United States. Don told me that, for the European leg, he had arranged with the musicians and crew to pay them per show instead of weekly. We had about 20 shows booked in Europe. While we were in France something strange occurred at one of the venues. We usually got the balance of the fees owing to the artistes before the show began. At this particular venue the promoter had not paid the balance up to showtime. Halfway through the show I went to the promoter's office and said to him, "I would love to have the balance for the artistes". He told me to wait. I got impatient and told him I was going to pull Jimmy Cliff off the stage. The promoter asked why I was antagonizing him for the balance when we got $20,000 for a show that had been cancelled.

Don Taylor had reminded us that one of the shows had been cancelled, so we would not be paid for that event. What he didn't tell us was that he had been paid in full for the cancelled show. The promoter went to Don Taylor, who was in the kitchen with Newton Merritt preparing meals for our team. He complained to Don that I was on his back for the balance. I said, "Listen sir, I don't care what you want to say but we normally get the balance for the show before we leave our hotel." Then I turned to Don and said, "He is complaining that I shouldn't be running him down for any money because he gave us US$20,000 for a show that was cancelled". Don Taylor's eyes popped. He had not expected the promoter to spill the beans. Don told me not to worry. He would deal with the matter. However, I was glad that I had been given the opportunity to let Newton know about the payment for the cancelled show. Newton said we should make sure that "Skipper" (Jimmy) knew about it.

Cliff and his band members on Table Mountain in Cape Town, South Africa. (Copeland Forbes Archives)

While we were driving to Marseille, the argument came up on the bus about the US$20,000 payment for the cancelled show. Don wanted to give the impression that he had informed me that he had received funds for the cancelled show and that he had advised me that he would be paying the band members for it. Don was trying to make me look bad, I blurted, "Jimmy I cannot work with this man. He is a liar. I am going home."

When we got to Marseille, I took my suitcase off the bus and asked how I could get the next train to Paris. Newton told Jimmy that I was in the lobby waiting for a car to go to the train station. Jimmy came down to the lobby and told me not to leave. He called Don to the lobby and spoke with him. Jimmy told Don he had to go. Don agreed. I stayed.

Don gave me the contracts and all the travel arrangements for the impending US tour before he left France. I soon noticed that two contracts were missing from the stash of documents Don had given me. I asked him about them. He promised to get them to me. He never did. I soon found out that those contracts were for two shows in Los Angeles and Miami which were being promoted by Don Taylor. That was why we had no contracts. Don had told us about dates at the Roxy Club where we had six shows and a guarantee of US$18,000 for the entire run. As we were heading to the West Coast, Don joined the tour. He stayed until we played the three-day (two shows per day) engagement at the Roxy Club in Los Angeles.

Don got news that Bob Marley had passed away at the Cedars of Lebanon Hospital in Miami. He immediately left the tour and headed for Miami. I stayed behind. I was going over the contract for the next show at the Old Waldorf Theatre in San Francisco, when I noticed that the capacity of the venue was the same as the one we had just played in LA. Ticket prices were the same, yet we were getting $15,000 for two performances in San Francisco and $18,000 for six performances in LA. I was curious and furious. I called Elmer Valentine at the Roxy Club in LA and said, "Elmer I'm doing my tour accounting and I misplaced my contract with you, please remind me what was the guarantee for the Jimmy Cliff performances?" Elmer responded, "You guys got $48,000 for the entire run". I told him thanks. I was shocked. Don told us $18,000 while Elmer said it was $48,000. Don had pocketed $30,000. I told Chinna and Newton and they advised me to inform Cliff immediately. I showed Jimmy the figures. He was mad. We were heading to Miami for the last show. I knew all hell would break loose. I asked Jimmy if he knew we had made a $35,000 bonus in Salvador, Bahia. He didn't. Don had not informed him.

Jimmy Cliff and Brazilian artiste Gilberto Gill toured Brazil together, 1980. (Lindsay Oliver Donald photograph)

We landed in Miami. Jimmy said he was going straight over to Don Taylor's office. I took the entourage to the hotel and checked in everyone. The Howard Johnson was packed. The passing of Bob Marley had created quite a stir. Many of Bob's family members were in town. Don Taylor's office was the hub for all Marley related activities.

While I was at the hotel, a gentleman told me that somebody was outside looking for "Jimmy Cliff's road manager". The gentleman said that the person didn't mention anyone by name but just wanted to find "the road manager". I walked to the front of the hotel. I wanted to see who was looking for "Jimmy Cliff's road manager". I saw a parked car with about six people inside. I could tell that they were Jamaicans.

I looked in the car and saw my old schoolmate 'Lip', the same person who had wanted to kill Don Taylor when I went to get Jimmy Cliff's tapes at Tuff Gong a year before. Lip told me he was looking for Jimmy Cliff's road manager. I started laughing and asked, "Colin, what you need him for?" He said Don Taylor had sent him to "deal with a matter" as the road manager was telling Jimmy Cliff bad things about him. At that point I told Colin (Lip) that I was the road manager. He was shocked. He blurted, "A you di bwoy Don Taylor want mi fi shoot?" Lip had a Glock 9 mm in his waist.

Lip jumped back in the car and sped off to see Bob's mother, Miss Booker. I called a taxi and went to Don Taylor's office. His door was open. He was sitting behind his desk with a cigar in his mouth. I hopped onto his desk and grabbed him by the collar. I threw him to the floor. I started to choke him. I quickly got a hold of myself and released him. I shouted, "Imagine you sent a man to shoot me. Suppose the man never know me?" I could not work with such a devious man. I decided to quit immediately.

I had received a call the day before from the management office of Peter Tosh in NY enquiring if I would be available to do the **Wanted Dread & Alive** tours. I spoke with Teresa Del Pozo who, along with Herbie Miller, managed Peter's affairs. I told her that I was available for the tours, I left the next day for New York.

While in NY I got a phone call from Jimmy Cliff. He was in Jamaica. I told him I had to quit as I could no longer work with Don Taylor. I informed him that I was going on the road with Peter Tosh. Don had sent a replacement road manager to Jamaica. Jimmy said he had never met the replacement before. He sent him back to Don in Florida. I told Jimmy about the hit Don had taken out on me. Jimmy was speechless. Jimmy promoted Flash Gordon who had been his stage technician to road manager. Flash had to do double duty on the road.

Working with Don was one of the greatest learning experiences I ever had. He taught me many things about the music business. Don Taylor was the driving force behind the success of Bob Marley after Bunny and Peter separated from their partner. Yet there was a disturbing side to his persona. Don seemed naturally predisposed to dishonest behaviour, a feature of his character which sullied what would otherwise have been an enormous legacy.

I will never forget the Cuban experience with Jimmy Cliff and Mutabaruka in 1981. Just before the group's departure date, Jamaica broke diplomatic ties with its communist neighbour and sent the Cuban ambassador home. As the tour and road manager, I had to seek advice from our foreign ministry and the then prime minister, Hon. Edward Seaga. I made a call to Olivia "Babsy" Grange, a close friend of mine who worked with the PM. I relayed our concerns to her and requested some advice. After two days of waiting, I received a call from Ms Grange. She pointed out that the PM said he was not telling us to proceed with our plans, and he was not telling us not to go.

We had a meeting with all members of our entourage including Jimmy Cliff and Mutabaruka. Jimmy Cliff stated that the movie *The Harder They Come* (he played the lead role of an outlaw named Ivan) ended with him trying to elude the security forces who were trying to prevent him from escaping to Cuba. Jimmy said he had not completed his mission on that occasion. In the movie, he had missed the boat in which he intended to make his escape. Jimmy said that he didn't want to miss the opportunity to visit Cuba and have life imitate art.

Cliff and Forbes in Havana, Cuba, 1981. (Copeland Forbes Archives)

We finally left Jamaica aboard the Russian Airline, Aeroflot, which had flights between Moscow, Russia and Kingston, Jamaica via Havana, Cuba once per week. We had a problem booking the return leg as the flight from Moscow to Jamaica did not operate on the date of our scheduled departure from Cuba. We would have had to stay in Havana for a few extra days for our return flight to Kingston. The promoter arranged for a charter plane to take the entourage back to Kingston to avoid our having to wait in Havana on the Aeroflot flight for five days.

We did two fantastic concerts, one at the Varadero Festival on the northern side of Cuba; the other in Havana. They were very well attended. The tour was very successful.

"Calls of nature had to be answered in an outhouse, called a pit latrine, which did not have the benefit of flushing. We had no choice but to keep our heads high if we did not want to endure the odour of the ordure."

▸ Pg 30. Chapter 1

CHAPTER 6
MAMA AFRICA: THE PILGRIMAGE

In 1980, Peter Tosh was caught up with the recording of his *Wanted Dread & Alive* album. He embarked on a European tour to support the album in 1981.The tour started in Scandinavia. I remember reaching Vienna, and hearing that the first single, "Nothing But Love" (a duet with Gwen Guthrie) had entered the Billboard Charts.

I started to hear grumblings on the road and by the end of the European tour Sly and Robbie, the Tamlins, and guitarist Daryl Thompson had quit the band .

One of the tracks on the *Wanted Dread and Alive* album was "Oh Bumbo Claat". Tosh claimed that the famous Jamaican expletive was a powerful incantation to ward off vampires and evil spirits. He was performing in New York when he requested that the song be included in his set. Keyboardist Robbie Lyn declared that he would not play on or provide harmonies for that song. We could not tell Peter this, so we decided to quietly drop the song from his set to avoid any discord.

Peter had an expectation of where the song was supposed to come in his set. When the band did not play the song. Peter said, "Stop it stop it, ah weh di bumbo claat do unnu, which song fi play now, nuh di bumbo claat song?" The band members all looked at each other and then drummer Santa Davis just went straight into "Oh Bumbo Claat". Robbie Lyn walked off the stage and went into the dressing room the moment the song started. He did not return to the stage until the song was finished. Peter did not notice that Lyn was missing. It was a close call.

By the time the tour was finished, Peter had decided that it was the end of the road for him and his management. He claimed that after the management had taken its commission, there was not much left for him. This is a perennial charge of artistes who often times do not understand the intricacies of the business of music and sometimes accuse their management wrongfully. Herbie Miller and Teresa Del Pozo headed Peter's management team at that time.

After much back and forth, it was decided that we would meet at the office of Bert Padell (Peter's business manager) in New York. The aim of the meeting was to finalise the separation between Peter Tosh, on the one hand, and Herbie Miller and his team, on the other. Those at the meeting were Mike Pantaleoni (Peter's lawyer), Paul LaMonica (ABC Bookings) Earl McGrath (Rolling Stones Records), Teresa Del Pozo (Peter's management team) and Herbie Miller's attorney. Herbie did not attend the meeting. Also present were Bert Padell, Peter Tosh and Copeland Forbes (Tosh's assistant).

Herbie's attorney requested that Miller be compensated for the remaining 18 months of the contract he had with Tosh. The attorney requested a settlement which was twice the amount of the management commission that Tosh had paid Miller in 1981. Padell requested a huddle with Peter and me for about ten minutes. Padell came up with a proposal and said he was going to make an offer that Miller's attorney could not refuse. Tosh was puzzled while Padell explained the details of the proposed deal to him. In fact, Peter seemed to have exhausted his entire catalogue of Jamaican expletives in the short meeting among the three of us.

We returned to the general meeting. Padell took the stand and made an offer to Miller's team. They whispered among themselves then asked to be excused so that they could consult with each other and, supposedly, with Herbie on the phone. They came back into the general meeting after about ten minutes and accepted the offer. The terms for the dissolution were settled. Miller would receive two payments as part of the deal. The first tranche (the larger) would be paid on the signing of the agreement. Peter would then be free to determine who would take up the mantle of his management. Tosh had completed his separation from Herbie Miller.

I was surprised to see Danny Sims when I went to Cuba with Jimmy and Mutabaruka in 1981 to do a few shows. He had come to talk with the Nigerian entertainer Sonny Okosun who was also in Cuba with us.

Danny told me he had met with Tosh in Jamaica and had struck a deal with him to manage his affairs. Peter had told Danny that I was his road manager. Danny wanted me to remain a part of Peter's team under his direction. Danny then had a meeting with Jimmy and made him an offer similar to the one he had given to Peter. Jimmy accepted. In one fell swoop, both legendary artistes were under the same management.

Danny Sims was a highly successful African American music producer, publisher, and promoter who came to Jamaica with R&B singer Johnny Nash, his business partner. Their publishing company, Cayman Music, controlled songs written by the members of the Wailers. Their JAD label released records from the Wailers on its imprint.

Danny lived on the twelfth floor of a building on East Central Park, a swanky part of Manhattan. His home was a hive of activity. He was, perhaps, the only person of his colour to live in that exclusive neighbourhood. Danny introduced me to his household which included his two brothers Paul and Eddie. Danny really wanted me to feel at home.

He also took me to his office, Copyright Services, which was located at 57th and Broadway. The company (as its name suggests) dealt with international copyright and related issues. Danny introduced me to Walter Hoffa, an attorney who spent a considerable amount of time in Florida where he also had a practice. Danny told

Tosh and Nigerian artiste Sonny Okosun in Nigeria, 1982. (Copeland Forbes Archives)

Danny Sims and wife, model Beverly Johnson. (Sims Archives)

me that Walter Hoffa was always there to provide me with any legal advice I needed. Danny also introduced me to Joey "Shorty" Armone, one of his Italian business partners. Joey was a straight shooter. He would pay regular visits to the Copyright Services offices and would hold meetings which I would attend at Elmer's in Little Italy,

I learned quite a bit from Danny about managing one's domestic affairs. He had two helpers, neither of whom spoke English. It was deliberate. Danny did not want them to understand what he was saying when he had meetings at home or was on the phone. Danny spoke very little Spanish, so it was always fun watching him trying to communicate with his helpers in his unique form of sign language.

I met Beverly Johnson, Danny's wife. She did not live with him. A top model, Beverly was the first Black woman to appear on the cover of *Vogue*. They had a daughter, Anansa. Danny named one of his labels after his daughter. Beverly would often drop off Anansa at Danny's apartment. It was during Bill Cosby's trial that I realised that when Beverly would leave Anansa for us to babysit, she had been going over to the comedian's house for auditions. During Cosby's trial Beverly claimed that she had been a victim of the comedian's unwanted sexual attention.

Peter wanted to go to Africa. He continued to experience constant headaches from the beatings he had suffered at the hands of the police in 1978. He wanted to see a bush doctor. In February of 1982, Peter and I left Jamaica for Nigeria. Sonny Okosun, whom I met in Cuba, had invited us to his homeland.

I was having a severe pain in my foot, the result of an injury I suffered in Cuba where I had fallen and pulled a ligament while riding a bike. Danny Sims took me to a Dr Auerbach in New York who told me that it would take some time to heal. Peter believed I should get some remedy for my injury in Africa.

We were finally on our way to the Motherland. We made a stop overnight in New York City to pick up some money from Peter's accountant Padell, Nadell, Fine & Weinberger. We collected US$10,000 for our trip. We forgot to call Sonny Okosun to let him know that we had stopped in NYC and would be arriving in Lagos a day late. We left the following day. Our plan was to spend a night at a hotel in Lagos and then locate Sonny with whom we would be staying.

After clearing immigration and customs at the airport in Nigeria, we got a taxi and headed into the city to book a hotel. On our way from the airport, we encountered several checkpoints, manned by soldiers and police. Each time we approached a roadblock and the members of the security realised Peter Tosh was traveling in the vehicle, they waved us through. Everyone wanted an autograph. I had some cassettes which I gave away at each checkpoint.

Things were very different at the eighth checkpoint. The police and soldiers greeted Peter politely. I gave them cassettes and autographed pictures. They took the cassettes and pictures, placed them under a tree, then picked up their M16 rifles and ordered us out of the car. Peter's unicycle was on the back seat. It could not hold in the trunk. Our suitcases and Peter's guitar were in the trunk. The soldiers told the driver that he knew that he was not supposed to carry luggage on the seat and started to beat him.

The senior officer directed the other policeman, "Take them to the station". The junior officer squeezed himself into the front seat beside me. Peter was in the back seat. When we got to the police station, the officer took the driver inside. I told Peter to wait outside. I went inside the station. I did not want Peter to get involved in the matter as I knew how easily things could get out of hand between him and the police.

Danny Sims and Copeland Forbes. (Copeland Forbes Archives)

I left Peter sitting on the sidewalk. I went out regularly to check on him. He seemed comfortable. He was surrounded by fans who were happy to be talking to such a huge star. I was in the station for over an hour when a policewoman came to me and asked if she could help me. I told her that Peter and I were visitors and that we were waiting on our driver who had been taken there by one of her colleagues. She almost choked when she heard the name Peter Tosh.

Peter Tosh outside the police station in Lagos. (Copeland Forbes Archives)

She asked where he was. I told her he was sitting outside the station. She looked outside and saw Tosh on the sidewalk surrounded by his fans. I told her that the police had arrested our driver for carrying luggage on the backseat of his car. I informed her that Sonny Okosun was supposed to have picked us up at the airport, but he was not aware that we had changed our travel schedule which was why we had to take the taxi.

The policewoman told me to give the arresting officer some money. I handed her a US$10 bill to give to him. She went inside a room and five minutes later the arresting officer came out and told us we could go. When I told Peter what had happened, he exclaimed, "Why the bumbo claat him neva say that from long time?" We left the police station and went to a hotel which the driver had recommended.

Peter was anxious to see a bush doctor. The driver said he knew a good one and he could take us to him. I thought Peter should have waited until we found Sonny Okosun but he insisted that he had to see a bush doctor as soon as possible. The driver took us to a bush doctor. When we got to the bush doctor's shrine, we sat and waited for him. He eventually came and greeted us. He took out a bottle of whiskey from a small refrigerator and offered us a drink. Peter declined his offer.

Peter Tosh and Sonny Okuson in Benin. (Copeland Forbes Archives)

I did likewise. Peter explained to the bush doctor why we had come to see him. The shaman assured Peter that he could find a remedy for his condition but that it would cost some money. Peter asked how much, telling the bush doctor that he did not want to waste any time. He wanted to get rid of his headaches.

The bush doctor asked if I had a pen? I told him yes and gave it to him. He started writing.

He did some calculations. He drew a line. He put down the total. I saw a six followed by a few zeros. I then realised the amount. He wanted 60 thousand naira. Peter agreed. I told Peter that we should wait until we found Sonny Okosun.

Before going to the bush doctor, we had visited a market where African mementoes and other paraphernalia were sold. Peter was fascinated with African art. He bought quite a few souvenirs. We had spent approximately US$1,800 at the market in Nigeria in less than a day. We were slated to stay in Nigeria for four weeks.

I asked the bush doctor if we could give him some of the money and then come back later to pay the balance. He said no. I told him I would go over to EMI Records and make a call to America and ask our accountant to send some money. We took

Tosh being interviewed by the press in Lagos, 1982. (Copeland Forbes Archives)

up our bags and were about to leave when he told us to go back inside the shrine. We complied. He took out a round board ringed with a raised edge. He threw some powder on the board. He had three crystal balls on strings. He told us to look at them as they spun. We watched the balls spinning. Suddenly, the white powder flew into the air and covered us. He informed us that the crystal ball said we should not go to the record company as it was not a good day to do business. I promised the bush doctor that we would return the following day.

When we left the bush doctor, I told Peter that we had to go over to the record company (EMI) as Sonny would be there looking for us. When we went over to EMI, Sonny had, indeed, been searching for us. He was there, ready to take us to his house where we would stay for the duration of our trip. We went back to the hotel to cancel our reservation and to see if we could get a refund, but they refused. Sonny's house was huge. He had about five wives living there.

I told Sonny about our visit to the bush doctor and how much the man was charging for his services. Sonny sarcastically asked if the bush doctor had planned to make a human being for that amount of money. He offered to take us to Benin to see a real bush doctor.

On the day of our departure for Benin, we drove around town to pick up food. We had planned to spend a week there. Peter was revolted by the sight of bread and other items of food (covered with flies) being sold to the public on the streets of

Peter Tosh and his unicycle were huge hits in Lagos and Benin, 1982. (Copeland Forbes Archives)

Lagos. He viewed this as an unfortunate legacy of colonialism. This gut-wrenching experience inspired the song "Not Gonna Give It Up".

As we were packing our belongings into Sonny's Range Rover, a little boy rode up on a bicycle and handed me a piece of paper. He said Doctor Ibo had told him to give it to me. I was wondering who Dr Ibo was when it dawned on me that it was the bush doctor whom we had visited two days before. The note said that Peter and I had to see the bush doctor immediately or we would face destruction. I showed the note to Sonny. I was nervous. Sonny crushed the paper shouting, "Rubbish". He turned to the little boy and said, "Tell the bush doctor to go to hell".

We soon started our long journey to Benin which was about five hours by car. Everything was going smoothly until about two hours into our trip when we heard a loud explosion and realised that our vehicle was skidding. I heard Peter shouting, "Jah, Jah, Jah". I was flung from the back and dropped into the front seat between Sonny and his brother who was driving. The vehicle continued sliding along the road while Peter kept shouting to Jah. I wondered whether we were experiencing the destruction that the bush doctor had threatened. The vehicle came to a halt after

Pope John Paul arrived in Benin during Tosh's visit. (Copeland Forbes Archives)

a long skid. It was filled with smoke. I tried to open the door, but I could not do so from the inside. I jumped through the window and quickly opened the doors from the outside. Peter abandoned the vehicle. Sonny and his brother followed him.

When the smoke had cleared a little, we saw that the right front and the left back tires had blown out. They were shredded. Sonny flagged down a vehicle and he and his brother went to purchase new tires. Peter and I stayed behind, sitting on the roadside. Sonny and his brother returned with the replacement tires after being away for quite a while. We got to Benin late in the night. We picked up Sonny's father who took us to a guest house. Sonny, his wife, and his brother spent the night at his father's house.

The following morning Sonny and his father came to pick up Peter and me. On the way to the bush doctor, they took us to meet some government officials who were all excited to see us in Benin City. They were, however, unable to spend much time to entertain us as Pope John Paul 11 was visiting and everyone wanted to attend the welcome ceremony.

Peter wanted to stop to take pictures of the villages through which we were passing. Each time we stopped and stepped out of the vehicle the residents would run away as soon as they saw Peter. I asked Sonny why the villagers were running away from us. He told me that they were frightened by Peter's dreadlocks and thought he was a witch. Peter was very upset that Africans were running away from a Rasta man while embracing the Pope.

Sonny's father introduced us to a bush doctor in Benin who took us into his shrine. It was a strange place with many unusual items, including the head of a bat. It was eerie. The bush doctor looked at Peter and said, "You are a smart man, people think you're crazy, but you are not. You have some poison in your head". He looked at me and said, "You my friend should never get involved with a yellow woman". He warned that I would face destruction if I did. I asked Sonny who was a yellow woman. He explained that the bush doctor was referring to light-skinned women.

The bush doctor asked the rest of us to leave the shrine so that he could attend to Peter. We obeyed him. While we were sitting outside in Sonny's vehicle, we heard a loud explosion coming from the shrine. I jumped out of the vehicle and ran back to the shrine. I peeped through the window. I saw a shirtless Peter standing on a big round stone with his hands outstretched. He might have gotten the inspiration for the cover of his *No Nuclear War* album from this experience.

The cover of Tosh's Grammy winning album *No Nuclear War*, a representation of his pose inside the bush doctor's shrine in Benin, 1982. (Neville Garrick photograph)

The bush doctor was feeding Peter some purple liquid from a bottle. He then poured the liquid in his hand and began sousing Peter's body. Peter said he felt as if his body was on fire. There was a gun on the table. I asked Sonny what exactly the bush doctor was doing. He told me that the shaman was providing Peter with protection. According to Sonny, if people tried to harm Peter with a weapon, he would simply become invisible to them, and they would not be able to hurt him. I went back inside the shrine. Peter asked, "You not going to make the man check out your foot?" I said, "Doctor Auerbach in New York already examined my foot and he told me that it was going to take some time to heal". Peter said, "No that is western doctor this is our culture". I was reluctant but Peter was insistent. I relented.

I told the bush doctor about the pain in my foot. He said that I should take off my socks. I did. He held my foot and started to rub it. He went to a cupboard and took out two bottles with liquid. He placed a basin before me and poured the contents of the bottles in it. I saw steam coming from the concoction in the basin. He instructed me to put my foot in the basin. He held my foot and put it in the "steaming" liquid. I thought the liquid would burn me, but my feet felt as if they had been immersed in ice. I was shocked. He gave me a bottle and said I should rub the contents on my foot each night before going to bed.

The bush doctor told Peter that he was going to give him something to wear around his waist. It was like a loincloth. The shaman advised him that none of the women in his life should see nor touch it. The bush doctor said that Peter had two women (one a foreigner) in his life. He added that one of them would cause Peter serious harm and would perhaps lead him to his grave.

After spending about five days in Benin we headed back to Lagos. Peter said he wanted to see Fela Kuti, a Nigerian musician whom Tosh admired and who lived in an area called Kalakuta. Sonny agreed. Peter wanted to smoke some of Fela's herb.

Fela Kuti is credited with being the prime mover behind the jazz, funk, highlife fusion known as Afrobeat. Fela's musical genius is not in question, however his radical political views not only placed him at odds with the Nigerian authorities but also with Western elites. Fela suffered as a result of his political stance, and it is believed that beatings he endured from the military authorities in Nigeria might have brought about his early demise.

Fela Kuti blew up a storm during our visit to his home in Kalakuta, Nigeria, 1982. (Sandra Izsadore photograph)

Saying Fela was unconventional would be conceding the obvious. Fela would have songs lasting for half an hour on an album and preferred to provide his audiences with brand new material (often performed for the first time) at his concerts. Fela sparked a musical revolution in Africa which is still being felt today. There are young musicians on the continent who embrace sounds from the West, including reggae and dancehall, infused with that which is essentially African.

Fela always had a large quantity of marijuana at his house. The residents of

US-born Afrobeat singer, Sandra Izsadore, with Tosh and friends at Fela Kuti's house, 1982.

the area would warn him whenever the police were entering the community. Everyone in Kalakuta seemed loyal to him.

Fela did not know we were coming to see him. He had been playing his saxophone when we arrived. He came out to greet us in his underwear. He and Peter hugged each other. He was happy to see us. Fela brought out some choice herb. Peter's eyes lit up. Fela and Peter rolled some gigantic cones. It would have been an insult to their size to call them spliffs.

We spent a wonderful evening at Fela's home. His close friend Sandra Izsadore, from California, dropped in while we were there. Fela was a fabulous host. He provided us with a wide range of edibles and beverages. Most memorable for me was the juice that Fela "ate". The liquid was so thick that it clung to the sides of the containers and had to be forcefully dislodged with a sharp spoon. Fela's house became a regular chill spot in the evenings during our stay.

A throng of people would come to Sonny's house to meet Peter during the days. One day Sonny told Peter that a high-ranking police officer would be visiting the house. Sonny told Peter that he would have to put away the marijuana while the policeman was there. Peter said, "No man, a Africa dis man what you talking about, me fi hide my herb, you must be mad". The officer came and they all had a good chat while Peter smoked his weed.

Peter was truly inspired in Africa. He composed several songs on that trip including: "Glasshouse", "Not Gonna Give it Up" and "Mama Africa". When it was time for us to leave Nigeria, we decided to go through London on our way back to Jamaica. Sonny flew to London with us. He had some business to deal with in Britain. I also had to take care of some matters in London, and Peter wanted to visit his son, Nabii, in Belgium.

We booked three studio apartments at 1 Harrington Gardens in Kensington. This was where Bob Marley & The Wailers stayed whenever they were in London. Peter spent five days in Belgium. I remained in London with Sonny and one of his wives whom he had brought with him from Nigeria.

When Peter returned to London, he wanted to buy a BMW for his girlfriend, Melody. Janet Davidson who resided in London and was a part of Peter's management team took us to buy the car. We shipped it to Jamaica. Once we had completed our chores in London we headed back to Jamaica.

The bush doctor had told Peter that when he returned to Jamaica he should go down to the sea and perform a particular ritual. We went down to Greenwich Farm by the sea and Peter followed the instructions the bush doctor had given him. I also did what the shaman had told me to do. We spent the morning fishing and did not leave the beach until about midday. We caught a reasonable number of fish. We went up to Peter's house in Sterling Castle and prepared some steamed fish with okra and crackers. I had become versed in the art of making that dish.

Tosh purchased many African souvenirs during his visit to Nigeria in 1982.

Peter and I were like brothers. We shared many things. I remember him telling me about his girlfriend, Yvonne, who had died in his arms after his car crashed with the both of them. He related to me another incident when a gas tank had exploded inside his house. He said he had left a man working in his house and had gone down the road to buy some goat milk. When he returned home, he saw a large crowd at his gate. When he went inside his kitchen, he saw pieces of the man's skin scattered all over the wall. The gas tank had exploded inside Peter's house, killing the man who was working inside the kitchen.

I have had great difficulty believing the story that Leppo, who killed Peter, had taken a rap for the Stepping Razor and had gone to prison to protect the artiste. Peter never mentioned anyone going to prison for him. I am confident that if this had been the case (given our relationship) Peter would have told me.

After Tosh returned from our private visit to Nigeria, Sims began recording an album with him. Danny chose Chris Kimsey, an engineer/producer for the Rolling Stones, to produce the album. Sims booked Dynamic Studio for the sessions. I remember the song "Johnny B Goode" was brought to the studio by Chris Kimsey and Donald Kinsey (Tosh's guitarist). They wanted Peter to cover the song. A smash hit originally done by Chuck Berry, it had sold millions.

Peter did not get to hear the song at first as he was just in and out of the studio. We laid down all the tracks and had some outtakes from the *Wanted Dread & Alive* recording sessions which we thought of using on the album. Peter's bass player, George "Fully" Fullwood, could not make the trip to Jamaica for the recording sessions. He was waiting on his green card and could not travel. We had to get another bass player, Leebert "Gibby" Morrison (a multitalented instrumentalist) for the recordings.

When I got back to the studio on the day Peter was scheduled to record the lead vocals on "Johnny B Goode" everything seemed to be at a standstill. I asked what was happening. Chris Kimsey told me that Peter (on Bunny Wailer's advice) had decided that he would not record "Johnny B Goode" and another song "Where You Gonna Run". According to Bunny, "Johnny B Goode" was written by Chuck Berry and "Where You Gonna Run" by Donald Kinsey and they both would not yield any publishing to Tosh.

I was very upset with Bunny for interfering with the project. I pleaded with Peter and told him the album needed different flavours. We were at the studio arguing when Bunny realised that he had run out of weed for his chalice and decided to go on the road to replenish his supply. As soon as he left, I went back to Peter who was sitting outside in his car and begged him to finish the song. I told him if he didn't like the song, he would not have to use it on the album. Peter finally decided that he would record the song but only in one take. I suspect he didn't want Bunny to come back and see him voicing the song. I ran inside the studio and told Chris Kimsey and Donald Kinsey to get the tape lined up as Peter was ready to voice the song.

I asked the security at the front gate of the property to alert us as soon as Bunny Wailer returned. We didn't want Bunny to come back and see Peter recording the song.

Peter looked through the lyrics and let fly a big expletive. He said he was not going to sing about Louisiana, and he was not promoting New Orleans, I looked at the lyrics of the original song, I changed them, deleting 'Louisiana' and inserting Jamaica. I took out 'New Orleans' and replaced it with 'Mandeville', a town in rural Jamaica. I made some other adjustments. I substituted "old hut" for "log cabin", and "reggae band" for "rock and roll band". I came up with the idea of letting the harmony singers do the "skana skana skana" ad lib to emphasize the guitar riff.

Chris started the tape. Peter began recording the song. He made a mistake at the end of the first verse. He stopped and told the engineer to take it from the top. I told Chris to keep that track. We went through this sequence several times. Each time Peter made a request to start over we put his voice on a different track. By the time we were finished laying the lead vocal we had used about seven tracks.

Suddenly the phone rang and the security at the gate told us that Bunny had returned. We stopped the recording immediately. Peter went back outside and sat in his car. Everything was quiet.

A Dagger for Jagger

During an interview on NBC in 1982, Peter made some threatening remarks to Mick Jagger. An angry Tosh said in the interview that he would inflict serious bodily harm on Jagger should he encounter him. Peter's publicist, Charlie Comer, called and said that Mick had heard about the threat and was traveling with a bodyguard who had been given strict instructions to take out Tosh if he came within 10 feet of Jagger. I told Peter that he shouldn't have made those remarks. Peter said he wanted to be released from Rolling Stones Records and that he needed to get the outstanding money the label owed him.

I was staying at Danny Sims' house in Manhattan when I got a call from Chris Kimsey who had co-produced Peter's album *Mama Africa*. I had not seen Chris since we had finished recording the album in Jamaica with Peter. Chris would be at the Hit Factory doing some work with Jagger later that evening and wanted me to come and hang out with them. I accepted his invitation. I didn't tell Chris that Peter was in New York. I immediately called Peter and informed him that Mick Jagger was in town and would be working later with Chris Kimsey at the Hit Factory. I told Peter that I wanted him to accompany me. I called Dennis Thompson, our engineer, and asked him to pick me up as Peter and I were going to the Hit Factory to see Mick Jagger. Carl T, Peter's cousin, would also be a part of our contingent.

Dennis asked if I had told Chris that Peter would be with me. He knew that Peter was not supposed to be within ten feet of Mick. If Chris knew that Peter was coming with me to The Hit Factory, he probably would have cancelled the session. I wanted to get Peter and Mick together to resolve their issues. However, there was no guarantee how things would turn out. It was a risky proposition.

We headed down to the Hit Factory. I rang the doorbell and identified myself. They buzzed me in. When we got out of the elevator Dennis and Carl T went to play pool in the recreation room. Peter and I went into the studio. Chris Kimsey looked up and saw Peter. He was shocked.

Peter went in and sat on a sofa in front of the mixing board. He was looking directly at Jagger voicing a track on the other side of the glass. Mick and Chris Kimsey had been the only ones there before we arrived.. Mick did not even have a bodyguard with him. When Mick looked through the glass and saw Peter sitting in the control room, he stopped singing. Chris Kimsey paused the tape. Mick opened the studio door and walked into the control room towards Peter.

Mick bared his chest, put his neck at Peter's feet and said, "I heard you wanted to kill me, if you're going to kill me, do it now". Peter who was still sitting said to Mick, "Hoy man get up off a di ground, you are a big man, and I am a big man, you're a musician, and I am a musician, you are a businessman, and I am a businessman, but is pure bumbo claat fuckry your company a deal with. I want my release from Rolling Stones". Peter had been getting offers from record labels but was stuck because he needed to be released from his contract with Rolling Stones Records.

Chris Kimsey got up from behind the console and went outside. I thought he had gone to the bathroom. Peter and Mick continued talking. I slipped outside to find Chris and saw him playing pool with Dennis and Carl T. I decided to leave Peter and Mick inside the studio by themselves. After a while, Chris went back into the studio.

Suddenly, I heard music with a distinctive guitar sound coming from the studio. I pushed the door and saw that Peter was playing a guitar. He was overdubbing the wah wah sound on one of Jagger's tracks. Chris Kimsey sat behind the console smiling. I ran outside, picked up the phone and called Charlie Comer. I told him to come to the Hit Factory immediately. "Mick and Peter are over at the Hit Factory together", I said. Charlie was frightened. He asked if they were fighting. I told him they were actually working on a song together. "I am going to send a reporter over there right away", said Charlie. Shortly afterwards there was a reporter from the New York Times who did not spend much time with us. The following day there was an article in the New York Times with the headline: "Peter Tosh and Mick Jagger a Hit at the Factory".

When they had finished recording, Mick told me that I should meet him at the Rolling Stones Records office in Rockefeller Plaza the following Monday at 5:00 pm. He informed me that he was going to meet with Earl McGrath, the president of Rolling Stones Records at that time. He said that if he had known that Peter had wanted a release from the label, he would have facilitated it. Mick emphasised that he loved Peter very much. He promised that when he and I met the following Monday, he was going to provide me with a copy of the release and a gift for Peter.

On the day I was due to meet with Mick I headed down to Rockefeller Center. I arrived at the Rolling Stones Records office at about 4:00 pm, an hour before we were scheduled to meet. Mick told Earl McGrath to draw a cheque to Peter for US$60,000. Mick gave me the cheque and handed me the release. As soon as we concluded the meeting, I walked over to 57th and Broadway to the office of Bert Padell, Peter's accountant, to apprise him of the development. As I entered his office Bert asked,

"Copeland what the hell is going on?" He told me that he had just finished a call with the "Italians downtown" who had informed him that Tosh had just received US$60,000, and that they wanted $10,000 as payment towards the money Peter owed them.

I called Peter and asked him to come down to Bert Padell's office. When Peter arrived, I told him that Mick Jagger had given me a cheque with US$60,000 for him. I told him that Mick had apologised for the delay and misunderstanding. Peter smiled and said, "Bwoy mi bredda, dat good man". I then told Peter that the Italians, who had advanced money to him through Danny Sims, wanted US$10,000 from the cheque. I still have not been able to find out how the Italians knew that we had received a cheque from Mick Jagger. Marlene, who had come to Bert's office with Peter, said, "No they must not get any money, mek dem go weh". I gently reminded Peter that the Italians had invested a large amount of money in him and needed their returns. My argument prevailed.

"I went down to Treasure Isle Studio on Bond Street for an audition. I was, however, unable to muster the courage to enter the studio. The intimidating figure of the gunslinging owner, Duke Reid, gave me second thoughts. I suppose I was just gun shy."

▸ Pg 32. Chapter 1

CHAPTER 7
MAMA AFRICA: THE ALBUM

Danny Sims was trying to secure a deal for Peter Tosh who had been released from his contract with Rolling Stones Records and was shopping around for a new label. Danny arranged with his friend, Dick Asher, vice president at CBS Records, to have a listening party in Manhattan. Peter had just finished recording his *Mama Africa* album which would be the focus of the audition.

Peter and I were on Mountain View Avenue in Jamaica on our way to the Norman Manley Airport when Bunny Wailer's Jeep pulled up beside our vehicle. Bunny's assistant, Chilbo, was the driver. He said that Bunny, who was at Jimmy Cliff's office on Lady Musgrave Road, wanted to speak with us. We went back to speak to Bunny, although we were running the risk of missing our flight and our meeting with Asher in New York.

When we reached Jimmy's office, Bunny began to interrogate us. He unleashed a barrage of questions and suggestions about the size of the advance we would be requesting. I really thought that he was being too inquisitive, but I answered his questions as it seemed that Peter wanted me to do so. Bunny was dismissive of the figures I suggested I would be proposing to CBS for the album. He described them as "peanuts". I tried to get from him how much we should request from CBS. He asked which one of us could type. My brother Patrick, who was driving us to the airport knew how to type so Bunny directed him to a desk with a typewriter and dictated a proposal to him.

Danny Sims and Peter Tosh at the Sheraton Hotel in Kingston.

I was becoming a bit concerned that we were going to miss our flight and our meeting. I looked over my brother's shoulder to see what was on Bunny's mind. He seemed to have had quite a bit on his chest – US$30 million to be exact. Bunny always thought in expansive terms. Confidence was one area in which he did not come up short. When I asked Bunny if he really expected me to seek the amount he proposed from the record company, he said that it was the kind of money RCA and Motown offered to the likes of Diana Ross and Stevie Wonder.

Bunny was drafting a deal for Intel Diplo (Peter's label) and wanted to be hitched to that arrangement. He gave me a cassette and told me that I should have the CBS executives listen to it. I asked what was on the cassette. He told me some of his songs were on it. I did not bother to listen to them. We were in a hurry. I took Bunny's proposal and his cassette and headed to the airport.

When we reached the airport, the check in counter had already closed. I begged the agent to allow us on the flight. I told her we had a very important meeting in New York with CBS Records on the following day. The representative spoke with her supervisor. They allowed us to board the flight, but we had to treat all our luggage as carry on.

Bunny had arranged for a lawyer to travel with us to oversee the proceedings, supposedly, on his behalf. When we arrived in New York, Peter went to stay at his own apartment. The lawyer and I stayed at Danny Sims' house.

The next day we all went over to CBS for the meeting. Dick Asher seemed to have invited his entire A&R Department to join him for the audition. They brought their writing pads and took copious notes. This was a serious matter. I had spoken with Danny Sims about the Bunny Wailer proposal before the meeting. Danny was very blunt in his advice, "Don't even open that fucking paper in the meeting". He repeated his instructions.

We gathered in a conference room at CBS Records for the listening party. The representatives from Columbia were enjoying the music Peter had presented. Bunny had laid down the rules that "Johnny B Goode" and "Where You Gonna Run" should be excluded from the album as Peter was not the writer of either of these songs. We were listening to "Where You Gonna Run" when Dick Asher turned to me and asked who the saxophonist was? He really liked the saxophone solo. I told him it was a young musician by the name of Dean Fraser. Asher said he had never heard of him before but thought the young Jamaican musician was amazing.

Cover of Tosh's album *Mama Africa*, 1983. (Peter Tosh Archives)

The next song on the tape was the magnificently produced "Johnny B Goode". The record company executives were rocking from the moment they heard the lush brass introduction. Peter poked me in the side and asked, "What about the cassette that Bunny gave you? Let them hear it." I told him to wait but he insisted that I should play the cassette. I took the cassette out of my pocket, stopped the tape with Peter's songs and I told my audience that they were about to hear music from Neville O' Reilly Livingstone a former member of the legendary trio, the Wailers which had also included Bob Marley and Peter Tosh. I really went to town on the introduction, and I believe even Bunny's insatiable ego would have been satisfied by the rhetorical flourish. I inserted the cassette in the player and pressed the start button. Dick

Peter Tosh and his mom, Alvera Coke, hanging out in Belmont, Westmoreland, Jamaica. (Lee Jaffe photograph).

Asher asked, "Is this a finished product? "I told him I didn't know but I could call Bunny to find out. I went into one of the executive offices to call Bunny in Jamaica.

When I got Bunny on the phone, I asked him if the tracks were finished. "You think I would give you songs that were not finished?" Bunny asked sarcastically. I then told him that the songs on the cassette did not last longer than 20 seconds. Bunny responded, "Then you think I was going to give you a full song? Mek dem bwoy swot dem, and mek dem White friend dem come record dem?" I responded, "How do you expect somebody to listen to a song for 20 seconds and make a determination on its suitability?" Bunny rebutted. I soon realised that we were going nowhere with our debate and ended the conversation. I went back to the conference room and told the group that I had not found Bunny. They removed the cassette from the machine and resumed playing the *Mama Africa* tape.

As we were heading out of the CBS office, the security called me and asked if we had just left a meeting with Suzanne de Passe. He requested that we turn back as there was an important call waiting for us upstairs. A representative from a rival record company EMI was on the line. He said he was aware that we were in negotiations with CBS but that EMI was willing to match or double whatever their rival label had offered. I was totally stunned.

Danny was impressed with the EMI offer but did not want to disappoint his friend Asher. Eventually, we decided to go with the deal from EMI. We chose a team to handle independent promotion. It comprised Bill Underwood, Fred DiSipio, Tommy Vastola, Morris Levy and Frankie Crocker. EMI gave us a US$200,000, non-recoupable advance for independent promotion.

Danny and his team had plans for a big tour with Jimmy Cliff and Peter Tosh. Danny wanted to show the world that despite their religious differences (Tosh, a Rastafarian, and Cliff, a Muslim), these two high calibre Jamaican artistes could work together. We also started the recording of Jimmy's album *Power and the Glory* which contained the hit single 'Reggae Night'. Amir Bayyan (from Kool and the Gang), Ronald Bell and Latoya Jackson were members of the song writing and production teams.

Danny had brought in a seamstress from New York to design and produce the outfits for the tour. Bunny Wailer would stop by at Jimmy's house regularly, which served as the hub for our preparatory activities. Bunny was there, ostensibly, to support Peter Tosh but we soon discovered that he had another motive. Sequoia, the seamstress whom Danny had brought in from New York, would become the mother of Bunny's children – Sensi and Asedenaki.

The tour began in California at the San Diego University amphitheatre in August 1982. It was scheduled to last 14 weeks. Everything was going according to plan. It was a great start. We had a date in Connecticut. When we got there, we realised that, contrary to the information in the itinerary, the venue was small. We were scheduled to play two shows for the night: one at 8:00 pm and the other at 11:00 pm. Although we had

Jimmy Cliff and Peter Tosh on tour, 1982. (Danny Sims Archives)

Peter Tosh at Reggae Superjam. His last concert, 1983. (Peter Tosh Archives)

reservations about the size of the venue, we went to the sound check and set up our equipment.

When we got back to the hotel, we had a meeting. We all agreed that we should not do the show. We decided that everyone should take the night off. A representative from the club came over and begged us to get the artistes to perform, noting that patrons were already in the club. The promoter spent about an hour pleading with us. He went away for about half an hour and when he came back, he was in a different mood. He was no longer pleading. His message was simple". If you don't play this gig, you don't get your equipment or your buses back".

I spoke to Jimmy and then to Peter. Jimmy said, "Let's just do this gig and get out". Jimmy realised that if the promoters backed up their threats the rest of the tour would fall apart. When I told Peter what Jimmy had said, he looked at me and asked, "Are you telling me we have to play as a ransom? I'm not in that business". I went with Jimmy's more pragmatic suggestion. We headed over to the venue and told the promoter that we would be doing one instead of two shows that night. He agreed. We did the show. It went well. The artistes returned to the hotel. I stayed behind.

I went downstairs to the promoter's office to collect the balance owing to us. The door was locked. I knocked. No one answered. I could hear people having a grand time inside. I knocked harder. The door swung open. A fellow weighing about 300 pounds and standing roughly six feet tall came to the door with a whiskey bottle in hand. He stood there glaring at me. "What the fuck do you want?", he shouted. I told him I was there to collect the balance on our fees. I explained that we had already received 50 per cent of our fees which had been sent to our booking agency and that I was there to collect the remainder. He asked what balance and swung the bottle at me.

I got out of the way and ran up the stairs. He came after me. I saw the security guard at the door, and I said, "Please, please I need some help, I went downstairs to collect the balance of my money and the promoter is chasing me with a bottle". The guard looked at me as if I was speaking a different language. He was employed to the promoter.

I saw a police car across the street. I ran towards the vehicle. I introduced myself. I explained my predicament to the police. The cop looked at his watch and said, "Let me tell you something buddy, this is Connecticut. Two o'clock is the curfew time. It is now 10 minutes to two. If you guys are still out here after 2:00 am, I'm gonna throw all your asses in jail". The cops were friends of the club owners. Clearly there was no one to protect us.

I left the scene and went to our hotel. I called Danny, who was in New York, and told him what had transpired. He asked me where I was. I told him. He asked me to hold the line while he made a call. Danny came back snarling, "Those motherfuckers don't know who they are fucking with".

Cliff, Tosh and entourage, 1982. (Peter Tosh Archives)

PETER TOSH
COMES TO
SWAZILAND - LIVE
SOMHLOLO STADIUM
Plus
– BRENDA FASSIE
– BABSY MLANGENI
– CARLOS DJE DJE
– UHURU
TOSH
HAS ARRIVED!
Dates:-
Saturday 17th
Gates open: 9:00a.m
Show starts: 12:00 noon
Sunday 18th
Gates open: 7:00 a.m
Show starts: 10.00a.m
Buy your ticket now:
EZULWINI
Lugogo Holiday Inn
Ezulwini Holiday Inn
Royal Swazi Spa
MBABANE:
Websters
MANZINI
SEE YOU THERE! SEE YOU THERE!
JAMAICA
PULSE
REGGAE SUPERJAM
NATIONAL ARENA - KINGSTON
DECEMBER 28-29-30,1983
DEC.28
Dennis Brown
Steel Pulse
Beres Hammond
DEC.29
Black Uhuru
Chalice
Leroy Sibbles
DEC.30
Peter Tosh
Gregory Isaacs
Skatalites
Give the gift of music.
GET YOUR TICKETS EARLY:
LIMITED CAPACITY
RED LABEL WINE
airJamaica
TICKETS NOW ON SALE

ON SALE NOW
Budweiser
Feyline and Budweiser present
Jamaica World Music Festival
NOVEMBER 25,26,27
Montego Bay, Freeport Zone, Jamaica, West Indies
NOVEMBER 25
Grateful Dead
B-52s
Joe Jackson
Gladys Knight & The Pips
Ronnie Milsap
Jimmy Cliff
Peter Tosh
NOVEMBER 26
Beach Boys
Aretha Franklin
Squeeze
Stacy Lattisaw
Skeeter Davis
Toots & The Maytals
Black Uhuru
NOVEMBER 27
Rick James
The Clash
Jimmy Buffett
English Beat
Bobby & The Midnites
Yellowman
Rita Marley and the Melody Makers
SHOWTIME 7:00 P.M. SHARP
Doors Open 5:00 p.m.
For Special Travel Packages and Ticket Information Call:
TRAVEL UNLIMITED/TOM LINTON
213-655-4252
A TIME TO TRAVEL
213-821-4324
$100 US (Includes all 3 nights)

Peter Tosh
AUSTRALIAN TOUR 1983 PROGRAM

I.T.S. Co-op. PRESENTS
YOUTH CONSCIOUSNESS
REGGAE FESTIVAL
PART.1
Featuring:
BUNNY WAILER
JIMMY CLIFF
PETER TOSH
JUDY MOWATT
MARCIA GRIFFITHS
with Special Guests Artistes
25th. DECEMBER 1982 NATIONAL STADIUM
KINGSTON JAMAICA
SHOWTIME: 6.00p.m.
THE MUSICAL EVENT OF THE YEAR

The Times OF SWAZILAND
'Yes Jah! I'm home again after 400 years' – PETER TOSH
STORMS! LIGHTNING! POWER CUTS
DON'T BE CAUGHT POWERLESS!
HONDA
SWAZILAND SUPPLY CENTRE
Hey, Rasta!
FOR SALE
FONTEYN
Half acre plots
Reasonable Prices
VJR AGENCIES

I later learned that some of Danny's associates had gone over to the club and given the promoters a vicious beating. The club was wrecked. Danny went down to Norby Walters' office and hit Richard Halem (the agent who had booked the tour) across his back with a chair. I don't know if that was Danny's way of showing the guy that he had his back. Maybe it was his way of breaking the back of a problem. Danny tried to throw Halem through the window from the fourteenth floor. Norby called me frantically asking what had happened.

Danny was quick to open doors for those he favoured and windows for those who crossed him. Defenestration, the act of throwing one's opponent through a window, seemed the punishment of choice for Danny.

The word got out to all the promoters across the United States that they should not mess with Danny's boys. When we got to the other cities, we were paid our balances by the time we checked into the hotels. We did not even have to wait for the customary sound check to secure our balances. Danny's reputation had preceded him. His presence loomed large even in his absence.

World Music Festival, Montego Bay

We attended the World Music Festival in Montego Bay 25-27 November 1982. Our booking agent was able to fit the festival into our tour schedule.

Barry Fey of Feyline Productions and Budweiser out of Denver Colorado were the promoters of the event. Feyline Productions was a promoter of big rock concerts. They told us that if we had any equipment in the US that we wanted to take to Jamaica they could get them in for us. They pointed out that there was a shipment going into Montego Bay from Miami for the concert. Peter had a good amount of equipment which he wanted to get down to Jamaica from New York. This was a golden opportunity. We got the equipment down to Miami and shipped them to Jamaica. We could have brought in anything we wanted in that container. It was not inspected on arrival in Jamaica

Peter was originally scheduled to perform on the opening night (25 November) of the World Music Festival, but his appearance was shifted to 27 November, the finale. The PA system broke down during the third song of his performance. Prior to Peter's taking the stage Aretha Franklin, English Beat, Rick James, Yellowman, Third World, and Rita Marley, had all performed without incident. Peter, at first, seemed unfazed by the technical glitch. He was joking with the members of the audience. However, his mood would soon change. He quickly became impatient and blurted out, "Hoy

hoy hurry up and fix it because you know I am a man when I draw my sword I don't play". He had a sword hanging from the waist of his white Kung Fu outfit.

Soon afterwards I heard Peter say, "What the bumbo claat dis? Imagine, heathen come to perform duppy come to perform, ghost come to perform, and when the Rasta man come to perform this system breakdown. Don't let me draw mi sword pon unnu bumbo claat". The problem with the sound was soon resolved and a rainbow appeared in the sky. Tosh gave a magnificent performance and an impassioned speech for the legalization of marijuana.

When he left the stage, Peter was surrounded by a throng of fans who were congratulating him on his stellar performance. He, however, suspected that I was displeased with his expletives. "Weh dem seh mi do now?" he asked sheepishly. I told him we would speak when we got back to the hotel. The following day I had a frank talk with him about the expletives in his performance. He apologised and promised to cease using them on stage.

After the festival we were due to head back to the US to resume the tour. Jimmy reported that he had hurt his back and couldn't continue the tour. We were left to proceed with Peter alone. Fortunately for us the tour was almost complete.

Rick James and Peter Tosh at the World Music Festival, Montego Bay, Jamaica. (Copeland Forbes Photograph)

During the tour we had been encountering a few challenges with regard to the sequencing of the performances. Jimmy said that he had been assured by Danny that he and Peter would alternate in closing the shows. Danny told me that although both Jimmy and Peter had equal billing it was Tosh who would bring the curtains down each night. Peter had closed the show in San Diego. Jimmy believed that he would bring the curtain down in Arizona. Peter was adamant that he should close all the shows. Jimmy reluctantly agreed. I could sense a distinct change in Jimmy's mood. He was deflated. He continued the tour, nonetheless. I believe that this development had a significant bearing on Jimmy's decision to leave the tour and Danny Sims' management.

Quite a bit of money had been spent on both Jimmy and Peter. In fact, I personally carried cash into the island for them both from Danny and his associates. Danny spent a considerable sum on recording and related expenses.

Danny faced a grave dilemma when Jimmy pulled out from under his management. How was he going to recover the huge sums that he had expended on Jimmy? He reached a deal with Jimmy. Cliff gave Danny the rights to the video recording of his live performances at the World Music Festival. Danny convinced his investors that the video had commercial value. The word was that a total of some three quarter million dollars had been expended on the projects to that point. While much of the expenditure was legitimate and justified, a significant portion of the funds was spent extravagantly.

Peter had one show left for 1982. It was Youth Consciousness which was being staged by Bunny Wailer at the National Stadium in Kingston on Christmas Day. This was Bunny Wailer's first show as a solo act since leaving the Wailers in 1973. I told Bunny that I did not believe Christmas Day was a good time to put on a concert. He didn't heed my advice. I estimated he had about 8,000 people in a venue with a capacity of 30,000. It was a well-produced event, nonetheless. I will never forget the scene after the show when Bunny exited the stadium in his pickup like a cowboy riding into the sunset with a huge plume of dust trailing behind him.

A few days later, Peter asked me if I had heard from Bunny since the concert. I told him that I had not. Peter was getting anxious as he needed to pay his musicians who had performed on the show. The situation was particularly urgent because two of Peter's musicians lived in the US and he needed to pay them so they could get their flights back home. Peter told me that he had tried calling Bunny and had gone to his office but could not find him.

The following day Peter came to my house. He had a machete in the front of his vehicle. He said he was going in search of Bunny. He told me he was going to drive to Kencot where Bunny loved to hang out with his soccer playing friend. Peter was right. When we reached Kencot, Bunny's orange Jeep was parked outside his friend's gate. Peter parked his vehicle and took up his machete.

Peter pushed the gate open and there was Bunny sitting on a piece of wood, smoking a chalice. Peter stepped towards Bunny who immediately stopped puffing. Bunny realised Peter was in a militant mood. Peter shouted at Bunny, "Hoy, hoy, you short ass midget with a high chest, weh mi bumbo claat money? I need to pay my musicians as two of them have to go away today. One week now and nobody can find you. What kind of bumbo claat business you a deal wid?" Bunny went into his briefcase and took out a cheque book. He asked to whom should he make the payment. Peter told him he should pay the cheque to me. Peter took the cheque and left while Bunny's friends sat in amazement.

When we left Kencot, I told Peter that we should stop by Bunny's office for a minute. When we got there, I saw a throng of people who had worked on the show and had not been paid. I told them that it was futile waiting for Bunny at his office because he was not coming there, given the circumstances. I told them Bunny was by his soccer-playing friend's place in Kencot.

Many of those whom Bunny had not paid knew where his friend lived. I showed them the cheque Bunny had given me. People started running to their cars and jumping on their bikes and bicycles. All roads were leading to Kencot. By the time I had reached the bank many of those who had been camping out at Bunny's office for payments were trying to cash their cheques. The line was long. I had to speak to the manager, or I would not have been able to get the foreign exchange to pay Donald and Fully so they could catch their flights back home.

The bank manager was most cooperative. He had attended the Youth Consciousness Concert. He arranged for the cashing of my cheque and the securing of the foreign exchange. When the manager came back to me with the funds he asked if there were others who would be seeking to cash cheques on the same account. I told him that many of those in the bank had cheques drawn on Bunny Wailer's account.

The manager told me that there might not be sufficient funds to cash all the cheques as there was only a small amount of money left in the account. I went out and told those who were waiting in line to be paid that they should not waste their time. There was no money in the account. I left the bank as I had to take Fully and Donald to the airport. I am not sure what transpired after I had left the bank.

In 1983, we embarked on a world tour to promote the *Mama Africa* album. It would kick off in Australia. I was, by then, spending more time in Jamaica and had acquired a house in Cherry Gardens.

Danny and his team managed to secure an appearance for Peter on the American Music Awards (AMA). This was a major coup. It required enormous influence on the part of the artiste's management to get an appearance on such a prestigious event. There was no denying that Danny had clout.

When Peter came to pick me up at the airport in Jamaica, I could see he wasn't really thinking about his scheduled performance on the AMA. When I got to his house, I saw that there was definitely something wrong with his girlfriend, Marlene. He said he needed to take her to a doctor, not a medical one. He wanted to go to a bush doctor in Westmoreland. I told him we were only going to be away for two days so he could attend the AMA and return to Jamaica to deal with Marlene. He was adamant that he wasn't going to leave her in that state by herself. "Boy, I can't leave", he said.

I called Danny to inform him that Peter wasn't going to be able to make it to the performance. Danny told me to do whatever I could to get Peter to change his mind. I tried but Peter wouldn't budge. I called Donald Kinsey the guitarist in Chicago and told him to stay put. I did the same with George 'Fully' Fullwood, the bass player in California.

Peter and Marlene journeyed down to Westmoreland to see the bush doctor. They did not find him. He was on vacation in Miami.

It was March. We would soon be ready to go to Australia for the first tour of the year. Peter fell ill. He had a pain in his lower back. He seemed to have dislocated his coccyx, or what we in Jamaica would refer to as his tailbone. I took him to a chiropractor who examined his back. The chiropractor, a Dr Officer, recommended chemotherapy. Peter refused stating that he did not want to suffer the same fate as Marley. There was an alternative which did not sit well with the macho image of Jamaican men. The chiropractor would have to insert his hand into Peter's rectum and straighten the coccyx. Peter went with the second option. The procedure was very painful.

We departed for Australia as soon as the procedure was done. We left Jamaica on the Wednesday and arrived in Australia on the Friday. We were slated to perform that night at the Horndern Pavilion in Sydney, a few hours after our arrival in Australia. We went straight from the airport to the venue for a sound check. We then rushed to our hotel, grabbed something to eat and got dressed for the show.

Dr Officer was a part of our entourage. He would not have allowed Peter to make the trip without his being there. We had made a deal to pay Dr Officer the

Tosh executes one of his karate moves, 1978. (Peter Simon photograph)

amount he would normally get from his practice for four weeks. He told Peter to refrain from doing his high kicking routine. Dr Officer stood by the stage for the first show. Peter started his performance sitting. However, when the music hit, he was feeling no pain. He started doing his karate moves. The doctor was worried. By the time we came around to the third show we were convinced that Peter had been sufficiently healed. I decided to tell the doctor that he could leave. The doctor had spent two weeks in Australia with us before we decided to send him back home.

We finished the tour on a high. Everything was going well except the relationship between Danny and his investors.

In early 1983, problems started to develop between Danny and his investors who needed justification for his expenditure. I was getting ready to go to Jamaica when Danny got a call from the investors in Little Italy. They needed us to attend a meeting at Elmer's. I didn't want to go and reminded Danny that I had a flight to catch. Danny said we had to go to the meeting. The investors sent a limo to Danny's apartment to take us to the meeting.

We went to the meeting which was convened in a very large room. There was a sizable gathering eating spaghetti and meatballs. Danny and I joined the table. Suddenly, I heard a voice from the other end of the table intoning, "Copeland all we need is what we laid out, not a penny more not a penny less". It was the voice of "Shorty", Joey Armone.

When we had finished eating, I started going through the accounts. I immediately saw some discrepancies. I pointed them out and Danny got mad. I thought he was going to kill me. He turned to me at one point and asked if I was with or against him. I told him I was not against him and that I was only pointing out that the artistes were being charged twice in some instances. Money had actually been legitimately spent but there was quite a bit of double billing.

I had hired a lawyer named Bobby Urban to handle Peter's affairs. On our way back from the meeting in Little Italy Danny and I stopped by Urban's office. Danny and Bobby got into a heated argument about the handling of Peter's accounting. Danny hit Urban over the head with a chair. I was scared, I didn't know if Danny was going to hurt me too. We had to find a way for the investors to recover their outlay. I arranged for EMI to give Danny and his associates a three-point override on Peter's deal with the label. Danny and his associates would have to recover, in full, the US$300,000 Peter had owed them.

I remember making a trip to New York and going to Danny's apartment hoping to meet with him. I could not find him. It was then that I realised that it was the investors who had owned Danny's apartment all along. They were looking for him too. Danny had fled

I would later encounter Danny (on one of his trips to Jamaica) while he was trying to resolve an outstanding issue he had with members of the Wailers. Danny had entered a publishing contract with the Wailers (Peter, Bunny and Bob) in 1968 through his company, Cayman Music. He alleged that the Wailers owed him. The Wailers had, reportedly, written songs under different names to circumvent the publishing deal they had with Danny. They claimed Danny owed them money for their publishing. According to the Wailers they did not receive any money from the publishing for their *Chances Are* album. They contended that this was in addition to other projects for which they had not been compensated. I suppose both sides eventually reached a settlement.

I didn't see Danny again until 1988 when I was selected to take charge of the African **Reggae Sunsplash** tour. We sat and talked for a long while. Danny told me what had happened and why he had to go underground. The next time I saw him was in 2012, when he came to Jamaica for the screening of a documentary on Bob Marley. We sat and talked, as was customary. It was the last time I would see Danny alive. He passed shortly after he returned to the US from South Africa. Norby Walters, the booking agent, ended up in prison. Tommy Vastola, the independent promoter, was also incarcerated. Joey Armone, the investor, also served a long time behind bars.

Bunny Wailer had introduced Peter to Marlene. Bunny had been having a relationship with Marlene's elder sister. Marlene was much younger than Peter and was quite attractive. They seemed to be very much in love and there was little that Marlene did that invited Peter's censure. Marlene's involvement in Peter's professional life grew, exponentially, over the years, but her impact seemed largely negative. Her contentious persona often caused the group embarrassment, and everyone was wary of getting a tongue lashing from her.

One of the early signs of things to come was an incident at the World Music Festival in Montego Bay. Rick James and Peter had become close friends. I remember we went to the venue with Rick during the festival and drove backstage although Peter was not scheduled to perform on that night. We were enjoying the show when we were alerted that there was a fight between Marlene and a security guard. Marlene was backstage selling T-shirts. The security advised her that this was not allowed. They offered her a stall. She refused. She saw nothing wrong with spreading her wares and displaying them atop Peter's vehicle. Others thought it was unsightly and inappropriate. Peter was furious and shouted to the security that they should leave his woman alone. Robbie Lyn, Peter's, keyboard player said it was a disgraceful scene and declared that he would be leaving the band at the end of the tour.

Peter had been talking to Claudette Kemp (Beres Hammond's then manager and lover), about purchasing a house for Marlene and himself. Kemp, who would later manage Capleton, was the architect of Hammond 's Harmony House label. She was also in real estate and insurance and had shown Peter a house at 5 Plymouth Avenue in Barbican which he loved. He took me to see it and told me that I needed to go to New York to pick up some money for the deposit on the house which was owned by Ronnie Nasralla, a prominent Jamaican figure in entertainment and media. Ronnie had told Peter that he could go ahead and occupy the house as soon as he paid the deposit. Peter was in a mad rush to get the deposit. He did not want to lose the deal.

Peter Tosh and his lady Yvonne who died in a car crash. (Lee Jaffe photograph)

I went to New York and picked up the money. However, the exercise would not be without incident. I had collected US$40,000 and I wanted to deliver it safely into Peter's hands. As soon as I got the cash, I arranged to leave New York. I was not able to get a direct flight to Jamaica on the day I intended to leave NYC. I had to take a flight to Miami and then catch another to Jamaica the following day. There was a US$10,000 cap on the amount of money one could bring into the island without having to make a declaration. I was carrying US$40,000 which was US$30,000 above that threshold.

When I reached the airport in Miami, I was in for a shock. The lady at the check in counter asked me for my travel documents. I opened my briefcase to retrieve my passport and realised that I had left the two envelopes, with a total of US$40,000, in the pillowcase at the hotel where I had stayed the previous night. I had put the money in my pillow and had slept on it as a security measure. In the rush to reach the airport, I had forgotten that I had slept on the money and left it in the pillowcase.

I dashed from the check in counter, jumped into a taxi outside the Miami Airport, and sped back to the hotel. I leapt from the car as we approached the hotel and darted inside. I ran down the corridor and into the room in which I had stayed. The housekeeper was at the door of the room I had earlier vacated. The door was open. I sprinted towards the bed and picked up the pillow. I felt the envelopes, much to my delight. I quickly took them from the pillowcase and ran back to the awaiting taxi.

I went back to the check in counter at the airport. The lady said, "Mr Forbes I asked you for your passport and you ran away from me". I calmly noted, "Miss if you

Melody Cunningham, mother of two of Tosh's children – Jawara and Niambe, on the **Mystic Man** *tour*, 1979. (Lee Jaffe photograph)

knew why I ran you would be very surprised. It had nothing to do with you". I didn't tell her why I had made a dash when she asked for my travel documents. I suspected that by telling her I would have invited unnecessary scrutiny.

I boarded my flight and put the two envelopes in my winter boots. If the authorities at the Norman Manley International Airport saw my coming from Miami in winter garb as an oddity, they certainly did not let on.

After clearing immigration and customs, I headed straight to Peter's house in Sterling Castle. When I arrived at his house, Peter was relieved. I took out the two envelopes and handed them to him. I told him to count the money. He refused. I left Peter's house as quickly I could. I was very tired. I needed to get some rest. When I got down to Red Hills Road, I realized I had given him the money without getting a receipt. I turned back so that I could get proof that I had given him the money. When I returned to his home, Peter was fast asleep on his living room floor.

The two envelopes were on the kitchen counter. I took them up and woke him saying, "How can you leave the envelopes on the counter, suppose somebody come in and take out some of the money?" He replied. "No man, nobody can touch that. Any man touch it hand drop off". I wrote a receipt and asked him to sign it. He did. I headed back down the hill.

The following day Peter went down to his mechanic on Maxfield Avenue to change some of the money. He discovered that three US$100 bills were missing. When I had gone back to get the receipt, I had seen a group of men milling around the yard by Peter's house. It is possible that one of them might have taken the money out of the envelopes.

Soon after Peter moved into his new house with Marlene, he had to make a quick trip abroad to deal with some personal issues. One of his friends decided to pass by the house, unaware that Peter had gone overseas. The friend was stunned by what he saw. Peter's two vehicles were badly damaged. Distressed, the friend (not able to find Tosh) informed me of his discovery. I immediately drove up to Peter's residence to see for myself.

I, too, was shocked when I saw the state of the vehicles. I asked Marlene who had damaged the vehicles. She boldly confessed that she had done it. Marlene had apparently taken a baseball bat to the windscreens, the rear-view mirrors and the headlights of Peter's Volvo. The BMW was also badly damaged as Marlene had pushed it to the edge of a cliff. I asked her why she had damaged the vehicles. She responded with a string of profanities. I left immediately and called Peter in New York.

I was very concerned about how Peter would react to the news. I had seen him chase his son Andrew (who had scratched his father's car) with a baseball bat. I

Peter and Marlene share a tender moment. (Peter Tosh Archives)

really did not know what to expect. Both Andrew and his brother, Dave, were waiting to see how their father would handle the matter. I went to meet Peter at the airport and took him to his house. When he viewed the wreckage, he removed his glasses and exclaimed, "Bumbo Claat, a wah dis." Then using his special name for her, he shouted, "Lene". She came down to meet him. He gently hugged and kissed her. Peter turned to me and said, "Rass claat, mi bredda just call Janet Davidson in England for me and order all the parts we need".

Janet's father worked with a Volvo and BMW dealer in London. Peter did not want to wait for the parts to be shipped from London. As soon as Janet ordered all the new parts I flew over to London to get them to Jamaica. It was quite a task schlepping these parts, in huge boxes and cases through the airports. I remember a customs officer saying to me, "You only need an engine to have a complete car". My problems were compounded by my itinerary: London, New York, Miami, Kingston. I returned to Jamaica and the vehicles were soon repaired.

I soon got a visit from Marlene. She wanted to retrieve the papers for the house Peter had bought "for her". She said she had heard that I was the person who was in possession of the documents. She gave me a tongue lashing with the obligatory expletives. She let fly that Peter had told her about the trip he and I had made to Africa. She said that Peter had told her that the bush doctor had predicted that Melody (with whom Tosh had been living at the time of his visit to Africa) was going to kill him. The bush doctor had said no such thing, at least not in my presence.

Another day, I went to Peter and Marlene's house. I did not see Peter's car. Marlene was wearing the loincloth which the bush doctor had given to Peter in Nigeria. She told me that he had gone to visit his mother in Westmoreland.

I got into my car and headed back to Lady Musgrave Road where I was staying while in Jamaica. I was traveling along East King's House Road when I saw Peter's Volvo approaching from the opposite direction. We pulled over and stopped near the house where Gregory Isaacs used to live. I told Peter I was just coming from his house where I had seen Marlene with the cloth, he had received from the bush doctor in Africa, wrapped around her head. He began to relate to me what had happened.

He said that just before he left his home for Westmoreland, he was in his bedroom putting the loincloth around his waist. Marlene called him to chop some coconuts for her. Peter said he hid the cloth under his pillow and went to chop the coconuts. He got a call from his lawyer to whom he spoke for a while and after the telephone conversation he drove out of the house forgetting that he had left the cloth under his pillow.

Peter claimed that it was after he had reached Westmoreland and was relaxing at his mother's house that he realised that he had not taken the cloth from under the pillow. He said he left Westmoreland immediately and had been heading home to find the cloth when he encountered me on the way.

He went home and tried to get the cloth from Marlene. She refused. She had become attached to it. There is a representation of Marlene with the white cloth around her head on the cover of the *Mama Africa* album. Marlene instructed the graphic artist that she wanted to be so depicted on the album jacket.

We were coming close to the end of the year, and we did a tour of the USA which not only included stops on the mainland but dates in Hawaii (Honolulu and Maui) before returning to Jamaica for a break. We had scheduled shows for Brazil, Swaziland and Jamaica to bring the curtains down on what was an incredible year. When we came back to Jamaica, Marlene had become even more assertive. Bunny was busy angling for more influence and these two forces were conspiring to determine the course of Peter's career in the ensuing months.

Both Marlene and Bunny agreed that Peter should not go to Brazil even though Tosh had already received payment in full for the date. The promoter had already bought the airline tickets and made the necessary arrangements for Peter and his entourage to make the trip. However, my argument held no sway. Bunny and Marlene prevailed.

I asked about the status of the tour to Swaziland and Peter told me that he would still be going ahead with it. Africa was important to him. I soon realized that Bunny Wailer had his own agenda for Peter. He wanted to establish his own version of the

Wailers. His aim was to assemble a group under the name Never Ending Wailers. The group would include Junior Braithwaite (original Wailer), Constantine "Dreamy Vision" Walker, Peter Tosh and Bunny himself. Bunny had booked time at one of the top recording studios for them to start producing tracks for an eponymous album. This move would have put a halt to Peter' s solo career which was on a roll.

The tour to Swaziland was on schedule; however, Peter did not seem to want to take Marlene with him to Africa. Perhaps he was trying to avoid the drama on the road. I had a few outstanding matters that I had to deal with in New York before the tour began so I took a quick trip up to the Big Apple. While I was in New York, I asked my brother Patrick in Jamaica to make sure that everybody received inoculations and tablets which were requirements for those visiting Africa.

Patrick called a few days later and told me that there was a little problem. He said he had gone up to Peter's house and had overheard the artiste on the phone telling his drummer, Santa, to hurry up and get his shot. Marlene was in earshot of Peter and realised that the trip to Africa was imminent and that she had not been included. She immediately accosted Peter about her exclusion from the entourage. He was not able to provide a suitable explanation for her omission.

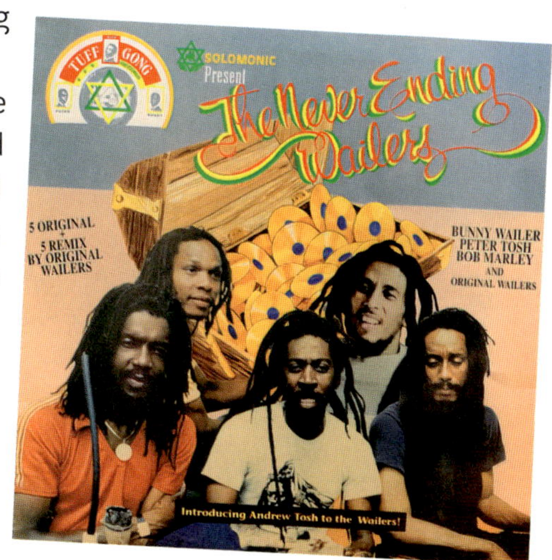

Album jacket *Never Ending Wailers*

Peter told Patrick to tell me to add Marlene to the entourage. I told Patrick that I did not believe that the promoter would be willing to underwrite the cost for Marlene's travel. I called the promoter, however, and told him that we had to add a technical person to the traveling party. I informed the promoter that it was essential that this person be included in the entourage. I had the promoter make the ticket in the name of M. Brown as I did not want him to know that it was a woman whom I was adding to the list, as I thought this might have aroused some suspicion.

Our entourage flew from Kingston to London and then to Germany. We went from Germany to Zimbabwe. The promoter had chartered four planes to take us from Zimbabwe to Swaziland. Peter had made it very clear that he did not want to go through South Africa. We would have had to go through South Africa to reach Swaziland, had we taken a commercial flight.

It was not, at that time, deemed appropriate for recording artistes to travel to South Africa as this was still the period of apartheid. Nelson Mandela was still in prison. Peter had refused many offers (paying huge sums) to perform in South Africa. He was afraid to even have a connecting flight through the racist nation as he knew that someone could take his picture at the airport and use it for propaganda purposes.

Earlier that year, Peter had done an interview with a journalist in New York who had asked him if he would perform in South Africa. He had said, "Yes, but the only way I would play is if I am performing for my people. Why should I keep my music away from my people?" The journalist distorted Peter's answer and published an article with the headline "Peter Tosh Said He Would Play in South Africa". It caused quite a bit of controversy. The misrepresentation angered Peter.

Things went relatively smoothly until we reached Germany. We were trying to get a connecting flight to Zimbabwe when a lady who was pushing a cart along the concourse accidentally hit Marlene from behind. Marlene had to be restrained from attacking the frightened woman. The musicians quickly left the scene. Fortunately, many in the airport were not familiar with the choice Jamaican fabrics (expletives) Marlene was unfurling in the airport or she would perhaps have been arrested.

There was a question on the Zimbabwean immigration form which asked how much money the traveller was bringing into the country. Marlene, apparently, had not answered that question. The immigration officer asked her why she had not answered the question. She told him that she did not need to travel with money as she was with her man. The immigration officer told her not to speak to him in that manner. She became irate. She berated the immigration officer who was ready to deport her. Peter intervened and the officer was taking steps to refuse both of them entry. A customs officer, to whom I had just given a copy of Peter's *Equal Rights* album, pleaded with the immigration officer telling him that we were in transit to Swaziland and would not be staying in Zimbabwe. The immigration officer relented but not before issuing a very stern warning to us.

It was a three-and-a-half-hour flight from Zimbabwe to Swaziland. We arrived safely in Mbabane, Swaziland (now Eswatini) and went quickly to the Holiday Inn where we had been booked. The hotel had an annex where Peter, Marlene and I were scheduled to stay. Carl T (Peter's cousin who took care of the artiste's food) also stayed in the annex with us. Tosh was slated to perform on Saturday 17 and Sunday 18 December at the Somhlolo National Stadium. People were walking through borders coming from South Africa and adjoining territories to attend the shows. Some patrons who had tickets for the Saturday show did not reach on time due to delays in getting processed at the border.

The security in Swaziland closed the borders due to the flood of people coming into the country from neighbouring territories. The promoters allowed those who had tickets for the show on Saturday (but were late) to use them on Sunday. The first night went very well. The Africans were thoroughly enjoying the opportunity of seeing one of their favourite acts perform on their own soil.

Suddenly the music stopped. Marlene was onstage talking to Peter. Tosh walked up to the microphone and told the audience that he would not be continuing the show unless the promoters opened the gates and allowed everyone on the outside to enter without charge. There were about 5,000 people outside wanting to see the show but could not afford the entrance fee.

I was stunned. How could Peter have made such a declaration? He had been contracted to perform at a paid event. His fees had already been sent to an escrow

Tosh on stage in Somhlolo Stadium, Swaziland, with his custom-made M16 shaped guitar, 1983. (Forbes photograph)

account. He had no right to determine what the promoters should charge. Peter was concerned that people had travelled many miles to see him, he felt that it was not right for them to be turned away because they could not afford the entry. Yet, Peter gave no indication that he would have been willing to waive his fees. Clearly, Peter wanted to engage in an act of charity but not at his own expense.

When the fans outside the stadium heard Peter's pronouncement, they broke down the walls and gates to gain entry. Thousands poured into the stadium without paying. Many ran with their fists raised straight towards the VIP area in front of the stage. The security could not restrain them

Peter was pumped when saw the crowd flooding into the stadium. He took up his M16 guitar and put the strap around his shoulder. The crowd went wild. He began performing the song "Apartheid". The stadium erupted. Everyone was in a frenzy as Peter sang, "We gonna fight, fight, fight, fight against apartheid". The entire stadium was singing and dancing.

The promoter came to me and said that he was going to sue for breach of contract. He was on solid legal grounds. "How could Peter have done such a thing?" he asked. The promoter said he was going to freeze our fees in the escrow account. He went away and then he came back and said "Mr Forbes, I thought about it. I know it's not your fault, but you have to tell your artiste that he cannot do these things".

The show went well. Peter had given another superb performance. The audience and the promoter were pleased.

During this time, I had managed to secure a merchandising deal for Peter covering southern Africa. I encouraged him to sign the agreement as there was an enormous amount of bootlegged merchandise (with his image) being peddled in the region. I informed him that going into a deal with someone from the region would help to stem the illegal trade in his image. Peter signed the contract and received US$10,000 in travellers' cheques on the spot. He handed them to Marlene.

We successfully completed our assignment in Swaziland. It was time for us to return home. While we were still in Swaziland the promoter explained that he was having problems getting everyone on the same flight from London back to Kingston. He said our entourage might have to wait until after Christmas in order to get everyone on the same flight from Heathrow to Norman Manley. Peter did not mind staying a few more days but some of the musicians did not like the idea. They wanted to be home for Christmas.

Our keyboard player, Keith Sterling, said he did not want to go back to Zimbabwe on a small plane. He was terrified on the flight from Harare to Mbabane and said he would not be able to make a return trip on a small craft. He noted that he would prefer to wait for a large plane which would take him to South Africa. We would have had to leave him in Swaziland as the plane to South Africa would depart later in the afternoon. Despite the fact that we were flying out early, Keith came to the airport with us.

While we were at the airport the promoter complained to me about Marlene. He said she was refusing to allow his pregnant girlfriend to travel on the same plane with us back to Zimbabwe. Marlene, he claimed, was degrading his girlfriend, who was Black, for being pregnant with the child of the promoter who was White. The promoter told Marlene that he was the one who had hired the planes. Marlene was unmoved. Patrick, who was the road manager, intervened and said he would switch planes with the promoter's girlfriend. Patrick would travel on the plane carrying Marlene, Peter, and me and give the promoter's girlfriend his place on the other aircraft. Peter sat quietly through the turbulence on the ground. Telling Marlene she was wrong would just not fly.

Keith Sterling looked around and realized he was the only person left at the airport. He felt afraid. Our flight was poised for take-off when our pilot brought the plane to a sudden stop. Sterling was standing in the middle of the runway waving at our plane. He had second thoughts about waiting on the large aircraft to South Africa. Sterling was afraid that a lion or some other animal might devour him while he was waiting alone at this eerie airport.

We landed safely in Zimbabwe with a frazzled Sterling. We headed to the Ambassador Hotel where we would spend the night before heading to London.

I soon heard a pounding on my door. It was Santa Davis. He told me that I needed to go up to Peter's room as there was a big problem. I hurriedly complied. The door was open when I reached Peter's room, Marlene and the hotel manager were screaming at each other. She was pointing in the manager's face and telling him to leave her room. I went up to them and said, "Excuse me! excuse me! what is happening here?" The manager said, "This woman is very disrespectful". The manager explained that the guests had been complaining about the smell of fish. Marlene was cooking fish in her room and the odour had permeated the entire floor. The manager said that he had gone to tell her that no cooking was allowed in the room. He had informed her that there was a kitchen downstairs where she could do her cooking. She had refused his offer. It seemed she just wanted to create a stink.

The manager turned to me and said, "Mr Forbes I lost seven members of my family fighting for the liberation of this country. I am not going to let a woman from the western world disrespect me in my own country. I want her out. Now!" The hotel manager left and headed downstairs. I followed him. He was mad. He said he wanted

Peter and his entire entourage out of the hotel immediately. He claimed that there was also a strong scent of marijuana on the floor. I pleaded with him to allow us to stay as we were leaving in the morning. Our keyboardist, Sterling, ran upstairs and brought back the stove and the utensils that Marlene had been using. Sterling wanted to show that the cooking had stopped. The manager was not impressed. He was insistent that we should leave. I managed to get a representative of the promoter to enter a plea for us. It worked. The manager relented. I later gave him a copy of *Mama Africa*.

We had to rush to the airport the following morning. Our ride was late. We managed to grab whatever seats were available on the British Airways flight from Harare to London. After the meal was served, there was a line of passengers waiting to use the restroom. Marlene jumped up from her seat and started pushing ahead of those in the line. A man who had been standing at the head of the line touched Marlene on the shoulders indicating to her that there was a queue. She spun around and delivered a left hook to his stomach. "What you want me to do stand up in line and piss up myself?" she vociferously queried. Everyone who had been ahead of her in line just stood back without a murmur.

We landed in London and boarded the flight to Kingston. It was a double decker plane. Peter and Patrick were sitting upstairs together. Marlene and I were downstairs. When the plane reached cruising altitude, Marlene started walking around looking for Peter. She went upstairs. She started arguing with the flight attendants who told her that she would not be allowed upstairs if she did not have a seat there. She pushed past them and went to the area where Peter and Patrick were sitting. She shouted, "Hey Copeland brother, what you doing up here with mi man? I am the one supposed to be up here". Patrick picked up his bag and switched seats with her.

We arrived safely in Jamaica about seven days before the Super Jam show was scheduled to take place. The promoter Kingsley Cooper was pleased to know we were back on the island in time for his show. However, Kingsley called me the following day, confused. Marlene had reached out to him saying that she wanted all the money (up front) for the show. This, he thought, was unusual. As far as Kingsley was aware, he was dealing with me on the matter. The standard procedure was for the promoter to pay the artiste 50 per cent of the fees on signing and the balance on the completion of the assignment. I told Kingsley that I was not able to explain what was happening. He asked what he should do. I told him to make out a cheque to Peter for the full amount and give it to Marlene. Kingsley followed my suggestion.

We had brought back a large number of T shirts from Swaziland. I told Peter that I was going to give one shirt to each band member. He agreed. Donald Kinsey requested an extra one for his wife. She loved Africa. Kinsey took up an extra shirt. Marlene began to berate him.

On the day of the show, Donald went up to Peter's house to talk to him. Peter was not responding. Marlene began cursing Kinsey again. Donald left for his hotel and told me he would not be playing on the show that night. I did not take him seriously. Donald Kinsey had been with Peter since Tosh had formed his first band – Word Sound and Power – after leaving the Wailers.

It was showtime, but we did not see Donald Kinsey at the venue. I remembered that he had told me he would not be playing on the show. I drove down to his hotel and pleaded with him to do the show. Don relented. Peter gave a stellar performance. Many said it was the best Tosh performance they had ever seen.

The promoter who had booked Peter for a series of shows in Brazil had spent Christmas in Jamaica. He went to the Super Jam concert. He saw Peter in full flight. The promoter was ecstatic, anticipating some outstanding performances from Peter in Brazil. There was, however, one snag. Bunny Wailer had other ideas. He thought Peter needed to rest. Marlene agreed. The promoter spent hours at Peter's house trying to talk to him. Peter totally ignored him.

Stepping Away from the Razor

I soon realised that things were taking a dramatic turn. Peter was becoming increasingly erratic, and it was time for me to remove myself from him. I decided to go New York and withdraw the outstanding commission which I had left in the Intel Diplo account. I had a tendency of not taking my full commission and would requisition only the amount that I needed at any particular time, leaving the rest to accumulate in the Intel Diplo account. When I needed money, I would fill out a form and sign it and Bert Padell would give me the funds I requested.

I went to Bert's office. As soon as he saw me, he exclaimed, "Copeland, I don't understand what is happening in Jamaica!" He then told me that he had received a call from Marlene instructing him not to release any money to anyone. Bert added that I should wait until Peter and Marlene reached New York to deal with any outstanding financial matters. They were scheduled to meet with him at his office the following week. I was annoyed. Bert was aware that I was owed my commission. He knew how much I was due. Nonetheless, I decided to wait until the following week as Bert had requested.

Peter, Marlene and a medical doctor turned up at Padell's office. I knew that the doctor also had an interest in the music business. I told Peter I was at Padell's office to retrieve my commission which I had left in the Intel Diplo account. I heard Marlene clearing her throat. I thought she had a cold. She walked over and spat at me. The doctor intercepted the mouthful of saliva with his face. I decided I was going to call the police. Peter remained quiet.

As I passed by my desk, while heading to call the police, I noticed that my typewriter, telephone and answering machine were missing. I asked the lady who sat in the office next to mine if she knew what had happened to all the gadgets which had been on my desk. She told me that the woman (Marlene) who came with Peter Tosh had taken them, claiming that they belonged to her. I continued in my attempt to call the police, but Bert pleaded with me not to do so as it could cause embarrassment to his company. I heeded his request. Bert promised to replace my equipment.

The meeting was rescheduled. I made sure to put some of my friends from downtown on high alert as I did not know what to expect for the next meeting and felt it was prudent to have some muscle in reserve.

As I emerged from the subway, on my way to the next meeting, I saw a sign announcing, "The Final Battle". I wondered whether it was an omen. The final battle was supposed to be between the forces of light and darkness. I had no doubt which side I was on. I went up to Padell's office. I sat waiting for the meeting to begin but nobody turned up. My friends waited discreetly outside for any signal of distress.

Bert came out and saw me and asked what I was doing at the office. I told him I was there for the 2:00 pm meeting. Bert was a little surprised noting, "Peter came here earlier this morning and said everything is cool, and that we should forget about the meeting. I thought he called you". Bert tried calling Peter's apartment but could not reach him. At that point I decided to head back to my hotel. Bert promised that he would call me as soon as he had made contact with Peter. I waited all day. No call came. I rang Bert the following day and asked him what was happening. He informed me that Peter and Marlene had left for Jamaica and had told him that they would deal with me when I returned to the island.

I returned to Jamaica, but Peter was in a state of confusion. He, at the behest of Marlene, had kicked out his sons, Dave and Andrew, from his home. It is alleged that Marlene had told Peter that the boys were making passes at her. Marlene knew that this was a fail-safe way of getting Peter to sever relationships and limbs if necessary. I decided that there was no point in chasing Peter for the release of my commission from the Intel Diplo account. I had other projects on my schedule. I was not going to allow myself to be distracted.

Peter had, allegedly, chopped his friend Ever Gordon, based on a complaint from Marlene. Interestingly, Ever confessed at a symposium that he had actually slept with Marlene. In his words he "had transgressed against Peter" almost suggesting that he deserved the wounds Peter had inflicted on him. Yet, Peter had wounded him for, allegedly, making a pass not a stop. If Peter had known "the truth" it would, perhaps, have been fatal. According to Ever, Marlene had been experiencing bouts of loneliness while Peter was on the road.

I was, at the time, preparing for a tour with Third World and went to Zinc Fence to monitor the rehearsals and engage in other preparatory activities. A fellow by the name of Jaco Thelwell, who worked with a number of the artistes, told me that "Bush" (as he referred to Peter Tosh) had just left the premises, threatening to do all types of damage to my person. According to Jaco, "Bush" claimed that I had gone into the safe in his New York apartment and removed US$150,000. I thought it strange. Peter did not have a safe in his apartment in New York, as far as I knew, and I had certainly not taken any money from him. I thought Jaco was joking. Peter told the people at Zinc Fence that he was going up to Jimmy Cliff's house to find me. Peter did not know that I was no longer staying at Jimmy's house.

I set out for Jimmy Cliff's house to meet Peter. I didn't want Tosh to catch me off guard like he did Ever Gordon. I heard that Peter was well armed. He was reported to have had a cutlass (machete), a sword, a baseball bat, a dagger and a nunchaku. He seemed to believe in overkill. When I got to Jimmy's house, he was standing at his gate. On seeing me, Jimmy exclaimed, "Copeland I don't understand, what is happening between you and Peter!"

Jimmy related that Peter had come to the house, with fire in his eyes, swearing that he was going to do grievous bodily harm to me. Peter had gone into Jimmy's home office and pierced the desk with his dagger saying that he was going to do the same to me when he found me. I decided that I was going to report the matter to the police. I went to the Matilda's Corner Police Station. They directed me to the station in Half-Way-Tree.

I told the police, who took my statement at the station in Half-Way-Tree, that I wanted to report that Winston MacIntosh was going around telling people that he was going to do me serious harm. I told the policeman that I didn't want to take any legal action against Mr MacIntosh.

When the policeman heard the name, it occurred to him that I was talking about Peter Tosh. "Why that boy won't behave himself?", the cop asked, rhetorically. "He remember what happened to him in that room?" the cop queried pointing to a

The Peter Tosh Museum at Pulse Headquarters in Kingston, Jamaica, opened 16 October 2016. (Copeland Forbes Archives)

cubicle in which Peter had suffered a life-threatening beating at the hands of the police.

I left the station and went down to a huge hardware store on Slipe Road almost immediately across from the complex where Penthouse Records and Shocking Vibes Production were located. I bought two machetes and two files to sharpen them. I was not going to be a helpless victim. I went back to Zinc Fence. I had work to do.

When I got to Zinc Fence, Bunny Wailer was there rehearsing for the second staging of the Youth Consciousness Concert. I went to the back of the compound to park my vehicle and sharpen my machetes. Bunny heard that I was on the premises and came around to see me. He asked what was the problem between Peter and me. He expressed shock and disappointment that Peter and I were at daggers drawn as, to him, we had been "like brothers". I told Bunny that I heard that Marlene had told Peter that I had gone into his New York apartment and taken out US$150,000 from his safe. Bunny was nonplussed. He didn't know of Peter having a safe in his New York apartment.

One day I was at home in Forest Hills, Jamaica, where my girlfriend, Diana, and I were living. She wanted to pick up a few things at the supermarket. The gardener had washed the car and removed the cutlasses. I did not remember that I had not

The Peter Tosh Mausoleum in Belmont, Westmoreland. (Copeland Forbes Archives)

put back my weapons in the vehicle before I drove down to the supermarket in the plaza at Meadowbrook Square to make our purchases.

I was parked outside the supermarket waiting for Diana when, suddenly, I heard a familiar horn tooting. It was Peter's. He had pulled up behind me in his vehicle. I was so frightened. This was the first time we were meeting since he had begun issuing his threats. I was unarmed. I looked across the street and saw the vendors selling yam and bananas. I spotted a big, long knife. I told myself that should the need arise, I would make a dash for it. Peter was alone. He brought down the window of his Volvo and asked, "Weh you a say mi brother?"

I responded, "Bwoy mi deh ya," meaning "I am here".

"You don't even come and check me", he continued.

"I am busy man. Doing a lot of work", I explained.

He told me about his *No Nuclear War* album and added that he wanted me to come and listen to the tracks. I said to myself, "Yeah a mi unno waan fi cum up deh fi do like weh unno do to Prof I". I had heard that people close to Tosh had beaten Prof I and trimmed his dreadlocks for his reported transgressions. Prof I had been Peter's chef.

Diana had finished her shopping and was coming out of the supermarket when she saw Peter and me in conversation. She froze. Diana would normally have been armed. Marlene had threatened her. However, like me, she had left home with nothing with which to defend herself. What would she do if we were attacked?

I continued my talk with Tosh stating, "Peter I want to ask you something". I went on, "It has been months now that I have been looking for you because I heard that you said I went to your apartment in New York and took US$150,000 from your safe". Peter retorted "Mi nuh have any safe a mi yard". I told him that I had heard the same story from various sources. He denied looking for me and said he didn't know what I was talking about. He again invited me to listen to his album. I told him I would. He drove away.

An Era Ends

Peter went to New York three years later to work out a deal with EMI for the *No Nuclear War* album. I was in California on tour with Third World when I got a call from Peter. He told me that he wanted to do a show at Madison Square Garden and was hoping I could be involved. I explained to him that my schedule was full and that I would not be available until later in the year. This was 1987. He said he was going to Jamaica shortly and asked me to look him up on my return to the island.

The tour with Third World was not without incident. While I was in Texas, a promoter pulled a 45 handgun on me when I went to collect the balance of the fee owing to the band. Marcia Griffiths and I were living together at the time, and we would speak to each other regularly. I related the incident to her. She implored me to be careful. The following day Marcia called me and told me that she had a dream (vision) in which she saw Bob Marley and Peter Tosh in a heated argument. She informed me that seeing the living and the dead (Bob was deceased and Peter was still alive) together in a dream meant an impending death. She warned me, again, to be careful and reminded me about the promoter and the gun.

It was Friday. The Third World tour had reached California. We had two shows booked in San Diego for that night. During the first show I saw our lighting director, Bobby Bascombe, running towards the side of the stage. Bobby asked me if I had heard what had happened to Peter in Jamaica? Bobby had called his wife in Miami, and she told him that Peter had been shot and killed. I asked, which Peter? He said Peter Tosh. I had spoken to Peter only two days before, after not being in touch with him for three years. I was shattered.

I called Marcia immediately. She was in Miami. "Copeland you heard what happened to Peter Tosh?", she asked. "That is why I'm calling you", I interjected. "I wanted to find out if it is true", I added. "Yes, it is true", she confirmed. I sat motionless for a while. I then walked towards the side of the stage. I broke the news to the group. Ibo Cooper was devastated.

Based on the stories of Santa Davis (Peter's drummer who was shot in the incident), the intruders had come to kill. According to the accounts of Santa and Marlene, herself, the gunmen blamed her as the cause of the friction which had developed between them and Tosh. The men thought they had killed Marlene. She was shot, but it was Peter, Doc Brown and Free I who had paid the ultimate price. Marlene lived to fight another day.

There are many who have criticized Peter Tosh for seeming to be too tolerant of Marlene's bellicose demeanor. The feeling was that Peter should either have been able to control Marlene or abandon her. Yet, I would like to believe that Peter might well have been ahead of his time and had recognized that Marlene might have been suffering from a mental illness. Peter, perhaps, understood that the Marlene, who so many people were finding cantankerous, was not the shy young lady whom he had first met through his friend Bunny Wailer. He might have concluded that something had gone awry and that the Marlene on public display was not the one he knew.

“Mick bared his chest, put his neck at Peter’s feet and said, ‘I heard you wanted to kill me, if you’re going to kill me, do it now’.”

▸ Pg 94. Chapter 6

CHAPTER 8
THE BLACKHEART MAN

In 2018, I was a speaker at the IRIE FM Lifetime Achievement Award in honour of "Bunny" Wailer at the Old Bournemouth Beach Club. I was asked to speak about a man I had known since our childhood. I reflected on the great things Bunny had done for the music and his career. "Bwoy I see you give the man good props, but you did not talk about the bad things that he's done," Mutabaruka stated after my presentation. I told him that I did not think that the ceremony was the appropriate forum to raise any concerns I had about Bunny.

Bunny was the most problematic of the vocal trio (Bob, Peter and Bunny) signed to Island Records. While I greatly respect his musical talents, I am of the view that his personality played a major role in his failing to have a greater impact on modern popular music culture. Many consider Bunny and Peter as being more articulate than Bob who was by far the most thoughtful and least confrontational of the trio. Bunny often made outrageous demands of record labels and promoters and frequently ended up pricing himself out of the market. I believe he made enemies of promoters which did not only do damage to his iconic status but had a lasting negative impact on how Jamaican and reggae acts have been perceived.

The Wailers did their **Catch a Fire** tour in 1973 to support their debut album with Island Records. At the end of the tour Neville, known as Bunny Livingston, was upset because he did not seem to understand the concept of tour support. According to Bunny, "How could I do a tour and when it is finished, I get a financial statement

1

2

3

4

1. Bunny Wailer's Lifetime Achievement Award Ceremony, hosted by Irie FM at Bournemouth Beach Club, Kingston, Jamaica, 2018.
2. Bunny Wailer receives Lifetime Achievement Award from Debbian Dewar, Irie FM's general manager and Andrea Williams, host of "Running African", 2018.
3. Sensi Livingston (Bunny's daughter), and Jean Watts, his common law wife. (Copeland Forbes Archives)
4.Bunny Wailer with Marcia Griffiths at his Lifetime Achievement Award ceremony.

showing that I owe the record company"? He claimed that he was the one who had worked not the label. He did not realise that artistes had to do unpaid shows for radio stations and personalities for promotional purposes. He did not seem to appreciate that record companies sometimes had to pay to get their acts on certain shows in order to secure exposure.

I remember him telling me that another thing that bothered him about the Island deal was the itinerary. According to Bunny, he had seen the itinerary for the **Catch a Fire** tour in the US and realized that most of the venues scheduled were hangouts for "freaks". Bunny was convinced that in no way would he be mixing with "reprobates".

Bunny quit the group and went back to Jamaica, claiming he was going to farm in Portland. Joe Higgs, who was originally associated with the group, as their voice coach, was brought in to replace Bunny, temporarily. After he left the group Bunny took the moniker Wailers. This created a bit of confusion among fans, but I doubt that it bothered Bunny. He was still earning money from Island through the *Catch a Fire* and *Burning* projects.

A Note on the Wailers

Bunny Wailer, born Neville O' Reilly Livingston, was the youngest, smallest, most formally educated and, arguably, the most vocally gifted of the Wailers trio which was signed to Island Records in 1972. Bunny was the longest surviving member of this terrific trio all of whom managed to secure one of the rarest and highest Jamaican national honours: The Order of Merit.

Besides their being members of the outstanding Wailers group, Bunny, Peter and Bob were linked in many other ways. Bunny Wailer and Bob Marley shared a sister, Pearl, who is the daughter of their respective parents, Thaddeus Livingston and Cedella Booker. Bunny's sister, Shirley Livingston, is the mother of Peter's son, Andrew Tosh.

Bunny fancied himself as the intellectual centre of the group. Yet, Peter was, in the estimation of many (including me), the most erudite of the group. I would say Bob was the smartest of them all. He was deliberate. He had a keen sense of when to step back and hold his peace. He knew when to attack and was, perhaps, the most fearless of the three.

Bunny surrounded himself with an aura of mysticism, positioning himself as a devout adherent to the priestly order. Many considered him to be the most spiritual

The Wailers at Island Rehearsal Studio, London, during the **Catch A Fire** tour, 1973.

of the three. Clad in his flowing robes he sought to convey the image of a shaman which, some contend, was at odds with his true persona which, they claim, was mean spirited and prone to financial entanglements.

Peter was the most outspoken and overtly political of the Wailers trio, though he was never known to be engaged in partisan matters. He was a passionate advocate for the legalization of marijuana, a cause which Bunny later appropriated. Bunny had the pleasure of witnessing the 2015 legislation which sanctioned the use of the herb by Rastafarians in religious ceremonies. Tosh was also one of the most visible opponents of the apartheid regime in South Africa and Zimbabwe. Despite seeming the least pious of the three, Bob was the most charitable and sympathetic of the group. He was always giving. Money seemed of little significance to him.

When Bunny decided to release his first solo album *Blackheart Man* in 1976, he dropped the "s" from Wailers and became known as Bunny Wailer. Ironically, when he released Blackheart Man he turned to Chris Blackwell (about whom he had said some of the most terrible things) to distribute his album.

The Wailers during the UK leg of the **Catch A Fire** tour, 1973. (Esther Anderson photograph)

Bob Marley passed in 1981. The following year, Bunny decided to stage an event inside the National Stadium on Christmas Day dubbed "Youth Consciousness". This was his first solo public performance since leaving The Wailers. It was an elaborate affair which lasted for hours. Bunny gave one of the greatest performances of his career which is still talked about today. It triggered a great demand for his appearance.

Bunny decided that he would work with Don Taylor. He felt that Don's vast knowledge and extensive contacts would give his career a boost. Don Taylor showed me a copy of a draft recording contract he had secured for Bunny Wailer from Solar Records. It was a four-album deal worth US$1 million. The contract had provisions for escalation if Bunny's sales figures were to exceed certain targets. It seemed like a good deal.

Don Taylor told me that Bunny Wailer came back to him two weeks later saying he wanted US$1,000,000 per album. Don went back to Dick Griffey at Solar and told him of Bunny's request. Dick and his team asked for Bunny's sales figures as a solo act. Griffey and his associates did their research on Bunny's record sales as a solo act. Griffey suggested that his initial offer of a million dollars for four albums might have been too generous, given Bunny's track record as a solo artiste.

Bunny soon made a deal with another record company. This time he took $50,000 for the album for which he had requested one million dollars from Solar. Incidentally,

Bunny threw in a video of his live performance at Madison Square Garden as a part of his new deal.

In 1982, Bunny produced the single "Electric Boogie" which he had written for Marcia Griffiths. It was a local hit. He went to Chris Blackwell to distribute the record. Chris told Bunny that record companies preferred to have an album to follow a hit single. Blackwell gave Bunny a large sum of money to produce an album for Marcia Griffiths with "Electric Boogie" as the first single. Bunny never completed the album. He held on to the advance Chris had given him claiming Blackwell had owed him money from the Wailers' album.

In 1989 (seven years later), I was on the **Reggae Sunsplash** USA tour with Marcia Griffiths when we got news that the song "Electric Boogie" had taken off and was a hit along the east coast of the USA. Some folks in Washington DC had created a dance called the electric slide. It gave the song, a new lease on life. We received a call from Gary Himelfarb (Dr Dread), CEO of Ras Records. He told us that he was the local distributor of the song in the Washington DC area and it was selling huge numbers without any promotion.

Doctor Dread asked me to include the song in Marcia's set when the **Reggae Sunsplash** tour reached DC. I got a cassette ready with just the TV (backing) track for Marcia to use in her performance and gave it to engineer Dennis Thompson. When it was time for Marcia to perform the song, we would just play the cassette and the band would pretend to be backing her. I saw almost 20,000 people dancing the electric slide at the venue in DC. The dance craze was spreading like wildfire. Soon, Marcia was being booked for graduations, weddings and major events. We called Bunny Wailer in Jamaica and gave him the great news. I told him that I thought he and Marcia should do a video for the song. He agreed. Bunny wanted us to return to Jamaica to do the video shoot as soon as our tour was finished.

Marcia was excited. She went to the Village in Lower Manhattan and bought quite a few outfits for the scheduled video shoot in Jamaica. She was also booked for Reggae Sunsplash in Montego Bay. We headed to Jamaica.

On the day of Marcia's performance at Sunsplash, she and I were heading to Montego Bay from Kingston. We were driving along South Avenue, off Constant Spring Road, in Kingston, when we spotted Bunny Wailer's Jeep parked inside the compound where the famed Mediamix studio (operated by filmmaker, Lennie Littlewhite) was located. I saw some people rehearsing what looked like the 'electric slide'. "I see some people doing the electric slide over there", I pointed out to Marcia. I drove into the Mediamix parking lot. Chilbo, was sitting inside Bunny's Jeep. I asked him what was happening. He said they were doing the video for "Electric Boogie". I said, "How come you're doing the video and you did not let us know?"

Marcia Griffiths, Chris Blackwell, and Copeland Forbes at Strawberry Hill, Jamaica, 2006. (Copeland Forbes Archives)

Chilbo seemed shocked. He thought we knew that Bunny was doing a video for "Electric Boogie". Then Chilbo said, "This is not the one with Bunny and Marcia, this is the one with him alone." I asked, "Which one with him alone?" He told me Bunny had re-recorded the song by himself. I said, "Hold on, the song that hit is the one with Bunny and Marcia, she did all of the lead on the verses. Bunny just did the line 'Dig Miss Kelly with the electric belly, she is moving with electric, she sure got the Boogie'." Bunny was, however, the producer, writer and the arranger of the song. He could do as he pleased with it. We took our time and drove down to Montego Bay. Marcia was very upset.

After Sunsplash, Marcia and I called Chris Blackwell in England and told him what had happened. He was shocked. He said we should meet him in New York in two days' time. We flew to NYC and met Blackwell along with Amy Wachtel, Jerry Rappaport and a number of other representatives from Island Records. Blackwell asked questions about "Electric Boogie". Jerry Rappaport told Chris that the song was moving about 50,000 to 60,000 units per week. Chris was stunned. He was also angry that the song was selling that number of units without any promotional support from Island. He then recalled that he had given Bunny Wailer some money to produce an album with Marcia.

Chris, however, decided he was going to do something different. He picked up the phone and made a call to some musicians in Florida who had worked with some top-notch acts, including Gloria Estefan. They called themselves "The Jerks". Chris asked the leader, Joe Galdo, if he and his band members were free for that weekend. They were. Chris sent a cassette with the song down to Joe and instructed him to create a new rhythm in the same key.

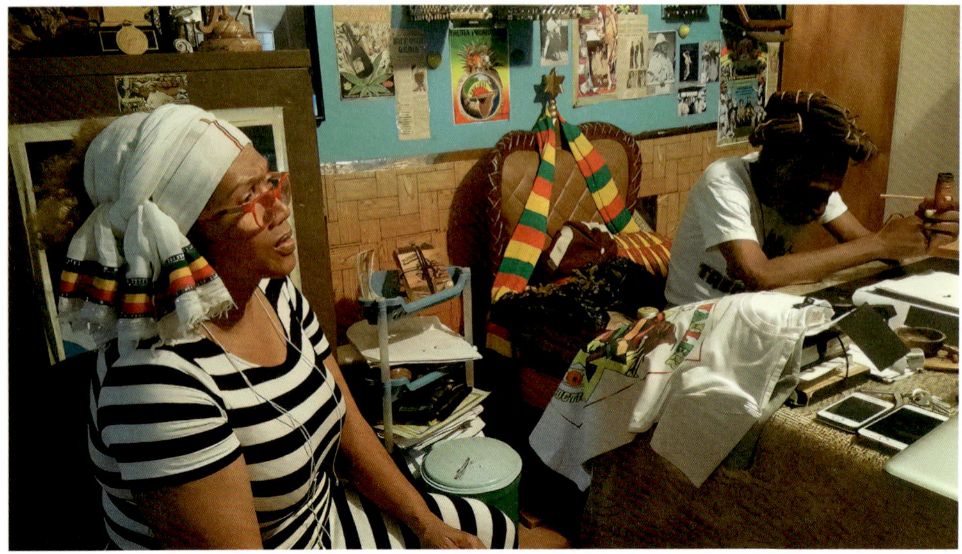

Griffiths and the Blackheart Man at the Wailer's Museum in Kingston, Jamaica, 2017. (Copeland Forbes photograph)

We went down to the International Sound Recording Studio in Miami, Florida where Marcia laid her vocal tracks for the new version of "Electric Boogie". The plan was to use Bunny Wailer's voice from the original recording performing the lines, "Dig Miss Kelly with Electric Belly, she's moving with electric she sure got the boogie" in the new version. Blackwell then decided against it. Bunny's role had now been reduced to just being the songwriter of that version of "Electric Boogie".

The producer auditioned quite a few people, including me, to perform the part Bunny had done in the previous version of the song. None of us met their expectations. Joe Galdo and Rafael Vigil came up with an idea to let Marcia insert a rap vocal to replace what Bunny had done in the original recording. "Diggla Misses Kelly with the bubbling electric belly, she's moving along with electric she sure got the boogie" was inserted to replace Bunny's vocals. I did the backing vocals, Danny Minto (Marcia's nephew) and Colin Forbes (my son) also provided background vocals. The three of us along with Rafael Vigil did the Spanish parts "don delo, don delo" and "Its Electric".

Chris Blackwell flew down to Miami to listen to the newly recorded track. He was very pleased with the results. Blackwell released the new version and pulled the original. The new version of "Electric Boogie" peaked at 51 on the Billboard Singles Chart. The original which Bunny Wailer produced became obsolete. Bunny Wailer had once again lost out on a great opportunity because of his indiscretion.

In 2007, Bunny was booked for four concert dates in Brazil. He was offered US$50,0000 per show. He got an advance. He never showed up for the concert. He didn't return the deposit. He claimed that the reason he did not turn up for the gigs was that there was a band with the moniker 'Tosh meets Marley' sharing the bill with him. Bunny said he was not going to perform on any show with another group using the name Wailers or Tosh.

His decision had a negative impact on the popularity of reggae in Brazil. Promoters became reluctant to engage reggae acts saying they were unreliable. It was not until Damian Marley released his *Welcome to Jam Rock* album that reggae acts would emerge from the doldrums in Brazil.

Marcia Griffiths congratulates Bunny Wailer at King's House on National Heroes Day, October 2017, where he received the Order of Merit. (Copeland Forbes photograph)

In 2010, Bunny called me and said he wanted to do a big world tour. He also asked if I could get him a date on one of the Bob Marley Festivals. I asked him how much he wanted. He told me US$30,000 for a show plus all expenses paid. I called the promoter Moss Jacobs in California and spoke with him about including Bunny Wailer on his bill. Moss called back later that day and told me he could get Bunny four shows at US$25,000 each plus all expenses. I told Bunny what Moss was offering. Bunny reiterated his original position. Moss said that was the best he could do. Bunny accepted the deal and asked me to get the deposit quickly.

I, however, wanted to secure my 10 per cent booking commission. I told the promoter that he should deduct my commission from the deposit and send the remainder to Bunny's account. Bunny told me that I was not due a commission from his fee because I did not get the amount he originally requested. He said the promoter should pay me a finder's fee. I called, Moss and told him what Bunny had said. Moss noted that in his over 30 years in the music business (as a promoter) he had never heard of such an arrangement. I told Moss I was out of the deal and informed Bunny I was no longer involved with his project.

Bunny Wailer meets Prime Minister Andrew Holness at Jamaica House in 2015. At right is Hon. Olivia "Babsy" Grange.

Marcia Griffiths, Bunny Wailer and former Prime Minister Hon Edward Seaga backstage at the Reggae Gold Award ceremony, Kingston, 2019. (Copeland Forbes Archives).

Later in the evening, I received a call from Moss. He said he had met with the members of his team, and they had made a unanimous decision to pay my commission on top of the agreed fee that was being paid to Bunny. They said that they would not go forward with the booking unless I was involved. They claimed they had heard of Bunny's reputation of collecting deposits and not showing up at concerts. Moss was now willing to pay more in order to have the show go ahead. I instructed Moss to send my commission directly to me. When Bunny saw the email I had sent to Moss asking him to send my finder's fee to me, he was angry. Bunny called me and asked who had authorized me to tell the promoter not to send everything to him. I told him I didn't want my money to go to his account. We got into a big argument. I told Bunny he could take the finder's fee and stuff it. Once again, I called Moss and told him I was not involved with Bunny and the booking.

I left Jamaica and went to Zimbabwe with T.O.K and the Live Wyya Band for a concert. While I was in Zimbabwe, I received a call from Jacobs asking me, "Who is Maxine Stowe?" Moss said he had received a call from Stowe who claimed that she represented Bunny Wailer. I told him I could not say whether or not she was authorized to act on Bunny's behalf. Moss was not interested in going forward with the deal.

Soon Bunny started calling people he knew who were associated with Jacobs, asking them to entreat Moss to reverse his decision. Peter's cousin, Carl T, who used to promote concerts with Jah B in San Francisco also received a call from Bunny asking him to speak to Moss.

I was in Harare when I received a call from Gary Himelfarb (Dr Dread) who was in Washington DC. He said that Bunny had called and asked him to speak to Moss Jacobs on his behalf. I brought Dr Dread up to speed with what had transpired. Dr Dread said he remembered what had happened with Bunny in Brazil a few years before and was sceptical about getting involved. He said he would speak with Moss. He said Jah B would have to give him a 20 per cent commission. He added that the deposit would have to be put in an escrow account until all the dates and obligations had been fulfilled. Doctor Dread called me an hour later and told me that Bunny had agreed to all the conditions he had laid down.

Bunny was not able to pay me a 10 per cent booking fee but was willing to give Dr Dread a 20 per cent commission.

In 2012, when Jamaica was celebrating its 50th anniversary, I joined forces with Rob Hallett, (vice president of international touring at AEG LTD UK,) to stage a two-week concert series inside the 02 Arena in London. Maxine Stowe, Bunny's representative, asked me to include Bunny in the 02 Concert Series. She also wanted me to arrange for AEG LTD to organize a world tour for Bunny.

I threw out the requests to Rob. He said that all would be fine as long as Bunny stuck to the terms of the agreement. During the months leading up to the show (in the 02 Arena), Maxine advised me that Bunny had 36 people in his entourage. She spoke of a performance with the new look Wailers, consisting of Kymani Marley, Andrew Tosh and Bunny Wailer. They had a single entitled "Butterflies". The Skatalites would also be a part of Bunny's performance.

I was surprised when I got an email from Rob asking me if Bunny had lost his mind. I called Rob and asked what had prompted that query. Rob said he received an email from Bunny and could not believe what he saw. He said Bunny was asking for huge deposits for the 02 Concert and the tour. I asked Rob what figure Bunny had requested. Rob said Bunny wanted a £1.5 million deposit.

I recalled then that in 1984, when Bunny was invited to play at Reggae Sunsplash at Crystal Palace Stadium in London, the promoters offered him £50,000. He told me to tell the promoters that he had to carry his football team, Solomonic Kickers. The promoter agreed. John Burroughs, David Rodigan and others from the BBC came to Jamaica to finalize the terms with Bunny. They waited for one week at the Pegasus Hotel without receiving a response from Bunny who said that he had to discuss the whole deal with his people before making a decision. When Bunny finally showed up,

Marcia Griffiths performing at the African Women's Ball celebrating President Obama's inauguration in Washington DC, 2009. (Copeland Forbes Archives).

he wanted £300,000, plus a bonus of one pound for each person who came through the gate at the event. The promoters nixed Bunny's invitation.

The event went through without Bunny's involvement. Over 56,000 people attended the concert to see Sugar Minott, Black Uhuru, Dennis Brown, Sly & Robbie, Aswad, Musical Youth, Maxi Priest and the Skatalites among others. The next time Bunny performed in Britain it was at the Brixton Academy for less than 50 per cent of what he had been offered for the Crystal Palace Sunsplash.

Bunny had great ideas but was not very good at execution. He often did not think through his projects properly. The idea of creating a box set to celebrate 40 years of Wailers music was a good one. However, Bunny was releasing tracks without securing permission from the owners of the masters (recordings). He ended up not being able to commercialize the venture. Such a pity.

CHAPTER 9
SOLIDARITY?

I started working with Black Uhuru (Duckie Simpson, Michael Rose and Puma Jones) in 1981. Our first joint assignment was a promotional tour in Europe to support their album *Red*. Black Uhuru was backed by Sly and Robbie and The Taxi Gang which consisted of Mikey Chung, Daryl Thompson, Keith Sterling, Franklyn "Bubbler" Waul, and Sky Juice. On that occasion, Black Uhuru toured the United Kingdom for two weeks. The group would return to Europe later in the year as the opening act for Kool & The Gang.

One of the highlights of that inaugural tour was an appearance on the *Rockpalas*, a hugely popular German television show featuring rock bands. Black Uhuru was billed to perform at three in the morning. They were sandwiched between two rock groups one of which (Mink De Ville) was from the USA. The members of Black Uhuru were worried (after all they were not considered a rock band) until they hit the stage. They gave an unforgettable performance which was carried live on television and radio across Germany to an audience of over 300 million. Over 30 million people. The performance was so outstanding that the promoter asked Black Uhuru to do an encore.

Duckie Simpson had wanted more money to appear on the show since it would be beamed across Germany to a huge audience. I had told him that given the potential size of the radio and television audience, the broadcast provided an outstanding promotional opportunity for the group. Duckie then dropped his demand, and the

Black Uhuru with Sly and Robbie beside their tour bus. (Island Records Archives)

rest is history. The impact of the broadcast was immediate. The tour was extended by another two weeks.

Kool & the Gang were fans of Black Uhuru and would watch them perform whenever they got the chance. One night both groups had a day off from touring and Black Uhuru was playing at a club in Sweden to earn additional income. The members of Kool and the Gang came to watch the show and were really impressed. I remember Kool (Robert Bell) and the lead singer James J.T. Taylor coming over to me and one of them saying, "I love that reggae thing man, we got to do some reggae thing." They went back to the US and recorded a reggae infused R&B song "Oh La La La" ("Reggae Dancing") which peaked at the number 7 position on the Billboard Hot 100 Singles Chart. When I learned of the success of the Kool & the Gang single, I went to Black Uhuru and said, "You see how influential you are? You impressed a big group like Kool & the Gang to do a reggae song which is now sitting on the top of the charts in the USA. That could have been you".

Black Uhuru was hot! They were touring with groups such as The Police, The Rolling Stones, Gil Evans Orchestra (featuring Jaco Pastorius) Herbie Hancock, Zap Rogers and King Sunny Adé to name a few. Their albums were getting significant media attention.

Black Uhuru were receiving a monthly retainer from Island Records to which they were signed. This meant that they were getting a monthly payment whether or not they were on tour. This financial gesture was designed by the head of the label, Chris Blackwell, to allow Black Uhuru to focus on their careers without having to deal with daily financial distractions. When the members of the group started to have problems among themselves, Blackwell decided to suspend the monthly payments until they could resolve the issues.

Blackwell came to Jamaica a few months later in an attempt to quell the unrest among the members of the group. He scheduled a meeting at the home of his accountant, Colin Leslie. One of the problems facing Black Uhuru was that each time they made a decision, Michael Rose would discuss it with his wife, Carole, who often overruled the agreements reached. It was decided that Carole should attend the meeting so she could make her input directly to the group rather than overturn decisions already taken.

In the meeting one of the three vocalists in Black Uhuru (Puma Jones) pulled out a long document containing rules governing the professional conduct of Sly and Robbie. Chris Blackwell had converted Black Uhuru from the original three-member

Sly Dunbar and top bassist Jaco Pastorius of the Gil Evans Orchestra, backstage the Black Uhuru Japan tour, 1984.

Jazz pianist Gil Evans and his orchestra opened for the Black Uhuru Japanese tour, 1984.
(Copeland Forbes Archives).

group to a five-member outfit by including Sly and Robbie. The original members of Black Uhuru insisted that Sly and Robbie should not be allowed to do independent work if they were officially a part of the group. Robbie made it clear that if he should be restricted from working with any other act apart from Black Uhuru, he would need a monthly retainer of at least US$10,000.

The meeting was adjourned until the following day to accommodate Rose's wife. The next day the meeting dragged on as a number of seemingly petty issues were introduced. Blackwell was fed up with the bickering. Island had just released the latest Black Uhuru album *Anthem* worldwide and it was getting quite a bit of attention. The album had a magnificent picture of all five members of the group on its cover. The first single, "Solidarity" written and originally recorded by Little Steven Van Zandt was making its way on to the playlists of many radio stations around the world.

An exasperated Blackwell, in an effort to bring an end to the contentious meeting, took out three envelopes bearing the names of the band members from his briefcase. Each envelope contained a cheque with four months' retainer which had been frozen due to the uncertainties surrounding the group. Duckie Simpson opened his envelope and looked at the cheque. When he saw the amount on the cheque, he put the envelope into his pocket. He turned to me and said, "Copeland just tell me when we leaving for the tour. I am ready right now. I don't want to hear no more arguments."

Cover picture of the Black Uhuru album, *Anthem*, 1984. (Island Records Archives).

The record company had organized an international tour for the group. It was slated to start in Europe. We would then move over to Hawaii where we were booked for three shows and would spend a week before going on to Japan for an exclusive tour along with Herbie Hancock, the Gil Evans Orchestra featuring Jaco Pastorius and a few Japanese acts.

We left Jamaica for London without any rehearsals. I arranged for the group to rehearse in London at the Shepperton Studios. Some of the members of the entourage decided to take their wives on the tour. I was never in favour of such a move. I believed the presence of spouses (whether male or female) in an entourage could be a source of tension.

When we got to London, I had a meeting with the artistes and the support crew and requested that they leave their wives in London as we headed to Europe. The plan was for the entire entourage (inclusive of the wives) to meet up in London after the European tour and then head to Hawaii through New York.

On our return to London, I was in my hotel room, prior to our departure for New York, when I got a call saying I should go down to the lobby immediately as a fight was about to break out between Michael Rose and Duckie Simpson. I reached downstairs just in time to prevent fists from flying. According to Duckie, he tried talking to Rose but would get no response from him as long as Carole was present.

Copeland Forbes dances up a storm at the Prince-owned Glam Slam Club, Minnesota, 1984. (Copeland Forbes Archives)

Those members of the entourage who didn't have their wives in London arranged to meet them in New York and then travel to Hawaii. We did three shows in Hawaii as planned. One night we were heading to a show in Hawaii and the bus was unusually quiet. Under normal conditions the bus would be noisy with the members of the entourage telling stories and teasing each other. That night, the members of the entourage were talking only to their wives. I took up the microphone and reminded the members of the crew that they were going to entertain their fans but that it seemed as if they were headed to a funeral. It was clear that the presence of the wives was having a chilling effect.

Normally, on reaching the venue everyone would head straight to the dressing room. This time the artistes walked off the bus with their wives and went in different directions. When the show was about to begin everybody scrambled from all sides to get on stage.

The plan was that after we had finished our engagements in Hawaii, the members of Black Uhuru and the production crew would head to Japan while the wives would return to their respective homes. Michael Rose came to me and said that he would like his wife to accompany him to Japan as he was a vegetarian with a special diet which she would prepare for him. I thought about it and considered the fact that he was the lead singer, and I did not want him to be uncomfortable. I reluctantly agreed to his request. It was a terrible mistake.

In Japan, things were going relatively well until Daryl Thompson, the guitarist, drank or smoked something which literally sent him over a cliff. We had to go down into a ravine, tie him with a rope and pull him back to *terra firma*. We then played in Yomiuri Land which was where we would have the first leg of the **Reggae Sunsplash** tour in 1985.

After fulfilling our obligations in Japan , we headed to Minnesota for the first leg of our American tour. We had a day off so most of the artistes and the crew were in my room chatting and watching Michael Jackson's *Thriller* video. Everyone was excited. *Thriller* was a monster and Jackson was the hottest commodity in show business at the time. My door was open. Somebody in my room made a comment that he heard that Michael was "a batty man" meaning he was gay. The person was referring to Michael Jackson. I got up and went to my door and when I looked outside there was Carole, standing in the hallway. I thought that if she had heard the reference about Michael's being gay, she might have thought it was directed at her husband.

The following day we went to do our sound check and I noticed that Michael Rose wasn't talking to anyone. It was showtime and they were on stage performing the song "Guess Who is Coming to Dinner". Michael was singing but the other vocalists were not able to follow him. They did not understand what he was doing. Duckie became upset and walked off the stage. Puma followed. I saw Robbie Shakespeare moving to unplug his bass when Sly shouted, "No, No Bya, it's gonna look bad. Let us continue". Michael continued performing while Puma Jones and Duckie Simpson sat on either side of the stage.

After this show, I called a meeting with all the band members and the crew. I asked each person to identify what was causing the problem in the group. Robbie chimed in and said the problem was Carole Rose and that she had to go home. Sly agreed with Robbie. Daryl Thompson the guitarist, pointed out that he would go with

Black Uhuru – Michael Rose, Puma Jones and Duckie Simpson – opened for the Rolling Stones' on one leg of the **Tattoo You** European tour, 1982. (Island Records Archives)

whatever Sly and Robbie said. Bubbler, the keyboardist, was reluctant to speak but conceded that it was obvious where the problem was. Sky Juice explained that he was the youngest one in the group, and he needed his job, so he was not going to say anything. I told Michael that he had to send his wife home. He decided to send her to New York to stay with her mother.

The next stop on the tour was San Francisco. We were off the following day so Michael decided that he would fly with his wife to New York and then meet us in San Francisco.

Rose headed straight to my room soon after he landed in San Francisco. He had brought back some receipts which reflected the expenses that he had incurred for taking his wife to New York. Robbie Shakespeare came into my room and saw the receipts. He asked about them. I told him that Michael was seeking reimbursement for the expenses he had incurred to take his wife to New York. Robbie was livid. He insisted that the group was not responsible for reimbursing Rose for taking his wife to New York. Michael took up all the receipts and went back to his room. We had a great show in San Francisco, although Michael hardly spoke to anyone except me.

As the tour went along things started to get better. All three singers were sitting together and having fun at the back of the bus. We shared billing with the group, King Sunny Adé, who was also signed to Island Records. Black Uhuru and King Sunny Adé were booked to appear at the 43rd Street Pier in Manhattan. Chris Blackwell was in town for the show. He placed a limousine at the disposal of the five members of Black Uhuru.

We were ready to go to the venue for the sound check but could not find our limousine. Someone told us that Michael Rose had gone over to Queens with the

Billy Idol flanked by Sly and Robbie at the Glam Slam Club. (Copeland Forbes Archives)

limousine to see his wife. The other members of the group and I had to take taxis to the venue for the sound check and back to the hotel.

Later in the night, I went down to the lobby to head for the show. Robbie Shakespeare was very upset. He asked me where was the limousine. I told him that it should be outside waiting for us. He said that there was a limo outside, but it was loaded with people. I went outside the hotel and asked a gentleman if the limo for which he was the driver had been booked by Island Records. He answered in the affirmative. I asked him who were the people in the limo. He explained that one of the entertainers had taken him to Queens to pick them up. They were relatives and friends of Michael Rose.

Robbie Shakespeare told everyone in the limousine to get out. They obeyed. I told the band members and singers to get in the limousine. They all did with the exception of Michael Rose. I suspect Rose and company had to take taxis to the venue.

Chris Blackwell was at the venue sitting in the VIP area with several of his staff members from Island Records. He came over to me after watching Black Uhuru perform the first three or four songs in their set and said that something didn't look right. I gave him a hint of what had happened. He shook his head. Despite the discernible discomfort among the members, Black Uhuru gave a superb performance.

We left Manhattan to continue the tour in Upstate New York where Black Uhuru was booked for a few shows, including one at the University of Buffalo. We then had an eight-day break. We decided that we would go back to Jamaica during that period.

We were about to leave Jamaica to resume the tour when I got a visit from Puma Jones. She told me that she had just left Michael Rose's house and that he was no longer a part of Black Uhuru. She said Rose's wife had told her that he was finished with the group. I was shocked. Rose lived a few minutes down the hill from me. I drove to his house to verify what I had heard. I knocked on the door at the Roses' house. Carole spoke to me from a window and confirmed what Puma had just told me. I asked her how she and Michael could make such a decision in the middle of a tour? She said Black Uhuru was a thing of the past. Michael said nothing. I left the Roses' house and went back home.

Duckie Simpson had heard the news and he decided to pass by my house to determine whether it was true. Duckie told me that he had a friend who could replace Michael Rose. His name was Junior Reid. He was from Waterhouse and was quite familiar with the Black Uhuru catalogue. Reid had a hit under his belt, "Foreign Mind". Duckie said they would just make Reid a member of the group and finish the tour. I told Duckie that I liked the idea but needed to bring Chris Blackwell up to speed on the development.

I called Chris Blackwell and gave him the news. He was shocked. I told him that Duckie had found a replacement and that his name was Junior Reid. Chris paused and then said to me, "Copeland if it's not Michael Rose, Puma Jones and Duckie Simpson I am not interested".

Blackwell was very upset. He had invested heavily in the group. He believed in Black Uhuru. When Bob Marley passed, Blackwell was searching for the next act to carry on the legacy. He was convinced that Black Uhuru had what was required to achieve that monumental objective. The dream had ended through a lack of solidarity.

I cancelled the tour, and all the remaining Black Uhuru shows for the rest of the year, including Reggae Superjam.

Black Uhuru was listed among the five nominees when the newly established Reggae category was announced for the Grammy Awards. Black Uhuru was declared the first winner in the Reggae Category at the 1985 staging of the Grammy Awards.

I later found out from Ducky Simpson that when Black Uhuru was nominated for the Grammy, Chris had tried to get them back together. Duckie said

Copeland Forbes, Island Records' Lister Hewan-Lowe holding his baby daughter, and Stephen "Cat" Coore at the Black Uhuru/King Sunny Adé Concert at Pier 84, NY City,1984. (Nancy Jonap photograph/Hewan-Lowe's Archives)

Robbie Shakespeare flanked by African stars King Sunny Ade and Hugh Masekela at the Glam Slam Club in Minnesota. (Copeland Forbes Archives)

that Chris sent envelopes to the three vocalists in the group and asked them to get back together if only to accept the prestigious award. That didn't work. Rose had decided against it. This was the end of Black Uhuru with Michael Rose.

Island Records dropped the group. Duckie and Puma agreed to continue with Junior Reid as Black Uhuru. They were later signed to Ras Records out of Washington DC and scored a hit, "Great Train Robbery". They were again nominated for a Grammy Award but came away empty handed that time. Puma Jones passed away in January of 1990 leaving Duckie Simpson to decide the fate of the group. Duckie prevailed in court over Michael on the ownership of the Black Uhuru name.

Some 15 years after Michael Rose had left Black Uhuru, Jay Z, who had then become the president of Island/Def Jam, decided to reunite the iconic group. Duckie Simpson informed me that Island/Def Jam was interested in signing them to the label. Island/Def Jam had controlled the Black Uhuru catalogue which included their Grammy Award winning album, *Anthem*. Jay Z perhaps believed that he would have been able to recapture the magic which had propelled the group to its iconic status before the split.

Much had changed through the years: Chris Blackwell had sold Island; Puma had died, Duckie Simpson and his, by then, ex-wife Marcia had a signed an agreement to share ownership of the Black Uhuru name.

Marcia had secured a 40 per cent stake in the group as a result of the funding she had provided Duckie in his lawsuit against Michael Rose and previous members to gain control of the Black Uhuru name. However, I recall Chris Blackwell asking Duckie, during one of our many meetings, "What really is the point of owning the name if there was no group?" Duckie owned the name, but it was Rose and his distinctive vocals which carried the claim to fame. Finally, it seemed that both Rose and Simpson had come to terms with the fact that they were better together than apart.

Duckie Simpson and Michael Rose in 2004 when they made an attempt at reunification.

Duckie and Michael were meeting regularly in Ocho Rios, in an effort to plan their grand reunion. It seemed to have come home to both men that their constant squabbles had brought one of the most promising musical projects to its knees.

I started preparing for the rebirth of Black Uhuru with the Sly & Robbie Taxi Gang. I contacted booking agent, Peter Schwartz to stage an American tour. Jay Z had just signed Rihanna and Island/Def Jam was poised for great things. The future was looking good for Black Uhuru.

Both Rose and Simpson agreed to a fifty/fifty split of all revenue less expenses incurred by the group. Duckie must have realized that it was better to have a piece of somethings than all of nothing. Both men decided that they would hire a replacement for Puma and that person would be paid a salary and not be a shareholder.

However, it was clear that things were not adding up. There was no way Duckie could have entered into an agreement to grant Rose 50 per cent of the earnings from the group without making an adjustment to the shares he and Marcia held. Duckie, realizing that he could not eat his cake and have it, asked Rose to reduce his proposed stake in the Black Uhuru name. Rose refused. If Duckie and his ex-wife had both reduced their shares in Black Uhuru by 50 per cent perhaps they would have earned far more from the new arrangement than from the original agreement they had between themselves. It was another missed opportunity.

However, to be fair, the share issue would not have been the only obstacle to reconciliation. Rose had some seemingly intractable immigration problems which had been dogging him since the heyday of Black Uhuru. These issues had posed numerous challenges to his efforts to visit and work in the United States. I believe, though, that had they been able to resolve the matter of the shares, they would have eventually been able to overcome the immigration hurdle.

Jay Z at the Tuff Gong studio with Tarrus Riley and Damian Marley in Kingston. (Timeline photos).

CHAPTER 10

HERE I COME

I met Dennis Brown when he was about nine years old and attending the Central Branch Primary School where he was a member of the Cub Scouts. I followed his early musical career before I left for the United States in the late sixties.

It was 1983, while I was managing Peter Tosh, when Dennis and his road manager, Horace "Mya Simeon" Campbell (from the Twelve Tribes of Israel), asked me to put Brown on the **Mama Africa** tour. Mya wanted Dennis to have the opportunity of playing at bigger venues than the ones for which he had been booked. They felt that touring with Tosh would provide such an opportunity.

I didn't know how to propose the idea to Peter. Dennis had already developed a reputation for being late and unreliable. I arranged for Dennis to meet me at Jimmy Cliff's house. I also invited Peter. We sat and talked about various things. I asked Peter if Dennis could join him as the opening act on the **Mama Africa** tour. Peter agreed but I knew he had misgivings and would want to discuss the issue with me further. Later that night Peter expressed his concern about Brown's reputation for being unreliable. I assured him that he had nothing to worry about.

I arranged to have Dennis and Peter get together in New York one week before the start of the tour in July 1983. I wanted to provide them with a chance to bond. They both enjoyed roller skating. They had a great time on the rink in the Big Apple. The tour was booked by FBI Booking Agency owned by Stewart Copeland, a former police officer.

Dennis Brown, his road manager Horace "Mya" Campbell and Sky-High "hold a trinity" backstage on the New York leg of the **Mama Africa** tour. (Heartnel Henry/Sky High photos).

The **Mama Africa** tour kicked off at the 43rd Street Pier in Manhattan. Dennis was present for the sound check but went missing by the scheduled time of his performance. He showed up some 10 minutes before the expiration of his allotted time to perform. He did two songs. We asked Dennis what had caused his lateness. I realized that he was having major problems with his management and told him he had to sort out his challenges very quickly.

The next show was at the Tower Theatre in Philadelphia. I sent Peter and the entourage ahead of me. I took the train down later. When I got to the Tower Theatre, I noticed that only Peter's name was on the marquee. I wasn't sure what was happening. I went inside the venue where I saw Steve Golding, the guitarist, who told me that Peter was upstairs and was upset. Peter's worst fear had been realised. Dennis was a no show.

I went upstairs with great trepidation. I found Peter. He was quiet. He gave me a harsh look but, did not utter a word. As soon as everyone had left the dressing room, he began shouting at me. "I tell yuh I doh wah dem man yah pon me tour"! he yelled. "Him was late for di first show and now him is a no show," he continued. I could not respond. Dennis dropped out of the tour. The promoters were disappointed. He was a crowd puller.

When the tour got to the West Coast, Mya and Dennis reached out to me. They wanted me to manage Dennis. I told them that I would not be able to take on that role unless Dennis got a release from his then management team comprising

Joe Gibbs and Larry Maxwell. In 1980, I had secured a deal for Dennis with EMI Music Publishing and Joe asked who had given me permission to act on Dennis Brown's behalf. I wasn't going to take any chances with Joe. I told Mya that once Dennis obtained a release, they should get back to me.

Peter Tosh
Dennis Brown
Burning Sensations
Friday August 19 8 P.M.
Berkeley Community Theatre
Tickets: $10.50/$11.50/$12.50 reserved
In assn with Bay Area Alternative Radio:
KALX / KFJC / KUSF

Peter Tosh and Dennis Brown sold out the Community Centre in Berkeley California on **Mama Africa** tour, 1983. (Copeland Forbes Archives).

Dennis and Mya returned with a 'release' from Joe. There was one hitch. The document did not mention the deal with A&M Records to which Dennis was, purportedly, signed. I told them to go back to Joe and ask about the A&M agreement. It was then that they realized that Dennis had not been signed directly to A&M. Joe Gibbs had a producer agreement with A&M. Dennis had a recording and management contract with Joe Gibbs.

Mya seized the tapes and masters of Dennis Brown's recordings from Joe Gibbs' studio. He flew with the tapes to New York and held on to them. By that time, I was making efforts for Dennis to join Peter in the last week of the West Coast tour.

I had Dennis fly in from England to meet with the team from A&M in California. Herb Alpert, co-founder of A&M Records, told me the label didn't want to have anything to do with Joe Gibbs. Joe was prohibited from pressing and releasing recordings covered by his agreement with A&M in the United States. He was not restricted (under the contract) from exporting recordings from Jamaica to the US. However, it was alleged that Gibbs had a plant in Florida and was pressing and releasing units in the USA which was in breach of his contract. Joe, allegedly, flooded the American market with recorded products (contrary to his agreement with the label) after which he gave the masters to A&M for them to do their release.

Alpert deemed this unethical. He said he was finished with Gibbs. He wanted to deal with Dennis directly. Joe's Miami-based lawyers called and said they wanted a settlement for the termination of the deal with A&M. Joe's lawyers requested US$30,000 cash up front and a three-point override on Brown's next album with A&M. The lawyers also requested that Mya return the master tapes he had taken from Gibbs' studio. I called Mya and told him what Gibbs' lawyers had requested regarding a settlement with Dennis. Mya decided to copy all the tapes he had seized from Joe's studio before returning them to Gibbs' lawyer. A&M quickly agreed to pay the cash.

Dennis toured the West Coast with Peter. EMI Music, the label to which Peter was signed, filmed the event at the Greek Theatre. It was an excellent show.

While I was in London, after completing a European tour with Dennis and the Lloyd Parks Band, I went over to the A&M office to meet with the president. He told me that if I could find a top-flight producer, A&M would give Dennis a good deal. I first thought of Stuart Levine who was very hot at the time, but he had so many projects and he would not have been able to touch ours for another two years. We needed to start immediately. I checked Eddy Grant. He was sizzling. He had a state-of-the-art studio in Barbados. The dealbreaker was that Dennis would have had to record in Barbados which carried quite a few restrictions.

"Are you ready to stand up and fight the right revolution" asked Dennis Brown during his magnificent performance on the **Reggae Superfest** 1990 European tour. (Fabrizio/ Roots & Culture Archives)

I then remembered Alex Sadkin who had done a considerable amount of work with Bob Marley. I called around to get in touch with Alex. I found out he was in New York recording with the rock group Foreigner. I jumped on a plane from London to New York and went straight to the studio where Sadkin was working. I will never forget that when I arrived at The Hit Factory, Sadkin and Foreigner were in the midst of recording the smash hit, "I Wanna Know What Love Is". I pulled Sadkin aside and told him I was looking for a producer for Dennis' next album with A&M and that I thought he was the best man for the job. I explained that we didn't have a big budget. He expressed his love for Dennis and told me that Marley would always ask him to listen Brown's music. He agreed to produce the album.

D. Brown and friends after a blistering performance at Reggae Jam Boogie in 1985. (Copeland Forbes Archives)

I felt elated but I wanted to hear figures. Sadkin said US$15,000. I almost fainted. Alex Sadkin, for US$15,000 dollars! I couldn't believe it. It was too good to be true. I took up my bag and was ready to head back to London with the great news. As I got downstairs, I realised that I needed to get Sadkin's commitment in writing. I went back upstairs to secure it. He wrote on a piece of paper and signed it. He asked me to get a demo on a cassette to him so he could take a listen to the songs and get started.

I flew back to London and went straight to A&M. I told the president I had found a producer, and it was Alex Sadkin. The president was excited. He knew Sadkin's reputation was huge. Alex had worked with some of the top artistes from A&M including Joe Cocker. When I showed the president the paper with the figure that Sadkin had written he was stunned. He just could not believe Sadkin would work for that kind of money. The A&M team got a handwriting expert and pulled out previous contracts they had with Sadkin to see if the signatures matched the one on the note that I had brought from New York. The signatures matched. A&M was ready to roll.

I called Lloyd Parks and his band. I told them to get ready as we were sending a vehicle to take them to the studio to do some demos with Dennis for his upcoming album. A&M had dispatched a Rolls Royce for Dennis and a van for the musicians. I stayed over at A&M to sort out the details of the new contract. I soon got a call from the limo company. The driver had been waiting on Dennis for two hours to take him to the studio and he was nowhere to be found. I was frustrated. I instructed the musicians to head to the studio while I tried to find Dennis. I called Castro Brown and a few other people closely related to Dennis. We went to the studio and waited for Dennis who showed up hours later with about 50 or 60 people in tow. One individual had a cardboard box with curry goat which he spilt on the recording console. It was frightening. I told Castro that we had to clear the studio. We chased everyone

The Dean Fraser led 809 band provided backing for Dennis Brown at the Reggae Jam Boogie, 1985. (809 Band Archives)

out and began recording. Dennis did three songs and then took the reel from the machine. He went into a bag marked "Yvonne Special", a record label in London which he had named after his wife. He took a tape out of his bag and used it to replace the one he had removed from the machine. He turned to Dean Fraser and said, "Rass Brass, I wah unnu put down some horns on this track for me." Dennis was using the rest of the A&M studio time to work on tracks for his personal label. Three songs were all I had to present to A&M. I was stunned.

The next day A&M called saying the songs we had recorded were not what they had expected. Dennis said he had the right songs in Jamaica. He claimed he had done some songs with Sangie Davis, the writer of the hit single, "Girly Girly". A&M decided to send Dennis and me to Jamaica to get the cassette with the songs. In Jamaica, Dennis got a cassette which, purportedly, had the songs for A&M. I took him, with the cassette, to the airport two days later.

I watched Dennis board the plane. I saw the plane take off. Dennis was scheduled to deliver the cassette to A&M in London the following day. A&M called asking me for Dennis. I told them, "He is in England". They had not seen nor heard from him. I called his wife in London. She had not seen him either.

Everyone in the UK thought Dennis was still in Jamaica. I told the people at A&M that I watched Dennis board the plane in Jamaica. I explained to them that I had seen the plane leave. Then something struck me. I remembered that the plane had to stop in Miami where Dennis had a girlfriend . I wondered whether he might have disembarked in Miami. I called his girlfriend. She told me she had met up with Dennis at the airport and was sure that he had boarded a British Airways flight for London. I called A&M and told them that Dennis was in Britain as I had spoken to one of his friends who had vouched that he had left Miami for London.

Dennis had been missing for two days when I came up with an idea to call my friend Hu Hu in Miami to see if he could locate Dennis. I gave him the address of Dennis' girlfriend and told him that he should dress as a delivery man and carry a package with the name 'Danish Brown' on it. My friend went to the house disguised as a delivery man. He rang the doorbell. A man opened the door. It was Dennis Brown.

My friend called me laughing, "Boss guess who come open di door, nuh Dennis himself". I asked my friend if he was sure. He said he was certain that it was Dennis who came out to him. He even described what Dennis was wearing – a pair of green shorts and a red, green and gold mesh marina. I called Dennis' girlfriend again to ask her if she was sure that Dennis had left for London. "I told you what happened already," she responded.

I admitted to her that I knew he was at her house. I went on to describe what he was wearing. She went silent. She then tried to cover the mouthpiece of the phone, but I could still overhear her telling Dennis that I knew he was there. Dennis asked her how I knew and eventually Dennis came on the line sounding quite apologetic. "I should be whipped with many stripes, I fucked up, I fucked up," he said. I told him to get on a flight and head to London that night. He agreed. I called Mya and told him I had found Dennis. Mya wanted to give Dennis' girlfriend a piece of his mind. I told him to wait until Dennis had gone on the flight.

Dennis got to London.I was so happy when A&M called and told me that they had picked him up at the airport. He went to A&M's office to play the cassette. A gentleman from the A&R Department called me and asked if we were joking. He went on to recount that Dennis brought a tape for them to audition and, "when we put it in the playback machine, we heard what sounded like a recording of pots and pans. They seemed to have recorded a smoking session". There was someone in the background of the recording shouting "my turn now".

The A&M representatives asked Dennis to fast forward and rewind the tape, but no music could be found on the cassette. The people at A&M decided that they did not want anything more to do with Dennis. They just could not understand how I could represent an artiste over whom I had so little control. Luckily, for Dennis, there was a clause in his A&M contract which stipulated that he would receive £60,000 should the label terminate the agreement with him.

Herb Alpert was sad. He really liked Dennis. I was so disappointed. Dennis lost one of the greatest opportunities to realise his enormous potential.

Despite the setback, I was still not prepared to give up on Dennis. In 1984, he performed at the Crystal Palace Stadium. Junior Lincoln had started to handle his management and Tommy Cowan was also a part of his team. In 1985, I decided to put on a show called Reggae Jam Boogie in Jamaica. Dennis was really in demand in Jamaica at the time. He was living in England and rarely came to Jamaica. When he did, it was surreal.

Some people said that I shouldn't have taken any chance with Dennis. They claimed that the previous year he was billed on a show with Chaka Khan and did not turn up for the event. Being the eternal optimist, I thought I could get Dennis to fulfil his obligations. Reggae Jam Boogie would feature three acts: Third World, Dennis Brown and Half Pint, along with the newly formed Dean Fraser-led 809 Band. Dennis said he wouldn't come to Jamaica for just one show. He suggested that I get him another gig. I got him another show in Negril at the Tree House Club, a very popular spot at the time.

"Piggy" Chung who was Sophia George's manager (and later her husband) was going to London to promote the song "Girly Girly" which had taken off in the UK. I gave "Piggy" the deposits, for the two shows, which he delivered to. Dennis who went silent after he received the money.

Reggae Jam Boogie was slated for 28 December, two days after Sting a major musical showcase in Jamaica. Many people said I could not compete with Sting which had so many acts while Jam Boogie had only three artistes on the bill. I wasn't concerned. I was not competing with Sting. I was going for a different segment of the market. I knew I had quality acts.

It was around Christmas Eve when word started to spread that Louise Fraser Bennett (an influential figure in the local entertainment business) was telling people that Dennis would not be appearing at Reggae Jam Boogie. Conventional wisdom had it that one should always pay attention to whatever Louise had to say.

Freddie McGregor called me with some advice, "Listen boss, yuh know Dennis like a book, nuhbody nuh know him like you and from yuh hear dem say him nah come, I think yuh should go England." I asked Freddie if he thought I should really head to Britain on Christmas Eve to find Dennis. He said yes. I booked a flight for Christmas Eve from Kingston to London which was like a ghost town when I arrived. I went to Victoria Station and got a taxi to take me straight to Dennis' house. I knew exactly where he lived. He had used the separation bonus he received from A&M to purchase the house. When I got to the house, Dennis' wife informed me that she had not seen him in three days. My head started to throb. I tried to make myself comfortable by taking a nap on the couch in the living room.

About a minute after midnight, I heard a huge noise. Dennis had arrived. I started laughing. He had no idea I was there. Dennis walked in, well dressed in a suit with two bottles of wine in his hands. He turned his attention to Yvonne and said, "Merry Christmas Mami". This was, by then, Boxing Day. Dennis seemed to operate on his own time. It hadn't dawned on him that his greeting to his wife was a tad late. When he saw me, he asked nonchalantly, "Wait, boss yuh deh yah?" I told him that his flight to Jamaica would be leaving at 11:00 am, later that morning. He said that he wouldn't be able to make that flight. We had to reschedule his flight for the following day.

The Crown Prince Dennis Brown in full flight on stage at the sold-out Reggae Jam Boogie concert at the National Arena in Kingston Jamaica, 1985.

ENTERTAINMENT

REGGAE JAM BOOGIE

DECEMBER 26, 1985
NATIONAL ARENA

A REGGAE CAREERS INTERNATIONAL PRESENTATION

Live IN CONCERT

THIRD WORLD
HEADLINES REGGAE JAM BOOGIE

DENNIS BROWN

HALF PINT

809 BAND

ONE SHOW ONLY
TICKETS ON SALE FROM MONDAY, DECEMBER 23, 1985

I informed Dennis that there was a big rumour in Jamaica that he would not be turning up for Reggae Jam Boogie. Barry G, the hottest radio DJ in Jamaica at the time, had suggested that I call him the moment I found Dennis. I called Barry G from Dennis' house. Barry had Dennis record a promo saying, "This is Dennis Brown and I'm now heading to Jamaica for Reggae Jam Boogie at the National Arena".

I felt a lot better. I had intended to stay by Brown's house until we were ready to leave for Jamaica. However, Dennis said he had to go on the road. I had to spend another night in London, so I decided to stay at a friend's house instead. I told Yvonne I would return to pick up Dennis the following morning.

I woke up early on the day of our departure and called Dennis' house. There was no answer. I was worried. A friend of mine took me to fetch Dennis who was still asleep when I reached his house. I had to wake him. Dennis got up and went to the living room to have coffee and watch television. He had not packed anything. I scrambled to find his clothes and stuffed them in a duffle bag.

We were on our way to the airport when Dennis suddenly realised that he had left his black and white shoes which were similar to the ones Michael Jackson wore in the *Thriller* video. Dennis loved to perform in them. I told him we couldn't turn back. He insisted that he needed his shoes and threatened to jump out of the car if we did not turn back. He started opening the door. We complied with his request.

When I got back to his house, I told Dennis to remain in the vehicle. I went inside to retrieve the shoes. He had told me they were under his bed, but he really had no idea where the shoes were. I eventually found them in a closet. Time was against us. When we got to the airport the check in counter was closed. The lady told us we could try our luck at the gate. I ran with a briefcase, a flight pack and Dennis' duffle bag to the gate. Dennis strolled along toting his guitar.

When I got to the departure gate there was no sign of Dennis. He had vanished. I searched a number of shops but did not find him. Suddenly, I heard a Jamaican voice on a phone call telling someone. "I soon come". It was Dennis talking to a woman, who I later learned, was at a hotel in Birmingham. I held him by the collar and took him straight to the gate. When we were seated on the plane, he said to me, "Boss mek me tell yuh di trute enuh, if yuh neva come, me wouldn't turn up enuh." I asked him why. He replied that he was just enjoying life. I asked him if he would have taken the deposits for both events and not show up. I cannot recall his response.

I was not able to find a direct flight from London to Kingston. We got on a flight to Miami. I figured if we got to Miami, we would be able to reach Kingston even if we had to swim. When we reached Miami there were no available flights to Kingston. We were on standby. Finally, one airline said they could seat us.

We were ready to take off, when we heard a loud noise. The plane shook and stopped suddenly. We were thrown into complete darkness. The plane had developed mechanical problems. They had to tow it back to the gate. The crew advised the passengers that they should remain in their seats until the problem was rectified. Dennis wanted to get off the plane.

I always carried a Bible. I gave it to him. I told him that we would remain on the plane and that he should read Psalm 121. Hours later they fixed the problem. We finally got to Jamaica. It was about 1:00 am on the morning of the show, when we arrived. The press which had been waiting for Dennis had already left.

Dennis had been scheduled to stay with one of his cousins off Molynes Road. I nixed the idea. I put Dennis in the guest room of my house. He went to sleep. We got up later that morning and went to JBC, RJR, and other media houses to let everyone know Dennis was in town. The undesirables searching for him by his cousin's house were unable to find him.

A friend of mine had left two of his vehicles by my house: a Porsche and a Benz. I gave Dennis the Benz to drive down to the show venue I followed him in the Porsche. The fans went wild when they realised Dennis had arrived. I had hired a top-notch security firm, headed by the wife of a legendary crime fighter, Keith "Trinity" Gardener. The criminals were crawling out of the woodwork to see Dennis perform. The police reported that they arrested 13 wanted men that night.

Dennis Brown greeted by fans on arrival at the National Arena for the Reggae Jam Boogie concert staged by manager Copeland Forbes seen snapping pics of the meet and greet. (Copeland Forbes Archives)

I had printed 10,000 tickets in Miami and gave away 1,000. The paid tickets were sold out and there were long lines of people unable to get inside the venue.. Dennis gave a scintillating performance. He disappeared soon after the show.

Dennis, An Enigma

Given all his indiscretions, how was one able to tolerate Dennis Emmanuel Brown? The answer is fairly straightforward, Dennis was able to disarm anyone with his ready smile and gentle manner. One would certainly be hard pressed to get angry with Dennis even when his behaviour sometimes attracted terrible consequences for others, including loss of property.

Dennis has been, arguably, the most imitated of Jamaican artistes. Many outstanding Jamaican acts started out sounding like Dennis Brown before they found their voices including: Luciano, Mykal Roze , Frankie Paul and Richie Stephens. It is widely known that he was a favourite of the legendary Marley. Many women swooned at the sound of his rich baritone.

Brown's catalogue is replete with reggae standards. No Jamaican party worthy of its designation would be complete without reference to Brown's rich collection of hits including: "Revolution"; "Wolf and Leopard"; "Promised Land"; "Here I Come"; "No Man Is An Island"; "Should I"; "Wichita Lineman"; "Love and Hate"; "How Could I Leave"; "Money in My Pocket" and "If I Had the World".

Dennis passed on 1 July 1999. He was only 42. He is buried at the National Heroes Park. He is the first Jamaican recording artiste to have been interred at the national shrine. His burial sparked a bit of controversy. Some of his close associates insisted that he had to be buried in the national shrine despite the fact that no official permission had been granted for the interment. Dennis is one of the most beloved artistes in the annals of Jamaican music.

Copeland Forbes, manager of Dennis Brown, visits the grave site of the Crown Prince at the National Heroes Park in Kingston, Jamaica. (Copeland Forbes Archives)

CHAPTER 11

NOW THAT WE'VE FOUND LOVE

My working relationship with Third World started in 1985 with the *Reggae Sunsplash* tour of the United States. Synergy Productions from Jamaica and Celebrity Concerts, a Californian outfit, headed by Eddie Haddad, were the promoters of the tour which also featured Dennis Brown and Gregory Isaacs. The acts were backed by Lloyd Parks and We The People Band. This was the first *Reggae Sunsplash* tour of the United States.

I had to book some of the artistes in the hotels under aliases in order to keep them away from the hustlers and hangers on who were constantly on their trail. Gregory Isaacs was registered as Paul Newman and Dennis Brown as Robert Redford. All went well until we reached Texas where the tour started to have financial problems. Tony Johnson of Synergy left the tour. He went to California. Ronnie Burke was brought in to replace him.

The financial circumstances on the tour had deteriorated rapidly and soon became too hot for Ronnie to handle. Ronnie left and Don Green came in to assume management responsibilities for the tour. We were asked to take a cut in salaries. The gate receipts in the Midwest were very low. The promoters said they would not be able to pay the weekly rates that had been negotiated. There was a week when the promoters cancelled all our shows. Dennis and Gregory went to Jamaica for the break. Dennis did not return. His friend Mya (who accompanied him on the road) did not want him to take a cut in salary.

Third World headlined the first US **Reggae Sunsplash** tour in 1985.

We spent a whole week at our hotel in Texas doing nothing. One of the promoters came to Ibo Cooper's room and complained that he was learning of some unusual and disturbing activities which were taking place in the hotel and which seemed to involve members of our entourage. The promoter noted that he had got wind of what was happening from the streets to which he was very close. He came to my room to deliver his warning. He was accompanied by a muscle-bound bodyguard. This behemoth stood threateningly over my bed while the promoter spoke of what he knew. The promoter urged me to keep the members of my team away from any wrongdoing.

The show in Texas went off without incident. The next stop was St Louis. Gregory decided to call it quits at that point. He had not been paid for over two weeks. He stated that he would be going no further until the promoter cleared the arrears which they owed him. Third World (then managed by Eulysses Lewis, the owner of the Paramount Theater in Seattle, Washington) decided that they had reached the end of the road. Third World had their own bus and headed back to California.

Some of the Synergy staff and crew took off for California in the other tour bus. Don Green, emcee Tommy Cowan and Carlene Davis made their way in the cab of a truck to the nearest airport leaving Gregory Isaacs, the members of the We The People Band and the production crew stranded. The hotel bills were outstanding. The hotel called the cops who arrived in no time. I explained to the police that Synergy was responsible for the bills and that they had left without alerting anyone. The cops told me that it did not matter who should have covered the bill as far as they were concerned anyone who slept in a room had to pay for it. More cops arrived on the scene, and it seemed as if things were about to take a turn for the worse.

Suddenly, I got a call from Eddie Haddad who had been a relatively inactive member of the promotional team. He said he would pay the hotel bill, take care of our other expenses and provide additional accommodation if we agreed to go to California and finish the tour with Third World. We conceded. He paid the bill. We all went to California and spent a week relaxing. The tour resumed with Third World and Gregory Isaacs. Steel Pulse replaced Dennis. The tour ended in San Francisco, and we returned to Jamaica.

In the fall of 1985, Third World and I embarked on a European tour which included a leg at the Wembley Arena where Chaka Khan was the headline act. Third World gave a performance which had Chaka Khan's crew on edge. Chaka's production team wanted to disrupt Third World's performance. They turned on the house lights and had to be restrained from unplugging the sound on the Third World performance.

In 1985, I took Third World to Suriname for a concert. The opportunity came up while we were performing in Curacao where I had met a guy who said he was from Suriname. His name was Raymond Tom and he wanted the band to perform in his homeland. We decided on a fee based on the capacity of a venue, in Paramaribo, which could hold 4,000 patrons.

On our way to Paramaribo, a flight attendant kept talking about the show. She said that the 20,000 tickets allocated for the show were sold out. She wanted us to include her on our guest list. The band members got curious and asked how I had told them that the venue could only hold 4,000 patrons and the flight attendant was saying that 20,000 tickets had been sold. I told them that as far as I was aware the venue had a 4,000-patron capacity. The flight attendant said the

Lloyd Parks and "We The People" backed Gregory Isaacs and Dennis Brown on the inaugural **Reggae Sunsplash** tour in the US, 1985. (Reggaeville Photos)

Dennis Brown and Gregory Isaacs (Helen King photos).

venue for the show had been changed due to the demand for the tickets. According to her, the original venue could only hold 4,000 but the promoters had to shift to the stadium which could accommodate 20,000 patrons. Having the band perform in a venue contrary to what had been negotiated would be a breach of contract.

A huge crowd awaited us at the airport in Suriname. We were taken to our hotel and before we settled in, I demanded that I see the promoter. I thought that the guy who signed the contract was the promoter. I soon realised that he was just an agent. I was taken in a limousine to see the real promoter to discuss the supposed breach of contract.

I was more than surprised to learn that the promoter lived in a palace. It was then that I realised that I would be speaking to the leader of the country and not just a regular promoter. The man who was really behind the show was the head of the military, Desi Bouterse, who would later become president of the South American nation. He politely asked, "What can I do for you Mr Forbes?" I calmly told him what I had heard from the flight attendant on my way to Paramaribo. He asked me what figure would make me and my team comfortable. I gave him the number. He asked if there was anything else that I needed. I told him that we had brought a large amount of equipment to Suriname at considerable cost and would welcome any assistance in defraying the charges for freight. He assured me that I had nothing to worry about. He tacked on an additional US$5,000 to our fees and provided a voucher valued at US$5,000 to cover the freight for the equipment.

Bouterse did not fit the image of a military strongman. He seemed kind and gentle. I went back to the hotel and told the group exactly what had transpired. They were very excited. On the day of the show, Bouterse walked through the bushes (surrounded by his bodyguards) and entered the stadium to loud cheers.

Copeland Forbes and then de facto leader of Suriname Desi Bouterse after Third World's performance in 1985.

Third World delivered an excellent set. The large audience was ecstatic. Mr Bouterse came to me after the show and said he would like to have another performance the following day. He explained that he needed another show for his cabinet members and government officials. The event in the stadium was for the people of Suriname, he explained.

Desi Bouterse was the de facto leader, though not officially the president of Suriname between 1980 and 1987. He had conducted a military coup. He was elected president in 2010 as the leader of the National Democratic Party (NDP) winning 36 of the 51 seats contested.

We continued touring the Caribbean after departing Suriname. While we were hopping across the region, Third World and I decided that we should do a concert for ourselves in Jamaica. We wanted to celebrate in fine style, so we came up with the idea to stage a concert at the National Arena in Kingston, Jamaica. Reggae Jam Boogie was to be a joint promotion between Third World and me.

Ziggy Marley and the Melody Makers performed at the Reggae Jam Boogie, 1985.

One week before the show I got a call from Rita Marley requesting that I put

The I-Three, who had not performed in Jamaica since the passing of Bob Marley in 1981, made a special appearance at Reggae Jam Boogie. (I-Three Archives)

Ziggy Marley and the Melody Makers on the bill. She promised that the I Three would also appear. The I Three had not taken the stage in Jamaica since the passing of Bob Marley. The curtains came down on Reggae Jam Boogie on 28 December. The show was a huge success. 1985 ended on a truly high note.

1986 was the year Third World was due to deliver their third album, *Hold On To Love*, to CBS Records. The group headed to New Jersey, USA where they encamped for a few months doing recordings, writing songs and engaging in brainstorming sessions.

While Third World was in Jersey, a huge concert was being advertised for the Giant Stadium in the Garden State. This event was an Amnesty International promotion, and it featured: Sting, Yoko Ono, Peter Paul and Mary, Joan Armatrading, Peter Gabriel and U2. The week of the concert I got a call from Bunny Rugs, Third World's lead singer. He told me that Ingrid Green (a friend of the group) had called him from the United Nations where she worked. She informed him of the impending concert and that U2 would be one of the featured acts. Bunny thought that she was telling him that Third World would be on the show. He had mistaken "U2" for "you too".

Rugs called me to find out how I had booked Third World for this show and had not said anything to them. I advised him that I didn't know anything about Third World being on the Amnesty International show in New Jersey. I told him I knew the artists who were advertised, and Third World was not among them. He suggested that I check it out. I placed a call to Bill Graham, the promoter, and asked him whether Third World would be appearing on the show.

Bill told me that Third World was not billed for the show. I told him what I had heard but he insisted that the group was not on the line up. He then asked me if I wanted him to include them on the show. I quickly answered yes. Bill and Third World were great friends. He put them on the show. He gave Third World a 25-minute slot. The Giant Stadium was full. The show was beamed live across the world. Third World rocked the house. It was one of their most impressive performances.

CBS released *Hold on to Love* in early 1987 creating quite a stir. I called Associated Booking Corporation (ABC), headed by Paul LaMonica, to arrange the tour which began in Japan. We spent 10 days and did about six sold-out concerts. Our next stop was the United States. I realised that the band had been generating a significant amount of revenue on the tour but had been spending a considerable portion of it on road related expenses. I came up with an idea for the group to save more money.

I got rid of the tour bus which was costing US$12,000 weekly. I replaced it with an RV with a price tag of US$1000 per week. I paid the driver of the RV US$700 per week. I then got a van instead of a bus to carry the crew. We were achieving huge savings traveling around the USA.

Due to the exposure, they had received from the Amnesty International concert, the group was in great demand across the globe. In 1987 they played to capacity crowds in New York five times. They sold out the 43rd Street Pier in NYC. They attracted a capacity crowd at Radio City Music Hall with Burning Spear as the opening act. They sold out two shows at the Apollo Theatre, two more at the Red Parrot on 57th Street, and another at the Roseland Dance City, a popular nightspot. We took a one-week break for Reggae Sunsplash in Montego Bay.

The group called a meeting in my room at the Howard Johnson before we left New York for Jamaica. I didn't know what it was all about. I noticed that the bass player Richard Daley had his hands behind him when he entered my room. I thought something might have gone wrong and they wanted to discuss it. They all filed in and then presented me with an envelope. I opened it. My jaws dropped. The envelope was full of cash: a bonus for the work I had done. I have been grateful for this gesture to this very day. Ibo Cooper said it was the first time they had taken home so much money

Third World on stage at the Amnesty International Concert at Giants Stadium, New Jersey, 1986. (Third World Archives)

since they began touring. It was the first and only time I had ever received a bonus from any act for my services.

We arrived in Montego Bay elated and ready to roll. Instead of booking rooms at a hotel , the promoters rented a huge house close to Hanover for the group to spend the entire week. The house was less restrictive than the hotels.

Third World gave a scintillating performance at Reggae Sunsplash 1987. I remember seeing David Coore, then deputy prime minister of Jamaica and minister of finance, sitting on the side of the stage watching Third World perform. He was the proud father of Stephen 'Cat' Coore, a founding member of the band. Mr Coore fondly remembered the band rehearsing at Vale Royal, his official residence for a number of years, while his son was growing up. He was overjoyed to see his son and band conquer the massive festival.

We went back to New York from Montego Bay and resumed touring, heading to Yugoslavia, a nation which has subsequently split into several different countries. The Balkans was virgin territory for Third World.

The Reggae Ambassadors gave a magnificent 90-minute performance at the National Stadium in Suriname, 1985. (Third World Archives)

Ibo Cooper had purchased a Kurzweil one of the most expensive keyboards in the world at the time. The only other person I knew who had one was Stevie Wonder. The keyboard was going for over US$30,000. One of the crew members forgot that there was a difference between the electrical cycles in the United States and Europe. In the US it is 120 and in Europe it is 220. This keyboard was manufactured in the United States. The stagehand plugged the keyboard into the electrical system in Germany, not remembering that he would need a transformer. The circuit in the keyboard was burnt creating a huge problem.

I had to get the manufacturers in Boston, Massachusetts to ship another keyboard quickly to us in Germany where we were slated to play at the Lorely Festival. Most of the programs for the performance were stored in the damaged keyboard and it would take a long time to restore them. The mishap had occurred just before the group was ready to leave the hotel for the venue to perform. We were in deep trouble.

The promoter kept calling, telling us that we had to leave for the venue. Ibo had headphones over his ears as he tried to transfer the programs to another keyboard as quickly as possible. He knew that going to the venue without the samples on the keyboard would be an exercise in futility. We tried all we could. The promoter came over to the hotel and started screaming that we had to leave.

We decided at that point that we would play it by air. We had no choice. Ibo (being the musician he is) was able to improvise as we went along. Third World put on a great show. We all breathed a sigh of relief and waited patiently for the replacement keyboard to arrive from Boston. We had a break the next day. The Kurzweil arrived and Ibo sat inside his room all night programming the keyboard. We travelled throughout Europe and then went to the UK. The tour ended just before Christmas.

Cat Coore hosted a huge Christmas party at his house. The entire first, second and third worlds were there. The album *Hold on to Love* was performing well on the charts and the single of the same name was soaring. Everyone was happy. We were ready for 1988 and partied as if it were 1999.

I pointed out to Third World that whenever they did a song about love they always had a hit. I showed them the evidence to support it. Their first hit was "Now that We Found Love", "Try Jah Love" (Stevie Wonder) was next. Then there were 'Hold On to Love", "Love You with a Sense of Purpose" and "How Can it be Forbidden if It's Love".

CHAPTER 12
HEY WORLD!

In 1986, Rita Marley asked me to put together the *Hey World!* tour for her children Ziggy Marley, and the Melody Makers. The Marley siblings were signed to EMI Records and had released their *Hey World!* album. Rita wanted a tour to promote the album. We had to make the tour attractive to promoters and sponsors across the USA. We added the I-Three (Rita Marley, Marcia Griffiths and Judy Mowatt) who also had a new album on EMI Records. We included Nadine Sutherland who was signed to Tuff Gong Records and Tyrone Downie, the famed keyboardist who co-produced the *Hey World!* album. The backing band was the star-studded 809, led by saxophonist Dean Fraser.

The tour was scheduled to run for a month in several major markets across the USA. I selected a top flight technical crew, while keeping the expenses down. I opted for people who were like family to the Marleys. We had Errol Brown as house engineer, Stephen Stewart as monitor engineer, Flash Gordon as stage technician, Gagie as technical assistant, and Neville Garrick as the lighting director. Others on the tour were Addis Gessesse, tour accountant, and Lorna Wainwright, personal assistant to the I-Three. We planned on having three buses, but as the tour date drew closer, the Marley children wanted another one. Their siblings, who were not members of the Melody Makers, would be joining them on the tour.

The tour got off to a wonderful start. We played at some famous venues including: Circle Star Theatre in San Francisco; The Felt Forum at Madison Square Garden in NYC; Front Row Theatre in Cleveland Ohio; and the Universal Amphitheatre in Los

Angeles. As we moved across the US and the word got out that the children of the great Bob Marley were on tour. Fans were lining up early to get the best seats in the house.

We had a show in Albany, New York which started at about 1:00 pm. It was over by 3:00 pm. When we got back to our hotel, Mrs Marley said we should pack up and drive to New York City for the show which was scheduled for the following day. I told her that if we did that, it would cost us another day of hotel expenses as we would end up paying for two hotels in one day. She was not concerned about the cost. I immediately called the Penn Garden Hotel in NYC where we were booked to stay. They were able to accommodate us for the additional day. We had an entourage of almost 50 people. The hotel needed payment for the rooms immediately. I relayed the message to Mrs Marley. She instructed me to call her accountant, Marvin Zolt in NYC to take care of the payments.

We later packed our belongings and started the six-hour ride to NYC. Everyone was happy to be heading into the Big Apple a day earlier than we had expected. Shopping was on everyone's mind. All four buses pulled up at the front of the Penn Garden Hotel which was located across from the MSG. I got off the bus and went inside the lobby to secure the keys and rooming list for the entourage. I got the keys and went back outside to distribute them. Mrs Marley said she didn't like the look of the hotel and didn't want to stay there. She instructed me to call the Waldorf Astoria and check if they had available rooms.

I reminded her that we had already paid for rooms at the Penn Garden Hotel, and they would not refund us if we didn't stay there. She said she just wanted me to check with the Waldorf Hotel. I did. They had rooms available. I told her that the rest of the entourage and I should stay at the Penn Garden and that she and the Marley family should go to the Waldorf Hotel. She agreed. I instructed Addis Gessesse, and the security personnel to go

The Melody Makers (Stephen, Sharon, Ziggy, and Cedella) headliners of the **Hey World!** tour 1986. (RMM/Tuff Gong)

The I-Three (L-R)Judy Mowatt, Rita Marley, and Marcia Griffiths on the **Hey World!** tour in 1986. (Copeland Forbes Archives)

along with the Marley Clan to the Waldorf. At the Penn Garden, I gave all those who would normally have shared accommodation a room of their own. We had rooms to spare. We called some of our friends and relatives in New York to occupy the rooms that were still vacant. The show at the Felt Forum in Madison Square Garden was sold out.

We then headed north to Hartford, Connecticut; Providence, Rhode Island; Boston, Massachusetts; and Portland, Maine. Things turned sour in Hartford. The venue was packed to capacity. A patron was recording the show and our stage manager, "Flash Gordon", warned him to cease and desist. The patron continued to shoot the concert. Flash took away the cassette and the recording device from the patron who

Nadine Sutherland one of the acts on the **Hey World!** tour.

Copeland Forbes and Ardie "Cuban" Wallace backstage at the Gregory Isaacs' concert in Hartford, Connecticut, 2006. (Copeland Forbes Archives)

complained to some off duty police officers. The police ordered Flash to return the items to the owner. Flash refused and went back on the stage to do his job. The two off duty officers then decided to arrest Flash. The officers attempted to handcuff Flash. He resisted. The patrons intervened. The off-duty officers called for backup. Over 25 cops arrived on the scene and overpowered Gordon. They cuffed him and threw him in the back of a police car. I ran and called the promoter, Ardie Wallace who tried to speak to one of the officers who shouted, "Shut the f*ck up, if you open your mouth one more time, you'll join your buddy in the car". Wallace said, "You can't tell me to shut up, I have my rights". As soon as he uttered those words two officers jumped on him, cuffed him and threw him in the car with Flash Gordon. Another cop turned to me and asked, "What about you buddy?" My lips were sealed. The police car then left with Flash and Ardie.

At the end of the show, I informed the Marley family about the incident. Ziggy, his brother Stephen and the rest of the Marley family were terribly upset. We all decided to go down to the police station. The Marley siblings, along with their assistant, Sky High, all loaded up in a pickup and drove to the police station. We got to the lock up at about 1:45 am. It was closed. We knocked on the door and windows. An officer opened the door and asked why we were beating down the door at that time of the morning. We told him that members of our entourage had been unfairly arrested and we would like to get them out of jail immediately. We explained that we had a concert in Miami the next day. The officer looked at his watch and said, "Buddy let me tell you all something, it's 1:50 am and curfew time in Connecticut is 2:00 am. I'm going to close this door and I'm going to open it in ten minutes, and if you guys are still on the road you all are going to join your friends in jail". He slammed the door.

Our driver was a resident of Connecticut. He advised that it was best for us to leave as the cops were very serious when it came to enforcing the curfew in the state. The Marleys insisted that we should stay. The driver suggested we return at daybreak. We took the driver's advice and left. When we arrived at the hotel,

Ziggy Marley and the Melody Makers album cover of **Hey World!** on Virgin Records, 1986.

Ziggy Marley on the Massachusetts leg of the **Hey World!** tour, 1986. (Copeland Forbes Archives)

Mrs Marley and two bodyguards were sitting in the lobby waiting for us. They were overjoyed to see us. However, they became angry when they learned that Flash and Ardie had to spend the night in jail. They wanted to go to the police station, but we advised them against it.

The next day we left for Miami while two of our colleagues faced the law in the state of Connecticut. Rita told me to let Addis stay back in Connecticut to handle the legal matters.

Ardie and Flash finally got bail and were released after a brief court appearance. Flash and Addis later arrived in Miami, while Wallace the promoter remained in Connecticut.

We did the final show of the fantastic **Hey World!** tour in Miami Beach. It was a fabulous finale. All the artists came on stage singing "One Love, One Heart Let's Get Together and Feel Alright". The next day the Marley siblings flew to Nassau, Bahamas to spend a few days. I, along with I-Three, went up to New York City to attend Bunny Wailer's first solo concert presentation at Madison Square Garden. It was a rare engagement for the Blackheart Man.

“Bunny fancied himself as the intellectual centre of the group. Yet, Peter was, in the estimation of many (including me), the most erudite of the group.
I would say Bob was the smartest of them all.”

▸ Pg 133 Chapter 8

CHAPTER 13
TAXI CONNECTION

The Sly and Robbie *Taxi Connection* tours were staged in 1986 and 1988. The 1986 tour kicked off in Miami, Florida. The bill included Yellowman, Half Pint, Ini Kamoze and the Taxi Connection Band. In addition to Sly and Robbie on drums and bass, the band comprised Winston "Bopee" Bowen on guitar, Franklyn "Bubbler" Waul and Handel Tucker on keyboards. The Rass Brass horn section with Dean Fraser on saxophone, Ronald "Nambo" Robinson on trombone and Chico Chin on trumpet completed the ensemble. This massive tour was the first of its kind to be staged by the world-famous Rhythm Twins and was scheduled to last three months – moving across the USA, Canada, Europe, England and Ireland. I was commissioned to take charge of the tours.

After the first show in Miami, we flew north to the Big Apple to meet our tour bus and the rest of our road crew which comprised: David Rowe (house engineer); Stephen Stewart (monitor engineer); Gregory "Flash" Gordon (stage and production manager); Brandon Nailor (stage technician and MC); Rabbi (personal assistant to Sly and Robbie); George Phang (security); and Winston "Tallman" Harriott (assistant to the tour management). We played to sold-out houses.

Earlier in the year, Yellowman had undergone an operation to remove a malignant tumour from his lower left jaw which had been diagnosed as cancerous. The doctor told us that Yellowman could not survive a three-month tour with the symptoms he was showing. Each week Yellowman had to fly from wherever we were playing back to New York to receive treatment.

The **Taxi Connection** tour (clockwise) Robbie; Sly Dunbar; Sly and Robbie; and Half Pint, 1986. (Copeland Forbes Archives)

The "Hot Stepper" Ini Kamoze delivering on the Sly and Robbie **Taxi Connection** tour, 1986. (Copeland Forbes Archives)

When the tour reached New York, Yellowman's doctor decided that he wanted to see the performance at the Ritz Theatre. The doctor stood at the side of the stage and watched Yellowman strutting his stuff. He turned to me and said, "Mr Forbes this is not the same Winston Foster that I have been attending to weekly, where did he get all this energy to be jumping around the stage like that?" The doctor gave us some guidelines to follow. He told us that we should instruct the lighting director to use soft and magenta lights during Yellowman's performances. He also advised that we should not use a bright spotlight while Yellowman was on stage.

We forgot to forward the instructions from his doctor to the lighting director for Yellowman's performance at the Universal Amphitheatre in Los Angeles. The house put the bright spotlight on Yellowman while he was at the front of the stage. He stepped off in mid-air and fell into the orchestra pit. Robbie Shakespeare and I rushed to the front of the stage while the band kept playing. Robbie and I looked down, but we couldn't see Yellowman. We only heard him. He was still performing. Flash Gordon helped Yellowman back on stage. Yellowman didn't miss a beat, his resilience was a source of amazement.

The next day the entourage left Los Angeles for London. When we reached Britain, we went to Dover to catch the ferry to Stockholm. We arrived safely in Sweden the following morning. Just before we disembarked the ferry, I met with the entire technical crew and warned them about speeding. I pointed out that the weather was very bad in Sweden. Ice covered the roads. The van transporting the technical crew and equipment came off the ferry first. It left the vessel like a rocket. The bus with the artistes and band members came off about 30 minutes later.

Yellowman on the Sly and Robbie **Taxi Connection** tour, 1986. (Copeland Forbes Archives)

We ran into a traffic jam after about 45 minutes of driving. We were moving slowly along the road. Suddenly, I heard shouting from some of the band members who had gathered in the front of our bus. They were calling my name in a tone which indicated that there was something seriously wrong. I heard the trumpeter, Chico Chin, shouting "Oh my God, that's our vehicle with the crew!" The van had gone over a precipice and was smashed almost beyond recognition. I saw fire trucks, and ambulances. The police were directing traffic. It was a dreadful scene.

I told our bus driver to pull over to the side so I could look into the precipice. I told the police officers that the van was ours and that the passengers were part of our entourage. I explained to the police that we were entertainers from Jamaica on a tour. I went through the bushes to find our injured colleagues. Engineer Stephen Stewart was shaking like a leaf, Brandon Nailor was covered in blood. According to Stephen, Flash Gordon (the driver) was badly injured and was lying on the grass being attended by the medics. David Rowe's speech impediment was exacerbated. He was speechless. Rabbi was in a daze.

I spoke with Stephen Stewart. He was still conscious. He said Flash Gordon had been driving at an excessive speed and was trying to overtake a vehicle. Flash, realizing that he couldn't overtake successfully, applied his brake to avoid a collision with an oncoming vehicle. The van skidded on the icy road and left the ground. Stephen said that while the vehicle was airborne it hit a high-tension wire and spun on its way down the side of the cliff. Flash Gordon was thrown forward into the steering wheel. He had to be rushed to the nearest hospital for treatment.

Copeland Forbes, Robbie Shakespeare, African soccer player, Freddie McGregor, Maxi Priest, and Dean Fraser. (Copeland Forbes Archives)

We abandoned the van. We took the crew members on the bus transporting artistes and headed to the hospital. While we were at the hospital, I called our booking agent in the UK and asked him to inform the rental company that the van had been involved in an accident and that we needed another vehicle as soon as possible. The hospital told us that they would have to keep Flash Gordon for a few days. We were booked for three concerts in Scandinavia. We left him behind. While we were in Berlin, Flash Gordon was released from the hospital in Sweden. He quickly rejoined the group.

We toured Europe for several weeks and then went over to the UK for a fortnight. We played two dates in Ireland where the tour ended. On our way to catch the ferry back to the UK, the vehicle with the technical crew broke down. It was early in the morning, so we were unable to get assistance. We had to abandon the vehicle and take the crew and the equipment with us on the bus once again. We called our booking agent's office and left messages with the vehicle rental company to retrieve the van. We all got to Heathrow safely with enough time for the entourage to get some shopping done before flying to NYC.

We arrived safely in New York and checked into the Howard Johnson. It was December. The tour would end in Florida a few days before Christmas. Yellowman and I met in Manhattan and went into an electronics store on 8th Avenue. Yellowman bought a 42-inch TV. This was long before the days of the flatscreen, so one can imagine its bulk. He also purchased four 500-watt speakers. I asked Yellowman how he planned to get the items to Jamaica. The tour was not scheduled to be completed for another three weeks. Yellowman decided that he would carry his purchases with him on the bus for the rest of the tour.

It was pandemonium when the delivery truck arrived at the hotel. The manager was surprised when he saw the huge boxes being brought into the lobby and called me to address the matter. I, too, was shocked when I saw the boxes. Yellowman had planned to keep the boxes in his room but they were so huge they couldn't fit inside the elevator. The manager agreed to let the boxes stay in the lobby. Although the TV was placed in a far corner of the hotel lobby, it was still visible to the guests. Members of the crew took the four speakers up to their rooms. The following day when we were ready to leave, we placed all five boxes in the truck along with the equipment for the shows. Moving the boxes around on the truck soon began to take a toll on the crew members. They started to complain. We had to find a solution.

We offloaded all the equipment from the truck and moved Yellowman's appliances closer to the driver. We tied them down. All the band gear was moved closer to the back door of the truck. This allowed the crew to access their equipment without having to move Yellowman's appliances. The tour ended in Miami four days before Christmas. Yellowman shipped all his appliances to Jamaica. The entourage returned to the island in time for the holiday celebrations and the annual party at my house.

The second staging of the Sly & Robbie **Taxi Connection** tours took place in 1988. Hurricane Gilbert had just hit Jamaica. There was no electricity on the island. This seriously affected our rehearsal schedule.

Freddie McGregor and Maxi Priest were the artistes on this tour. The band members were the same as for the previous tours with the exception of Bubbler Waul who was replaced on keyboard by Herbie Harris. I arranged to accommodate the entire entourage in Florida for two weeks of rehearsals. Some members of our delegation stayed at my house in Florida, and a few at the Holiday Inn, not far from my home.

As we trekked across the border into Canada, at the end of the first week, there was a misunderstanding. One of the principals of the tour had made an observation which did not go down well with another member of the team. It created a bit of tension, but the tour continued playing to sold out audiences.

When we got to Cleveland, Ohio, Maxi Priest told me that he was very concerned about performing in the UK. He advised me of a potential confrontation between himself and a well-known "British bad boy", popularly known as Keithy Axe, who was aware that Maxi Priest was on the tour which had been heavily advertised in the UK. I told Maxi that the idea of his not doing the UK leg would not fly. I explained to him that the show had been billed with only two acts to perform and that we could not change the line up without creating problems with the promoter. I apprised Maxi of the steps we would put in place to guarantee his security.

We flew to Athens, Greece for the first show of the European tour. We did two magnificent sold-out concerts, not far from the world-famous Acropolis. We were in high spirits. From Greece we flew to Rotterdam, Holland, where we started the trek around the European mainland which lasted three weeks.

We took the ferry from Calais in France across the English Channel to Dover in the UK. When we arrived at Dover, I noticed that Maxi Priest had taken up all his

"Rass Brass" horn players (L-R) Ronald "Nambo Robinson, Junior "Chico" Chin and Dean "Cannon" Fraser live on the **Taxi Connection** tour, 1988. (Copeland Forbes Archives)

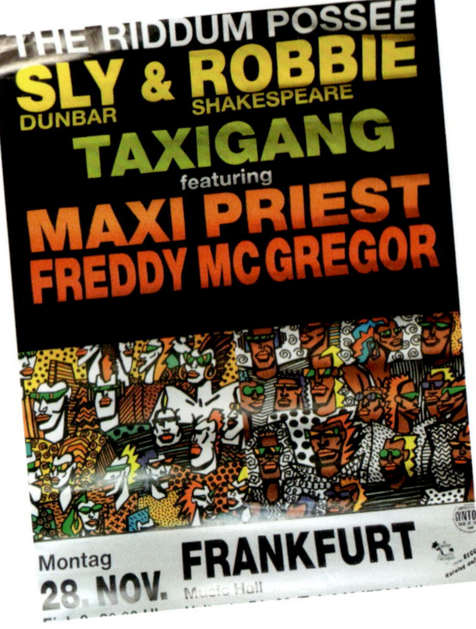

Poster for the German leg of the Sly and Robbie **Taxi Connection** tour, 1988. (Copeland Forbes Archives).

belongings and was leaving the bus. I asked him where he was going. He said he was leaving the tour because he was afraid of a confrontation with Keithy Axe. Robbie Shakespeare saw Maxi collecting his luggage and asked me where Priest was going. I told Robbie what Maxi had said about Keithy Axe waiting on him to get back into the UK. Robbie got very upset and went outside to speak to Maxi. Robbie told Maxi that if he left the tour there would be very serious consequences. Maxi returned to the bus and took his seat.

I sat with Maxi and explained that Robbie had arranged with some of his men to provide security for the entire entourage while we were in Britain. Maxi's manager, Alan Edwards, also secured the services of a well-known tough guy, Messam, to be Maxi's bodyguard throughout the UK tour. When we got to the hotel, the security detail was already there. We checked in the entourage and the extra security and started the preparations for the concert later in the evening. After we were checked in, Maxi came to my room and complained of a pain in his throat which, he said, was affecting his singing. He wanted to see a doctor. I thought it was an issue of mind over matter, but I called a doctor who came to the hotel and examined Maxi. He detected what looked like fungus at the back of Maxi's throat. The doctor suggested we let Maxi rest for the night.

We had to rearrange the entire show. We decided to let one of Maxi's backup singers, Barry Boom (a well-known artiste and songwriter in Britain), open the show for Freddie McGregor. Barry had written such hits as "Should I" (Maxi Priest); "In the Springtime" (Maxi Priest) and "Mi God Mi King" (Papa Levi).

Our next stop was the Hummingbird Club in Birmingham where we were scheduled for two days of performances. Keithy Axe was from the Birmingham area. We hired extra security. Everyone was looking out for Keithy. There was no sign of him. When we went back to our hotel, Maxi said he was going to stay with a friend for the night stating that he would feel much safer doing so. He promised to find his own way to the Hummingbird Club the following day. I acceded to his request.

Keithy Axe did not turn up so most of the security went down to London the following day. Everyone was relaxed. When we were ready to leave the hotel, Messam was the only security with us. We called Maxi and told him we were leaving for the venue so he should start making his way over to the club.

L-R Robbie Shakespeare, Freddie McGregor, Sly Dunbar and Maxi Priest at the JFK Airport at the start of the 1988 **Taxi Connection** tour. (Maxi Priest Photo)

We got to the club about 20 minutes before show time. Maxi turned up about five minutes after we arrived. The show kicked off with a set from The Taxi Gang. Maxi Priest went on and performed for about 45 minutes. Freddie was next and had the audience eating out of his hands. Coincidentally, as Freddie began performing "Push Come To Shove" one of the roadies came running to tell me that Keithy Axe was in the house with about six of his enforcers. I quickly made my way towards the stairs leading up to the dressing rooms. When I looked at the door, I saw Messam fighting off a group of men trying to gain entrance. I ran to the stage and shouted, "Robbie, Robbie! Keithy Axe and his friends are here and going towards Maxi's dressing room!" Robbie immediately handed his guitar to Steve Johnson, the stage technician (who himself played the bass), telling him to get on with the show. Robbie headed towards the dressing room. Messam was fighting like a tiger.

I ran over to the owner's office to inform him of what was taking place. Lloyd Blake, the proprietor of the club, took a shortcut through the boiler room. I followed him closely. Lloyd and I entered the dressing room from the back just in time to see Keithy coming from the other direction followed by Robbie Shakespeare. Messam was still busy holding off Keithy's friends.

Maxi's former manager, Erskine Thompson had, allegedly, taken a deposit from Keithy for the artiste to perform. Maxi failed to honour the commitment. The show never took place. Keithy also contended that while he was doing time in prison,

Freddie McGregor's PDA (Psion).

Maxi was having an affair with his girlfriend. Maxi confirmed both allegations. Maxi agreed that he would refund Keithy his deposit for his no show. He did not, however, give any indication, as to how he would make amends for sleeping with Keithy's woman.

The tour ended and we were ready to depart London for Jamaica, connecting through New York. We were originally scheduled for a late afternoon flight. Trombonist "Nambo" Robinson asked if we could change to an earlier flight as he, like other members of the group, wanted to do some shopping in New York before our departure for Jamaica. It was too late to make the changes so the travel agent suggested that we should get to Heathrow Airport as soon as we could as they had a flight leaving at around 11:00 am which would arrive at JFK in the early afternoon. This would give us more time to shop when we reached New York. Sly, Robbie, the Taxi Gang, Freddie McGregor and Maxi Priest were booked for the Sting concert in Jamaica slated for 26 December at the National Stadium. Sly, Maxi and his two backup singers decided to stay in London for an extra day to take care of some personal business. Robbie Shakespeare had decided to go back to the hotel to get some rest (after the show) and had promised to meet us at Heathrow for the flight to JFK.

We later learnt that when Robbie got back to the hotel, he wanted to change from the PanAm flight on which the entire group had been booked. Our itinerary was Heathrow – JFK – Miami – Kingston. Robbie wanted to go to Miami (where he lived) directly from London. PanAm would not allow the change as there were several restrictions on Robbie's ticket. Robbie purchased a direct ticket from London to Miami on British Airways.

The rest of the group went straight to the airport as our travel agent had instructed us to do. When the PanAm counter opened, I went to the clerk and enquired about getting on the earliest available flight to NY. Luck was on our side. The PanAm representative told me that there were seats available on a flight that was scheduled to leave at 11:00 am. We took it. I checked in everyone. Some of the members of the entourage almost changed to the later flight on which we had been originally booked.

Freddie McGregor had bought a Psion personal digital assistant (PDA). At the security check point they told Freddie that he had to put the gadget through the scanning machine before he could take it on to the plane. Freddie objected saying the radiation from the scan would damage the memory of his machine. He told me that he would be prepared to take the later flight on which we had been originally booked. The argument escalated. They summoned the supervisor. We explained that Freddie did not want to take the chance of ruining his PDA by passing it through the X-Ray machine. The supervisor assured us that it would be safe to do so. Freddie insisted that I take him off that flight. The supervisor told us that changing flights would not prevent the airline from scanning the gadget. I was able to convince Freddie to place the Psion on the security belt as it was mandatory for them to scan the gadget. Freddie finally complied. The Psion went through the scanner without any damage.

We waited a long while before the plane left the gate. It was winter. They had to de-ice the plane. I started hearing shouts and complaints from some members of our team saying that we should have stayed with our original flight as they considered the de-icing to be a bad omen. The calls grew louder, I finally jumped up and told them that all those complaining should relax and read Psalms 91 and 121. After a prolonged period of de-icing, we finally pushed away from the gate. We were on our way to JFK, New York.

Everyone was delighted when, after an uneventful flight, we landed at JFK. We noted that the mood in the terminal building was sombre as soon as we disembarked. People were crying. Something was wrong. We soon learned that the Pan Am flight 103, on which we had been originally booked, exploded shortly after take-off, and had crashed over Scotland in a town called Lockerbie. Two hundred and seventy people were killed. I immediately thought about Robbie Shakespeare, who had gone back to the hotel after the show and had promised to meet us at the airport. After clearing customs, I found the nearest telephone booth and made a call to Sly. I was overjoyed when I heard Sly's voice. I asked him for Robbie. Sly told me

Scenes of the crash site of the Pan Am flight 103 in Lockerbie Scotland.

that Robbie had bought a ticket on British Airways to fly directly from Heathrow to Miami.

We tried to contact our loved ones in Jamaica to reassure them that we were safe. I called Barry G, (the top radio DJ in Jamaica at the time) and did a live interview with him from JFK airport telling the entire island that we were all safe through "the powers of the most high" and were ready for Sting 88. I could not help thinking that Freddie could have gone to Zion in an effort to protect his Psion.

CHAPTER 14
WHO COLT THE GAME

It was 1987, promoter Don King brought quite a number of world-famous boxers including Muhammad Ali, Simon Brown, Mike Tyson and Mike McCallum for a grand black-tie affair in Kingston, Jamaica. King had also brought civil rights activist, Reverend Al Sharpton, Joseph (Joe), father of the great Michael Jackson, Dexter Scott, son of Martin Luther King Jr, and tennis champion, Arthur Ashe. Many Jamaican celebrities and political representatives from both parties (Prime Minister Edward Seaga and the Head of the PNP, Michael Manley), attended the event. There was an entertainment package comprising the I-Three and Carlene Davis. They were accompanied by the Dean Fraser-led 809 band. It was a lavish affair at the Wyndham Hotel in Kingston.

King and Ali called me aside at the event and said they wanted to do an international reggae tour. King noted that he could get sponsors to underwrite the expenses. I thought he was joking. I quickly realized that he was very serious. We soon settled on the acts for the tour. We agreed to keep it in the Marley family. We chose Ziggy Marley & The Melody Makers, The I- Three, The Wailers and Nadine Sutherland, who was signed to Tuff Gong Records, for the tour. We also added former Wailer, Tyrone Downie, as a special guest who would be accompanied by the 809 band. King gave me a list of prospective sponsors: Pepsi, Jeep, Panasonic, and Nikon. We agreed to a US$3 million guarantee for the tour.

A few months later there was a World Heavyweight Boxing title fight in Las Vegas. Don King and Rev. Al Sharpton invited us to be their special guests at the fight which was being held at the Hilton Hotel. We accepted the invitation. Marcia Griffiths,

Don King (in white) at the Wyndham New Kingston Hotel singing "One Love", flanked by (L-R) Carlene Davis, Tommy Cowan, Marcia Griffiths, Mike Henry, Olivia "Babsy" Grange, Rita Marley, and Judy Mowatt, 1987. (Copeland Forbes Archives)

The I-Three performing at the VIP reception for Don King at the Wyndham New Kingston Hotel, Kingston, Jamaica, 1987. (Copeland Forbes Archives)

Rita Marley, Addis Gessesse and I flew to Las Vegas. Judy Mowatt had a solo engagement and was unable to make the trip. We were in the company of Red Foxx, Sylvester Stallone, New Edition and a host of other celebrities. Jamaican promoter, Lucien Chen, and the then Minister of Culture and Sports Edmund Bartlett were also in attendance. The Jamaican delegation received a standing ovation when we were introduced. We were royally treated.

Copeland Forbes and Don King backstage at the Mike Tyson-James "Bone Crusher" Smith fight, Las Vegas, 1987. (Copeland Forbes Archives)

Soon after we returned to Jamaica, I received a call from Don King's office in NYC. They wanted us to come up to New York to receive the deposit for the tour. We were slated to pick up a cheque for US$1.5 million. On hearing the good tidings some of the band members started looking for houses to purchase. Dean Fraser and the drummer Mikey "Boo" Richards called me saying they had found houses and were awaiting my return to Jamaica. Everyone was looking forward to what was shaping up to be a magnificent tour.

Addis Gessesse and I were chosen to go to New York to collect the 50 per cent advance. On the day of our departure, we were picked up by Marcia Griffiths and taken to the Norman Manley Airport. I already had my ticket in hand, but Addis did not have his. The line at the airport was very long so I checked in Addis' luggage under my name. Addis could then pick up his ticket at the Air Jamaica counter.

While I was waiting for Addis to get his ticket, I saw three policemen coming through a door shouting "Who is Forbes?" I raised my hand and identified myself. The police were dressed in army fatigue. They asked me to follow them. I did. We went into a room strewn with luggage. I saw a police dog holding on to Addis' flight pack. The police asked if the flight pack belonged to me. I told him, "Not really". The officer asked me for the owner of the flight pack. I told them he was outside. We all went to the check in counter. Addis was in the line. I shouted to him "Addis come here". He said "No". He was afraid that if we came out of the line we were going to miss our flight. I told him not to worry about the flight, as we had bigger issues to address.

Addis came out of the line and followed us to the area where there was a pile of luggage. He saw the dog holding his flight pack in his mouth. He asked why the dog was holding on to his flight pack. One of the officers told him that there was, perhaps, something in the bag which should not have been there. They wanted to search the bag. I ran back outside the airport and shouted to Marcia Griffiths, telling her not to leave. I told her that the sniffer dogs might have found contraband in Addis' flight pack.

Marcia and I went back inside the airport to the area where the police were searching Addis' flight pack. They emptied the bag of all its contents. They didn't find anything. They threw the bag to the other side of the room to see if the dog would pick it up. The dog went and grabbed the flight pack again. Still, they came up empty handed. At that point the police asked Addis where he worked. He told them Tuff Gong. One officer exclaimed "Jesus Christ, that place has more ganja than anywhere else in the world". I told the officer that I could swear that Addis didn't smoke cigarettes nor marijuana. Marcia Griffiths told the officers the same thing. The officers searched and still could not find anything. They took the flight pack and tossed it away from us. They set the dog loose again. The dog went sniffing. He held on to the flight pack and pulled it outside and waited for his handlers to approach him.

The police decided to rip the flight pack apart. Suddenly, I heard one of the officers shout, "Bingo". There were three huge spliffs (blunts) inside a concealed pouch of the flight pack. I asked Addis to explain why brought the spliffs in his flight pack. He admitted that he had borrowed the flight pack from, the appropriately named, "Sky High" who was Ziggy Marley's security on tour. Sky High had put the marijuana spliffs in the flight pack and didn't remember to take them out. We explained to the officers that Addis had borrowed the flight pack without searching it. The officers believed us. They gave Addis a break. However, our flight had already left.

We stayed at the airport until we could find another flight. We finally did. We got to New York late that evening. We checked in at the Essex House Hotel and headed straight to bed. It had been a harrowing day. We were spent.

Don King and Rev. Al Sharpton were the first to arrive for our meeting the next morning. They were soon followed by representatives from Pepsi, Panasonic, Jeep, and Nikon. We gathered inside the conference room. Spirits were high. Expectations were great. Everyone seemed prepared. It was all systems go.

Rev. Sharpton got up to go use the restroom. On his way back he stopped by the newsstand in the hotel lobby and picked up a copy of the *Village Voice*, a weekly newspaper in New York. The headline caught his attention: "Rita Marley Charged for Fraud in the Marley Estate." He bought the newspaper and brought it into the meeting. He threw it on the conference table and asked, "Fellas, did you guys see this?" Everybody started reading the paper. I noticed the cheque books started to close. Everybody took turns reading the article. When the last person had finished reading, they all looked at each other. "I think we should wait until tomorrow before we make a final decision. We have to discuss this matter with our legal department," one of them said. The meeting was adjourned.

Don King and Rita Marley backstage at the Mike Tyson- James "Bone Crusher" Smith heavyweight title fight at the Hilton Hotel, Las Vegas, Nevada, 1987. (Copeland Forbes Archives)

Everyone left and went their separate ways. I told Addis, that things didn't look good. Addis and I went out on the town to eat and to attend a Broadway play. "Tomorrow would be a better day" we thought. We waited until late in the afternoon the following day to see if we would have heard from Don and his team. Nobody turned up. I was puzzled. When darkness descended, I told Addis that I didn't think Don and his team were coming again and suggested that they must have changed the meeting time to the following day, Wednesday. I wondered whether they might have needed more time to discuss the matter with their legal department. Another day went by without a meeting. We went to bed, without knowing what the future held.

On Wednesday morning we got up bright and early. We figured that by this time Don and the sponsors would have cleared everything with their legal departments. We were sure that we would see everybody at the Essex House Hotel for us to convene and finalise the deal. We waited to no avail. When I saw that it was afternoon, and we still had not heard anything about the meeting, I decided to walk over to Don King's office, which was just five blocks away from our hotel.

When we got to Don's office, his secretary asked if she could assist us. She recognized us as the gentlemen from Jamaica. She seemed confused.

"I thought you got the news already", she said to us.

"No, what news?", I responded.

She broke the news that the sponsors had decided that they could not go forward with the tour, and it would have to be postponed or cancelled. She told us that Mr King had left on Monday evening for Florida. We were absolutely heartbroken.

We did not know whether we should call Jamaica and tell them or wait until we returned home to do so. We did not know how to break the news to them. Everyone would be so disappointed. I decided that I was not going to wait until I got to Jamaica to break the news. I called Marcia Griffiths and told her that the tour was off and that she could go ahead and inform the band members. I initially told her that I would not give her the details over the phone. I soon changed my mind. I told her the full story. I had her promise that she would keep the additional information to herself.

Addis and I flew back to Jamaica the following day. We called a meeting at Tuff Gong with Mrs Marley. We broke the news to her. She said she had heard. She was quite stoic. She handled the matter with calm and dignity. The worst part was telling the musicians and technical crew members who were expecting a big pay day to secure a roof over their head. Some asked if the tour couldn't be postponed. I told them it was a highly sensitive issue.

Rita Marley was eventually freed of all the charges brought against her. The reaction of the sponsors brought home to me just how brittle corporate support can be. In the boardroom the principle of innocent until proven guilty did not seem to apply. Rita had not been convicted of anything yet the sponsors were willing to abandon us. They bailed at the first sign of adversity and what would have been a historic tour came asunder as a result of corporate timidity.

CHAPTER 15
TUNE IN

Gregory Isaacs went on a tour of Europe with the Ryddim Kings Band in 1989. The tour started off with a 16-hour ferry ride from Dover in Britain all the way up to Stockholm, Sweden. All the members of our entourage had cabins, but nobody (except Gregory) wanted to sleep. We spent the entire night swapping stories and having a good laugh.

In the mornings, when we had to drive to a new location for the subsequent leg of the tour, I would let the rest of the entourage go ahead of me as I always had to wait for Gregory. He was never able to wake up on time. I kept the key to his room for every hotel at which we stayed on tour. It was quite a task getting him ready in the mornings, but he was putting on excellent performances and the fans were enjoying the shows.

After our stint on mainland Europe, we returned to Britain to continue the tour. Our first show was slated for Brighton. On the way to Brighton, Gregory wanted to stop in Brixton to visit a friend and get something to eat. We got to a street in Brixton and Gregory told the driver to stop the car. He alighted while we remained behind in the Rolls Royce waiting for him. One hour passed and there was no sign of Gregory. After two hours, I went in search of him. I eventually found him asleep at a friend's house. We roused him from his slumber and managed to arrive just in time for the show in Brighton.

In order to avoid the undesirables who would be dropping in on him, I didn't book Gregory at the Colombia Hotel where the rest of us were staying. I got a luxury

Gregory Isaacs and Copeland Forbes on tour in Europe, 1989. (Helen King photos)

apartment (Lees Flat) near the US Embassy. Gregory's wife, June, had come to London and she was staying with him.

I soon got a call from the property where Gregory was staying. They told me to get there as quickly as possible. Something had gone terribly wrong in Mr Isaac's room. I dashed over to Lees Flat. When I got there, I saw water running down to the front desk, from Gregory's room. I rushed up to Gregory's apartment and thought I was in a swimming pool. Everything was upside down. The bathtub was overflowing. Gregory was shaking like a leaf. June was holed up in a corner and there was his friend, Jubba, who seemed out of touch with reality.

I ran into the bathroom and turned off the tap. While I was there trying to assess the extent of the damage, Jubba told me that Gregory wanted £10,000. Gregory chimed in saying he wanted the money immediately. I told them I didn't have that amount of money and that they would have to wait until I saw the booking agent in the morning. Gregory told me that if he didn't get the money on the spot, he would not be performing at the show in Huddersfield that night. June shouted at me saying I should not give them any money. Gregory started chasing her through the apartment. I told him that if he harmed her, he would go to jail. Gregory asked me who I was protecting. He was shaking violently. "You," I told him. He said he was not afraid of being arrested. He explained that he had gone to jail 40 times and the forty-first would not be a problem.

Then there was Jubba imploring Gregory, "Hitla, just say the word, if head affi fly fi di 10 grand". Gregory was called "Hitla" by many of his friends for his supposedly fearsome demeanour. Jubba was reassuring Gregory that he was prepared to kill on his behalf, and I seemed the likely target. Gregory asked for his passport. Luckily, I had it in my briefcase. I handed it to him. Gregory said If he did not get the money, he would be going back home to Jamaica.

Jubba kept promising Gregory that he was ready to kill. I saw a meat chopper in the kitchen. I went closer to it, pretending I was going to drink some water. I wanted to be able to defend myself should Jubba decide to pounce. June was cowering in the corner. Gregory swung at her each time she spoke. I told her to keep quiet. Suddenly, we heard a knock on the door. "Who dat?" Gregory asked. It was Denise Brown, the lawyer from New York whom Don Taylor had brought in to negotiate a new record deal for Gregory. She had come to hang with us that evening. The promoter had sent a Rolls Royce to transport Gregory. It was parked downstairs.

Gregory Isaacs and Ken Williams who was the first promoter to take the "Cool Ruler" to perform in the USA, 1975. (Reggae Global Photos)

When Gregory opened the door to let Denise into the room, I wanted to tell her to get out of the way so I could make a dash to my hotel and catch a flight back home. She asked me what was happening. I told her Gregory wanted £10,000 and that he stated he would not be leaving for the show until he got the money. I told Gregory I would go downstairs and ask the receptionist to call Don Taylor to get the money. Gregory locked the door, took out the key and put it in his pocket. He told me that I should use the phone in his room to call Don.

While talking to Denise, Gregory began to calm down. Denise asked how much money I had with me. I told her £1000. She said she had £500 and wondered whether he would accept £1,500. I told her I didn't know as he kept saying he wanted £10,000.

Denise told Gregory that she and I only had £1,500 between us, but we would give him the remainder the following day. He was at first reluctant, then he agreed. We handed him the money. Denise then reminded him of the show and that the car was downstairs waiting to take him to Huddersfield. Jubba said he would be driving his own car and would be taking Gregory with him. I agreed.

After Jubba and Gregory left, I called Robert 'Chuckles' Stewart, our production manager and told him that he should start the show without me, as soon as Gregory got to the venue. Normally, I would have been the MC for the show, but I had to stay behind to clean up Gregory's apartment. I had told the driver of the Rolls Royce that Gregory would find his way to the venue and that he should wait on me.

I finally reached Huddersfield at about 2:00 am. It was roughly a three-hour ride from London. I told myself that with a bit of luck we would have caught the closing of the show. When the driver pulled up to the venue, we saw about a thousand people milling around outside. I heard people saying, "See him ya". I sensed something was wrong.

The promoter asked me for Gregory. I told him Gregory had left hours ahead of me and should have been at the venue at least two hours before I arrived. The promoter informed me that the patrons were irate. Fights had broken out and people had started to steal equipment.

The promoters took the car keys from my driver. We couldn't move. When the crowd started to gather around me, I explained to them that Gregory had left me hours before in London on his way to Huddersfield. I told them I had no idea where he was. The promoter was mad.

They called the police who arrived in full riot gear. I was talking to the owner of the venue when one of the cops came over to us and asked who was in charge. Everyone was looking at me. The cop expressed concern about the safety of the patrons and asked who would refund them. I told him I didn't know. On hearing the question about refunds, the promoter slowly disappeared. People began to surround me. They were pointing in my face and threatening me. I told them I didn't have their money.

One fellow took out his knife and demanded his money back. I looked at him and said, "Let me tell you something, I spent six years in Vietnam and all I was trained to do was to kill. If you touch me, I will take out your throat with my bare hands right now." I was in my army fatigues. He pulled back and put the knife into his pocket. I called his bluff, though I had a weak hand.

The "Cool Ruler" Gregory Isaacs in Rio, Brazil, 2007. (Copeland Forbes Archives)

Gregory Isaacs and the Ryddim Kings in Amsterdam, Holland, during his European tour, 1989. (Helen King Photos)

While we were arguing, I saw the members of the Ryddim Kings band coming towards me. I heard "Doctor Paul", the leader of the band, say "Y-O Y-O". I asked him what he meant. "You are on your own", he replied. He told me he saw a man with a shot gun in the dressing room making threatening noises.

Doctor Paul instructed the musicians to take their time and leave one by one. He advised them that their driver had parked the bus further down the street. When the police asked who was in charge I pointed to the owner of the building. While the cop was talking to the owner, I bent down pretending to be tying my shoelaces and shuffled backwards for about 20 yards. Then I slipped away.

The entourage was booked at the Novotel Hotel in Bradford, but the show was held in Huddersfield which was about 13 miles away. I started walking on the highway until I saw a sign which read: "This way to Bradford".

By then, the tour bus had departed with the musicians. Their instruments were left behind at the venue. I walked until I got to the Novotel Hotel. When I got to the hotel, the members of our entourage were in the lobby. They thought I had been killed. I explained what I had to do to escape. I told them I saw people stealing the instruments and equipment. It was like a horror movie.

While we were still in the lobby, I saw a convoy of about 20 vehicles coming up the hill towards the hotel. We were all concerned, wondering whether the mob had found our location. The members of our entourage all scampered to their rooms. I ran into the hotel restaurant and hid under a table.

I heard a noise. I saw a throng. I spotted a man sporting a fedora and a white unbuttoned shirt with a mesh marina. It was Gregory. I heard him ask for his room key. They gave it to him. I got from under the table and went to the front desk. The receptionist asked if she could help. I explained to her who I was. She told me some people were looking for me. I asked her where they were. She said they went to Mr Isaacs' room. I was not sure what was happening. I called Gregory's room from the front desk. A man answered. I asked if I could speak to Gregory. He replied, "No, he's in a meeting and can't talk". I tried again, the same person answered, "Breddrin yuh nuh hear me say we inna a meeting and cyaa talk". I made a third attempt and the voice said, "Hol on deh bredrin," then he asked, "who dis?" I told him. He asked my location. I informed him that I was in the lobby. He hung up the phone. Within minutes six elevators opened in the lobby. Gregory suddenly appeared.

He was surrounded by a crowd. I asked him, "Why you didn't turn up for the show in Huddersfield?" He replied, "Boss mi don't know what happen to Jubba, we drive and drive till we see peenie wallie (Jamaican name for fireflies)." According to Gregory, Jubba thought the show was in Leeds.

Gregory Isaacs and his personal assistant Beecher Barrett on the **One Love** tour in the US, 2006. (Copeland Forbes Archives)

The promoter aborted the show in Huddersfield and suggested that we reschedule for the following Tuesday. The promoters of the Birmingham leg of the tour had heard about the debacle in Huddersfield and had driven up to Bradford to get Gregory to go on the radio to confirm that he would be doing their show in Birmingham.

The promoters from Huddersfield wanted Gregory to do an interview on a station in their area to confirm that their show had been rescheduled for the following Tuesday. The men from Birmingham wanted him to leave so that he could do their interview.

The men from both camps had a heated argument before going to the restaurant to get something to eat and calm things down. When they were finished, I was left with a tab of £1,000. We went to two radio stations in Huddersfield. By then the men in Birmingham were getting upset because they wanted Gregory to leave so that the patrons in their area would know that he was in town.

The promoters in Huddersfield finally agreed to let Gregory leave for Birmingham. By then, the Ryddim Kings Band had gone ahead of us. When we got to Birmingham it was 9:00 pm. Happily, there was a radio station which aired a reggae show until midnight. Gregory was able to do his interview and head to his hotel to get himself ready for his performance. There was very little time to spare. Showtime was midnight.

When we were ready to leave for the venue, I told Gregory and Jubba to get in the car with me. Jubba insisted that he would drive himself and would take Gregory with him. I told them to drive ahead of me. Jubba's driving was beyond dangerous, and I had the risky task of following him. It would have been unwise to let them out of my sight.

As was to be expected we were pulled over by the police. I quickly got out of my vehicle. I did not want Jubba or Gregory to interact with the police. I made sure I was the one doing the talking. The cop asked if we were drunk. I told him we were in a rush to get to a show. He asked where was the show. I told him by the Hummingbird Club. He asked if it was the Gregory Isaacs show. I told him yes. He confided that his wife had wanted to go to the show. He was in awe when I told him, Gregory was traveling with me. He signalled me to follow him. We were given a police escort to the Hummingbird. Jubba's and Gregory's bad behaviour seemed to have paid off. When we reached the Hummingbird, Gregory got out of the vehicle. I still didn't want him to go near the police. Gregory was shaking. The police wanted an autograph. I had Gregory sign one of his CDs which I had in my briefcase. I gave the CD to the cop and thanked him.

Gregory put on an amazing show. Josey Wales was in town and joined him on stage. They brought the house down. When he was finished Gregory asked me how I felt about the show. I told him that it was an impressive performance. He immediately asked for money.

We were booked for a show at Exeter University the following night. I told Gregory that we should return to base in London. He opted to stay in Birmingham and said that he would find his way to Exeter. I gave him £1,500 and headed back to London with the crew. The following day, I called the hotel in Birmingham to ensure that all was well with Gregory. I did not want any foul ups in Exeter. Jubba answered the phone and said he had not seen Gregory since the previous night. I kept calling but Jubba said he could not find Gregory.

Time was running out. I took the last train to Exeter. When I got to the campus people were walking out of the venue. I stopped some of the patrons and asked why they were leaving. They pointed out that the show had been cancelled. Gregory had not turned up for the gig.

The promoter seemed resigned to the outcome. "It is just one of those things in show business" he said. He refunded all the patrons. We went back to London. Why had Gregory missed the show in Exeter? According to a source at the Hummingbird, Gregory had gone back to the venue under the impression that he was performing there. He did not remember that he had played there the night before and was due to be at the Exeter University. Gregory would not have been able to reach Exeter from the Hummingbird for a performance at that time. Exeter was quite a distance from Birmingham.

When we got back to London, I called the agency about the car that Don Taylor had promised to buy for Gregory. Dave Betteridge told me that Don Taylor had left for the USA and had taken all the money with him. I didn't know how to face Gregory with the news that Don had not left any money for him and that he had not bought the vehicle he had promised. When I told Gregory what had happened, he was furious. He decided on the spot that he was not going to Huddersfield. This meant that we would have to leave the UK on Tuesday instead of Wednesday.

Chuckles said he would go with the band to the airport early and try to get on a flight.

When we went to check out at the front desk, the hotel staff confiscated our bags and hid them in a storeroom. Our bill had not been paid. I had no money. Danger was looming. When I asked the hotel staff if they would allow us to go if they received a fax from the agency promising to cover the bill, they agreed. The received the fax and released the luggage. Chuckles and the rest of the crew went to the airport. I had to stay back with Gregory.

I was having difficulty waking Gregory. I told him that if he did not hurry the promoters from Huddersfield might find him and he would end up having to do the rescheduled show for them. He got ready quickly and we left for the airport.

When we got to the airport Chuckles had already secured our passes. We boarded the flight and left Britain. It was a narrow escape. The British Airways flight made a stop in Nassau. I got off the plane and placed a call to Don. He told me that Valerie Cowan would be waiting for us at the airport in Jamaica and that she would give me £30,000 on our arrival.

Live Wyya band bassist Carl "CPhat" Edwards and Gregory Isaacs backstage during the **One Love** tour, 2006. (Copeland Forbes Archives)

When we got to Jamaica the musicians grabbed their luggage and hurriedly left the airport. Gregory and I waited behind. There was no sign of Valerie. I tried calling Don but got no answer. He seemed to have gone into hiding. Gregory and I headed to our respective homes in Kingston.

I called Gregory the following morning, he asked if I had heard from Don. I told him that I had not. He assured me that he knew what to do and that I shouldn't worry myself. He said he had a plan which he did not reveal to me. I would soon realise what Gregory had in mind.

I received a call from Don Taylor's girlfriend who operated a boutique at the Mall Plaza in Kingston. She asked me to come and see her immediately. I complied. She told me that someone had left a crocus bag at her door with a note which read, "Please find yuh man Don Taylor, so me can get me money, or put yuh self inna this bag."

I suspected that it was Gregory who had left the threat. I told her that I believed that it could have been Gregory who had left the note. She called Don immediately and related the incident to him. Don got the message. He told her to give him a minute and he would call back. He was true to his promise. Don told me that I should go to the office of a prominent attorney and get the Jamaican equivalent of £30,000 from him. Gregory drove behind me. We went to the lawyer's office and got a cheque. The Cool Ruler had prevailed. Score one for the wily Gregory and nil for the shifty Don.

Gregory Isaacs was very shrewd. Quick witted, he would always be ready with a response to put his rival on the back foot. Gregory was also very careful in the handling of his money. While some of his earnings would be devoted to frivolous activities, Gregory was always one to ensure that his money was invested in the acquisition of real estate and other valuable assets.

Gregory was able to create a song on the spot often without written lyrics. The Cool Ruler had a loyal throng of followers who seemed enamoured with his tough guy demeanour. His confessional "Hard Drugs" is considered a classic which many believe only Gregory would have had the musical chutzpah to deliver.

June Wyndham-Isaacs, widow of Gregory, inspecting the headstone at his resting place at Dovecot Memorial Park to mark the 70th anniversary of his birth, 15 July 2020. (Gregory Isaacs Foundation)

CHAPTER 16
AFRICA UNITE

The *Reggae Sunsplash* Africa tour was a project originally spearheaded by Synergy Productions (out of Jamaica) and supported by a group of promoters helmed by Keith Wilson from Liberia. A popular Jamaican businessman, Bunny Francis, was assisting them in their efforts. Representatives from Synergy spent three months traveling across some 16 African countries to ensure that the requisite systems were in place for the staging of a tour of such a magnitude. An impressive line up of artistes was booked including: Chalice, U Roy, Judy Mowatt, Third World, King Sunny Adé, Fela Kuti, Kotch and Burning Spear.

Negotiations between the Jamaican and African organisers of the tour broke down some three weeks before the artistes were due to leave for the Motherland. Tony Johnson of Synergy had requested that the Africans make a deposit of US$1 million to his account prior to his leaving Jamaica. The Africans did not agree to his request and Tony Johnson and Synergy pulled out.

I was at the Bob Marley Museum chatting with Ziggy Marley and his brothers when I saw a packed car enter the compound. I took a good look. I immediately recognised two familiar faces, Don Taylor's and Danny Sims'. This was quite unusual. These men did not normally travel together. Something was afoot.

They alighted the vehicle and told me that they had been looking for me and had heard that I was at the museum. They spoke to me about an impending African tour and informed me that Synergy, originally slated to manage the tour had dropped out. They futher explained that they needed someone with the appropriate expertise to replace

Synergy and that they thought that I was the man for the job. I told them that the project would be a major challenge for me as I did not have the requisite organisational infrastructure. They requested that I accompany them to the Wyndham Hotel where they were staying. I complied. They asked me to put a team together.

On the way to the hotel I started thinking about persons I would approach to be part of my team. I thought about my brother, Patrick Forbes. He had worked with me on the Peter Tosh tours. I also considered Steve Johnson. He and his wife were both very knowledgeable about tours. Danny and Don made three telephone calls as soon as we reached the Wyndham Hotel. First, they called Liberia and spoke to Keith Wilson. They introduced me to him on the telephone. He was very pleasant and promised to provide me with whatever I needed. Wilson called the Meridian Bank in The Bahamas which would guarantee the expenses for the tour. Danny Sims made another call to some of his Italian friends in NY and had me speak to them.

It was still fresh in my mind that in 1982, Mutabaruka, Steel Pulse and some other reggae acts had gone to Nigeria for a tour and had been left stranded there. I was a little wary about going forward. While I sat with Danny and his friends at the hotel, I recalled how I had to go to the then Jamaican Minister of Tourism to devise a plan to get the artistes and musicians out of Nigeria. The travel agents had not been paid in full and had cancelled the return leg of the airline tickets for the artistes. I, along with the Minister of Tourism, arranged with the Nigerian High Commissioner to Jamaica to have the artistes transported from Lagos to New York. The High Commissioner was instrumental in getting the Nigerian national airlines to be a part of the mission. The Jamaican consulate and the Jamaica Tourist Board office provided food and accommodation for the artistes once they landed in New York.

The Reggae Sunsplash Africa Tour

I told Danny and Don that my fee for the tour would be US$50,000. They immediately agreed. They responded so quickly that I wondered whether I should not have given the matter a bit more thought.

They told me that I should arrange for the artistes to sign the contracts which were already prepared. The payment schedule in the agreement was quite generous: 50 per cent on signing; an additional 25 per cent one week before departure and the final 25 per cent on arrival in Africa. The artistes readily agreed to the terms.

I noticed a clause in the agreement which said, that "if one should receive 50 per cent or more of his fee and the tour was not completed the promoter would not be

Fela Kuti and Copeland Forbes during the **Reggae Superfest** tour, 1989. (Copeland Forbes Archives)

"obligated to make further payments". I was uncomfortable with that provision and discussed it with all the artistes. They seemed unperturbed saying that they did not believe anything would go wrong to bring the tour to a premature end. I decided that I would change the potentially problematic clause in my own contract. I was adamant that I should not be penalised for matters which were beyond my control. The promoters and I agreed that I would get a flat fee regardless of the outcome of the tour.

Third World did not sign their contract, insisting that they wanted more money than the promoters were willing to offer. The promoters instructed me to find a replacement act. Third World was out.

I was at home when Robbie Shakespeare stopped by, as he normally did on a Sunday. I jokingly asked him If he would like to go to Africa? He said, "If the money's right". I told him of the situation with Third World and pointed out that the band had asked for more than the promoters were prepared to pay. Robbie asked me how much was the original offer. I told him. He immediately said "yes". He called his friend, producer George Phang, and asked him for the whereabouts of Yellowman.

Phang told him that Yellowman was attending a Stone Love session at the House of Leo. Robbie went in search of Yellowman. He soon returned in the company of Yellowman and George Phang. I made a call to Liberia, and I told them that Sly and Robbie, the Taxi Gang along with Yellowman were available as a replacement for Third World.

I was still harbouring some doubts about the tour despite the fact that I was making all the arrangements for it to become a reality. I wanted to find out why

Synergy had dropped out. I called Ronnie Burke of Synergy and asked him why they had pulled out of the tour?

He gave me the story that Tony Johnson had wanted a guarantee of a US$1 million paid to the Synergy account before he and the entourage would leave for Africa. Ronnie told me that he would not advise me whether I should go or stay. He emphasised that it would have to be my decision whether I wanted to take the risk. I decided I would give it a shot.

I assembled a crew with some of the best engineers and technical support personnel I could find. This group included: David Rowe, Mervin Williams, Robert "Chuckles" Stewart, Franchot Henry, Trevor Brown, Bugs from Chicago, Brigga and Bobby Budhal. They had all worked on **Reggae Sunsplash** concerts in the past. I also recruited Popcorn, Flash Gordon and Bird from the USA. I brought in Zola Burse who had worked as production manager on all the previous Reggae Sunsplash tours and events. We had an entourage of over 120 people.

One week before our departure, I received a call from the Ministry of Health requesting an immediate meeting with me at their office on Marescaux Road in Kingston, Jamaica. I went. They took me into a conference room where I faced about ten doctors and nurses. The spokesperson for the health workers told me that they had knowledge of our plans to take an entourage of 120 people to Africa. They informed me that as a precautionary measure the Ministry of Health would provide us with

Copeland Forbes and Yellowman on the **Reggae Sunsplash** African tour. (Copeland Forbes Archives)

some condoms to take on our journey. I agreed. They asked how long we would be staying in Africa? I told them three months.

When I reached home, I saw several large boxes on my veranda. I soon realized that the boxes contained the condoms which the Ministry of Health had promised. Clearly the ministry expected us to be very busy on tour as 10,000 condoms were left on my porch, according to the document which accompanied the boxes. I am not sure how they arrived at the figures. I, however, had some explanation to do as my other half was wondering why we needed ten thousand condoms to go on a tour?

I realized that I wouldn't be able to take all of the condoms with me on my flight, so I decided to take half of the amount and ask Bunny Francis to bring the rest with him when he joined the tour later. I called some of the band members and told them about the condoms. Everybody laughed. They thought I was joking.

We travelled in two separate groups. I went with the second batch. We were headed to Monrovia, Liberia where the tour was scheduled to begin. Sly & Robbie, along with the members of their group, were also in the second contingent. They had been late in signing up for the tour and so they were behind in satisfying the necessary conditions for the trip. I had to stay back in Jamaica with them so that they could complete their medicals and secure their deposits.

The portion of the entourage which comprised Chalice, Burning Spear, U-Roy, Judy Mowatt, Kotch Band, the technical crew and MC Tommy Cowan (Mr Yes Indeed) was on the first of the two flights from Jamaica en route to Liberia. The Jamaicans were due to join the Nigerians King Sunny Adé and Fela Kuti who were already in Liberia.

I flew to Miami, with the remainder of the entourage, and decided to stay there until the issue of the deposits (for Sly & Robbie and Yellowman) was resolved. We then left for New York, en route to Monrovia. Everyone on our flight was on a high when we landed in Liberia. Some members of the entourage, who had never been to Africa before, kissed the ground when we disembarked. They were filled with gratitude for being able to visit the Motherland.

The promoter, Keith Wilson, met us at the airport. When we reached the hotel, those members of our entourage who had gone ahead on the first of the two flights were already quite at home having fun. Some were playing football. Alla from Chalice was riding a horse, others were in the lounge jamming with the house band and dancing up a storm.

I went to the promoter's office the following day to discuss my remuneration after coming to the realisation that the fees I had charged for my services were woefully inadequate. I had underestimated the scope of work. I needed more money.

I explained to him my position that the budget I had been given was inadequate. He asked me how much more I needed. I told him. He agreed.

He asked if I needed some local currency to do some shopping. He pointed me to a room filled with boxes bursting with Liberian dollar coins. He told me I could take as much as I needed. Technically, we could not take much as one hundred dollars' worth of coins was quite a load to carry around.

The Liberia Show

The first show started at 8:00 pm sharp the following evening. Everybody was eager to perform. The opening acts were local. Chalice was the first overseas act to perform. Everything was going well until about two hours into the show when we heard a commotion at the gate. I walked to the main entrance and couldn't believe what I saw. There was a large contingent of soldiers in their camouflage outfits who were obviously in a dispute with the members of the promoter's staff. They were all speaking in a language I didn't understand. I picked up that the disagreement might have had something to do with money. The soldiers and police soon took control of the gates and started collecting money from the patrons while putting the cash in their pockets.

The promoter and his team were helpless. I remembered that the day before I was at the promoter's office when a representative from the Minister of Culture came and requested 20 complimentary tickets. I heard Keith Wilson sending a gross message to the minister. He was quite graphic in his instructions. He told the bearer to tell the minister to "fuck off". I asked Wilson how he could give such a message to the representative from the Ministry of Culture. Wilson complained that all they wanted was "money, money, money".

After some two hours the police and soldiers left. Things quickly returned to normal, and the show went on until about ten the following morning with Fela Kuti and Africa 80 bringing down the curtains on the event.

We all headed to our rooms to get some rest after the show, as we would be leaving Liberia the following day. Next stop was Ghana, or so we thought. Later that evening the promoter called me to his office for a meeting. He told me that we would not be going to Ghana but to Zaire claiming that they had switched so that they could get hard currency. I followed the instructions of the promoters and informed the members of our entourage about the changes.

The following day we all left for the airport at about midday. It was an eight-hour drive to the airport where a chartered A300 was supposed to have been waiting on us.

When we reached the airport, we had to wait another three hours for our plane to arrive. Everyone was relieved when it did. We boarded the airplane as soon as it reached the tarmac. We had a four-hour flight to Zaire.

When we entered Zairean airspace, the airport was closed. There were no air traffic controllers. We were all then very angry as the plane was circling around while the pilot tried to locate the air traffic controllers and other important members of the airport staff. We were flying into a country which was supposedly unaware of our presence in its airspace. It was a frightening experience. We circled the airport numerous times before the runway lights finally came on and we were given clearance to land. We finally touched down. Everyone was awake and anxious to deplane. We quickly disembarked and went inside the terminal building but would have to contend with another delay. We could not find anyone in customs or immigration to process our travel documents. We were forced to wait for the customs and immigration officers to report to work.

I boarded a bus as soon as I cleared customs. I was anxious to reach the hotel to ensure that proper arrangements were in place for the accommodation of our entourage. According to my itinerary, we were booked to stay at the Red House. There was a word (N'sele) written in small print (beside the name of the hotel) on the itinerary. When I told the driver that we were going to the Red House he looked puzzled. He started shaking his head. He formed his hands in the shape of a gun, suggesting that shots would be fired at us. He spoke French and some tribal languages which none of us understood. He did not seem to understand English. I signalled for him to drive as I really wanted to get to the hotel to make arrangements for the entourage.

After we had driven for about 45 minutes, the driver stopped some distance from a building and started shaking his head indicating that he was going no further. I decided to walk towards the "Red House". On approaching the building. I saw soldiers armed with guns at the entrance. I wondered why this hotel would have armed soldiers on the property. I went up to one of the soldiers and introduced myself. I asked him to show me to the front desk. He spoke no English, so I struggled to explain to him by making signs.

After a few minutes, an officer who spoke a little English passed by and asked if he could help. I told him that I was looking for the front desk so I could check in my entourage. He looked at me as if he thought I was crazy. He led me through a building where I saw machine guns, grenade launchers and an array of artillery. I was thinking to myself that the hotel was a veritable fortress. He took me into a room where some soldiers and officers were in a meeting. When I walked in, they looked uncomfortable. Their privacy was being invaded.

The soldier who led me to the room spoke in French to an officer and tried to explain my plight to him. The officer, whose chest was covered in medals, asked me in English how he could be of help. I repeated my story that I was booked to stay at the Red House and was trying to find the front desk so I could check in the members of my entourage. I showed him my itinerary and informed him that I had some 120 persons who had been traveling for more than a day and needed to rest. He looked at my itinerary and began to laugh.

We were, indeed, at the Red House, but it was the home of the president and not the hotel. The Red House (the hotel) where we had been booked to stay was located in N'sele, some 20 kilometres from the home of the president where we had gone. I apologised to the soldiers, grabbed my bag and ran back towards the bus.

Outside, I saw that Sly & Robbie, Burning Spear, Judy Mowatt, U-Roy, King Sunny Ade and members of the management team were standing at the gate with their suitcases waiting to get to their rooms. I told them that we had made a grave error and that we were actually at the home of the Zairean president which shared the same name as the hotel where we had been booked. I told them that our hotel was actually in N'Sele, some 20 kilometres from where we were.

On our way to the hotel in N'Sele, the bus broke down. We, as a result of the language barriers, were unable to determine what was the cause of the vehicular malfunction. The members of our entourage who had not slept for more than a day were letting their displeasure known in very explicit terms. I tried to flag down a vehicle to take us to our destination. My greatest fear was that those members of our team whom we had left behind at the airport might have reached the hotel and were causing a commotion if they had not been given the keys to their rooms.

Finally, the driver of our bus indicated that the mechanical problem was resolved. We were ready to resume our journey. After about an hour of driving we were caught in traffic and were moving very slowly. I heard a noise coming from the other side of the highway but could not determine the source as there were trees planted along the median. I picked up the sound of Jamaican patois coloured with expletives. I realised that the rest of our crew was nearby. I signalled to them that we had heard them, and we were going to turn around and join them.

When our vehicle pulled up behind the parked buses, all the crew members were already outside their vehicles. They were hopping mad. They said that they had gone to the Red House in N'Sele and it was a derelict YMCA building. I remember Chuckles Stewart saying that the mosquitoes at the Red House were so big they could lift a man. I didn't ask him how many mosquitos would have been needed for the task.

Amidst all the commotion, Tommy Cowan was in the bus sleeping. He finally woke up and came out of the bus sporting thick locks which reached below his waist. The populace in many parts of Africa were not familiar with locks. The local people who had gathered to investigate what was happening ran into nearby bushes as soon as they saw Tommy.

Judy Mowatt (of the I-Three), was the only female act booked on the **Reggae Sunsplash** African tour, 1988. (Judy Mowatt Photos)

I checked my itinerary to see where the promoter might have been staying. He had travelled separately and had arrived in Zaire before us. I soon realised that he was booked at the Intercontinental Hotel in Kinshasa. We boarded our buses and headed for his hotel.

We arrived at the Intercontinental, where I presumed that the promoter was staying. I was concerned that the front desk personnel would panic on seeing such a large number of strange sounding people alighting from buses and invading the lobby. I told our driver that the vehicles should not be taken up to the front door of the hotel. Initially, I would be the only person from our entourage to enter the lobby, everyone else should remain on the buses which were parked at a reasonably good distance from the front desk.

I asked the receptionist if there was a Keith Wilson staying at the hotel. She informed me that he had left a "do not disturb" request at the front desk. I told her that it was an emergency and I had to speak to him. She called his room. She told him my name. He said I should come to his room.

I went up to his room where I found him half asleep. "Keith I can't understand how you are here sleeping comfortably in your hotel room while we have been stranded for over two days," I said. He asked if we had gone to our hotel. I told him that when some members of the entourage turned up at the Red House, they realised it was a derelict YMCA building. Keith claimed that he knew nothing of the deplorable conditions of the Red House. He told me to check with the front desk of the Intercontinental to see if they could accommodate the entourage. I did. They had rooms for the entire contingent.

Robbie Shakespeare was the first to approach the lobby with his suitcase. They gave him the key to his room. He was followed by Sly who was also granted access to a room. Soon the rest of the entourage was in the lobby waiting to be

Burning Spear one of the featured acts on the **Reggae Sunsplash** African tour, 1988. (Burning Spear Music)

assigned rooms. After some two hours of processing everyone except me had secured a place to stay. The receptionist told me that she would speak to the general manager to get permission for me to stay at the exclusive annex which housed major celebrities when they were in town.

The following day the entire technical crew, led by Zola Burse, went to look at the venue. One of the most important challenges we faced was the issue of voltage variations across the different African territories. All the sound equipment and the stage gear including lights came from the United States which is on 110 -120 voltage. We did not have any issues in Liberia which operated on a similar system to the one used in the USA. Zaire was different.

We heard that they had a huge generator at the venue so the technical crew decided to check whether it could be brought into service for the occasion. The crew worked tirelessly but was unable to secure operability between our equipment and the generator.

While we were at the venue a man approached me asking what was my mission. I told him that we were connected with the Reggae Sunsplash event which would be held at the venue the following day. I added that we were setting up from the day before to ensure the smooth running of the event. The man expressed concern that we were busy setting up for a show and had not made payment for the use of the venue. I told him that I found his allegation strange but explained that I was not the person responsible for making the payment. I went back to the hotel and told Keith Wilson about the matter of the rental for the venue.

Keith and I went back to the park to meet the man who had demanded payment. Keith asked him to provide the rate for the rental of the park. He told Keith that it was half a million Zairean francs. Keith paid him. He handed Keith a receipt. Keith and I left the park and went to the municipal office to complete some paperwork.

When we got to the office, we told them that we had already paid for the park as the gentleman in charge had demanded that we did.

The workers in the office were shocked when they heard that we had paid a fee for the use of the park. They explained that the government (which owned the park) had waived the rental for the show. They asked if we knew the man to whom we had made the payments. We told them we did not.

We had the lingering problem of the electricity supply on the day of the event. The technical crew worked tirelessly. Darkness was descending on the venue and so, too, were the patrons many of whom had paid for their tickets in advance. We reluctantly took the decision to tell the waiting patrons that due to technical problems we had to postpone the show. We promised that the tickets purchased for the first night would be valid for the second night of the scheduled three-day event.

Meanwhile, during the days female fans were flocking to the hotel to mingle with the artistes. This led to the management of the hotel having to beef up security. The overwhelming presence of the women led to a precipitous drop in our condom supplies. I was not quite sure if the members of our entourage were giving away the condoms as the rate of depletion was rapid, indeed.

We spent the entire Saturday calling all over Kinshasa trying desperately to find generators. However, we would suffer the same fate as we did on the Friday. There was no electricity at the venue when the gates were due to be opened at 6:00 pm. Fans would have to be denied entry to the venue for the second consecutive day.

We remained at the hotel as we thought it would have been pointless for us to go down to the venue unless we were assured that the technicians had identified a reliable electricity supply for our equipment. Once again, the promoters had to tell fans that the tickets they were holding would have to be used for the following night.

While we were at the hotel (waiting to get word that there was a compatible power supply at the venue) someone told us that the US Embassy in Kinshasa had over 150 generators. I realised that I would have to find the address for the ambassador's residence as he would not have been likely to be in office on a Sunday. I collected the passports of the US citizens in our entourage and put them in my bag. I told the Americans in our group to accompany me to the ambassador's residence.

It was 10:00 am on the Sunday when we arrived at the ambassador's residence. Two military personnel were on duty at the gate. We identified ourselves. We told the guards that we wanted to speak to the ambassador. The guards informed us that it would be impossible for us to see the ambassador on a Sunday, adding that we would have to visit the US Consulate in Kinshasa the following day in order to have audience with him. The ambassador spotted us from his veranda and rang the guards to find out why we were at the gate. I overheard the security telling the ambassador who we were and that we needed to speak to him urgently. The ambassador agreed to see us. They escorted us to a conference room in the residence.

I explained our plight to the ambassador. He asked if we had a truck. My heart leapt on hearing the question. A solution was now in sight. He then asked which artistes were billed on the show. I started listing their names. When I mentioned Fela Kuti from Nigeria, the ambassador's expression changed. He whispered to his assistant who was taking notes. After a few more minutes of discussion, he promised to get back to us later in the day. I left the meeting feeling quite upbeat. We were going to have a show after all.

I told our production manager, Zola Burse, to check out a truck so that we could pick up the generators and take them to the venue as soon as the ambassador gave us the green light. I sat in my room all day as I did not want the ambassador to call and not find me. My phone rang at about six in the evening. It was the front desk telling me that some people from the US embassy were there to see me. I told the front desk to send them to my room. I was overjoyed. Things were falling into place. We would have a show or so I thought.

Two representatives from the US Embassy (a man and a woman) came up to my room. Both had been in our meeting with the ambassador earlier in the day. My heart sank as the man said that the ambassador had asked him to tell us that he was sorry he would not be able to grant our request. I can't recall if he said anything after that as my mind went blank.

I had already sent Chalice down to the venue with the expectation that they would be performing. The lady from the embassy pulled me into my bathroom. I was taken aback. I soon realised that she wanted to share something confidential with me.

She explained that the US Embassy did have the generators in their storerooms but pointed out that the Americans had an issue with Fela Kuti. There would be no show. Fans who had waited three nights to see their favourite acts perform would have to settle for a refund. I got the message down to Zola Burse at the stadium that he should pack up the equipment as we would be leaving Zaire the following day.

Next stop Lagos, Nigeria. We sent the containers with the equipment to the airport and loaded them on to the chartered plane.

On the morning of our departure, I received a call from the representative of the local light and power company who told me that he had found out that we needed some specially configured generators and that he was able to provide five of them for us. He was suggesting that we could put on the show that night. I told him that train had already left the station. We would be flying out later in the day and our equipment was already on our plane.

We made allowance for the members of our entourage to do some shopping and a little sightseeing before we left Kinshasa for Lagos.

We were cruising at 37,000 feet when Fela Kuti decided that he wanted to go higher than the plane . He took out a huge joint and started smoking. Soon he was joined by other members of the entourage whom he supplied with some huge marijuana cones. The aroma of the marijuana permeated the entire cabin, and everyone was flying under a cloud. The flight attendants were unable to find their way down the aisle. Thanks to Fela everybody and everything we had to eat. or drink was smoked.

The Lagos Heist

When we landed in Lagos, Judy Mowatt was walking out of the terminal building to the curb when she slipped and fell. I was walking ahead of her so I put down my luggage and went to assist her. I managed to get her back on her feet. I turned to pick up my belongings. I could not find them. I thought a member of our entourage had taken them up and had carried them to the bus.

We left the airport and headed to the Holiday Inn in Lagos. After reaching our destination I checked all the luggage which accompanied our entourage. I reluctantly concluded that my suitcase and briefcase had been stolen.

Yellowman and I had a friendly rivalry to see who had more Travel Fox shoes. I had about 12 pairs of Travel Fox shoes in my suitcase and several items of great value in my briefcase: US$5,000, a gold watch, my US alien card (green card) and 56 airline tickets. Luckily, I had my passport in my pocket.

I went to the United States Embassy in Lagos to report the loss of my green card. They told me that I first had to get a police report before they could begin the process of replacing my card. When I got to the police station, I remembered that I had been there six years before with Peter Tosh when we visited Nigeria as guests of Sonny Okosun.

I had to get a copy of the report signed and stamped by the senior police officer to take back to the embassy. I asked for the senior officer. They told me that the superintendent (the senior officer) was down the road in a bar drinking with friends. I decided to go in search of the superintendent. I found him and told him what I needed of him. He listened and then continued drinking as if I did not exist. I gave him a US$10 bill and told him to buy himself a drink. He asked me for a piece of paper and a pen. He quickly wrote a short message for me to take back to his secretary.

I went back to the police station and gave the note to the superintendent's secretary as I had been instructed. She was supposed to type and stamp the report about the missing travel document so that I could take it back to the bar for the superintendent to sign. She took the note from me and put it on a desk. I quickly realised I was not on her list of priorities and handed her a US$10 note. She immediately went to the desk and quickly typed and stamped the report. I took it back to the superintendent. He promptly signed it. I gave him another US$10 bill and headed straight to the embassy where they asked me to fill out a few documents and take some passport size pictures.

They gave me two envelopes at the embassy; one was addressed to the airline informing them that I was a legal US resident whose green card had been stolen; the other was to the US Customs and Immigration Services (USCIS) advising them of my circumstances.

On my way back to the hotel I decided to stop by a roundabout to purchase a few pieces of clothing as I had nothing to wear except what was on my back. I was also trying to see if I could spot anyone who might have been trying to sell any of the items stolen from me.

I stopped at the radio station where they had scheduled an interview for some of the artistes in our entourage. I told the DJ to announce that anyone who found and returned my briefcase would be given an all-expense paid trip to Reggae Sunsplash in Jamaica. They made the appeal on radio and television. However, no one came forward to claim the trip.

We were booked to perform for three consecutive nights in Lagos at Tafawa Balewa Square. King Sunny Ade and Fela Kuti requested large dressing rooms. I had to ask the authorities of the Tafa Balewa Square (which was a government-owned complex) to give us a large room for Fela and his entourage. They readily complied. Everything went well on opening night.

The next day I got a call from the gentleman in charge of the venue complaining that we had left the place reserved for Fela in a deplorable condition. The official said he was disappointed. He took me into the room which they had allocated for Fela's entourage the previous night. There was an awful stench coming from the room. I was shocked to see what had been done to the room. It seemed to have been a form of political protest. I didn't know what to say.

Meanwhile there was a large surge in the demand for the rapidly dwindling supply of condoms. The musicians and artistes were having a great time in Lagos and so, too, it seemed were the Nigerian women. It was a grand reunion of Africa and the diaspora. It was love and harmony.

On the third and final day of the concerts in Lagos, Keith Wilson decided that he should do a leg of the tour in Benin, a city in the south of Nigeria. MC Tommy Cowan, who had been very close to the promoter, went to Benin to help make the arrangements for the show. Tommy was a huge star wherever we went. Posters with his image featured prominently in all the cities in which we played.

Tommy Cowan (Mr Yes Indeed) was a big hit on the **Reggae Sunsplash** African tour, 1988. (Copeland Forbes Archives)

It would be a five-hour road trip from Lagos to Benin. Given the size of our entourage we had to charter four buses for our journey. On the eve of our departure from Lagos, I went downtown to a "bus company" to make our booking. We were scheduled to leave at nine the following morning. The "bus company" told me that I had to pay for the vehicles in advance since we were leaving so early in the day. I paid for the buses. I got a receipt and went back to my hotel.

The next morning, we checked out of the hotel and were waiting in the lobby for the buses to arrive. We were ready for Benin. We waited until after 10:00 am. We didn't see the buses. I went back downtown with the intention of finding out from the "bus company" what had been the cause of the delay. No one could tell what had happened to the bus company. It had disappeared into thin air. Another business had sprouted at the very spot from which the bus company had been operating. I had been robbed.

I was now forced to book four more buses. I went to another "bus company". I paid for the buses. This time though I kept an eye on the guy to whom I had made the payment. I noted that he was packing up his bags and heading outside after he had collected my money. I asked him where he was going. "I am going home" he replied. "Who is going to take care of the buses?" I queried. "Don't worry the drivers are coming with the buses", he assured me. "If you have my money, you are not getting out of my sight", I informed him.

I held on to him and told him he had to wait until the drivers with the buses arrived. He kept saying he had to leave as he was late for an appointment elsewhere. I told our security, Sugar Bear, (a burly 6' 3" man from out of California) to hold on to the man who had our money and not to let him go unless he paid the drivers the full amount (on the spot) for the return trip to Benin.

The guy from the bus company spoke in a different language to some men who were standing close by. The men went to some buses which were parked nearby. I told the man from whom I had booked the bus that he should pay the drivers in full for the return trip. He refused. I instructed Sugar Bear to grab him and throw him in the bus in which I would be travelling. I told the driver to head to our hotel. The three other buses followed.

"The collector", as he referred to himself, kept saying he had to go to a meeting. I told him he could return our money and be on his way. He insisted on holding on to the money and we refused to let him go. We all left for Benin with the 'collector' as our reluctant guest.

We were about an hour into our journey when "the collector" asked us to stop so that he could pray. He was a Muslim. It was midday. We stopped by the roadside. He came off the bus and took a little mat from his briefcase. Burning Spear shouted a warning that I should keep an eye on "the collector". Sugar Bear escorted "the collector" to prayer.

"The collector" kept saying that his family didn't know he would be going to Benin. He claimed that his relatives would be frantic when they could not find him, I again reminded him that he would have been free had he returned the deposit for the buses to us.

"The collector" would repeat his prayer ritual several times along the journey much to the distress of the members of our crew who wanted to reach Benin. We decided, after a while, that he would have to shorten his prayers. When we saw that it was getting dark, we told him that he would have to wait until we reached our destination before he could engage any further in his rituals.

Benin

We got into Benin late in the evening. Tommy Cowan had been in town before we arrived, and had ensured that everything was in order. We checked in easily and had a brief meeting with the promoters. The local organising team in Benin was led by Mr T, a thug with a menacing aspect. I suspect he earned the moniker through his striking resemblance to the title character of an American television show. He had a small army. He was notorious.

Shortly before the show on the next day, I had a visit from our production manager, Zola Burse. He informed me that he had called Los Angeles and his wife had told him that she had checked the account in which the salaries for the technical crew members should have been deposited. There was no money. In fact, nothing had been lodged to the account for over three weeks.

The crew members decided that they were not going to work unless they were paid the entire balance they were owed. One of our crew members, Flash Gordon, was throwing a tantrum. He was screaming, hurling things across the room and smashing objects against the wall. He wanted his money. I had a growing mutiny on my hands. I told Zola to get hold of the promoter. Everything had suddenly ground to a halt.

Some 30 minutes later, I looked outside and saw the promoter coming towards my room. Mr T, accompanied by about 30 thugs armed with pieces of wood, was behind him. They all came into my room. They said they had heard that we were not going to do the show. I said to Keith Wilson the promoter, "It is almost three weeks, and no money has been deposited to the account to pay the members of the technical crew. What are we to do?" He had no response.

I asked Keith and Mr T to give us ten minutes to sort out the issue. Mr T and his gang went outside. They did not care whether or not we were paid. They just wanted a show. I had a quick meeting with the crew. I told the members of our entourage that I had not come to Africa to be killed by a mob. My advice was simple, "Let us do the show and try to get our money afterwards". Most of those present agreed with me. Flash insisted he was not working and headed to his room leaving a trail of expletives in his wake.

Mr T and his men returned to my room and asked whether we were going to work. I told him "Yes". We got ready and left for the venue. When we reached the stadium it was already packed.

The concert went smoothly. The large crowd was ecstatic. The Jamaican acts delivered.

Fela Kuti and Egypt 80 put on a magnificent show. Our joy would soon turn to despair as nobody could find the promoter when the show ended. We packed up our equipment and headed back to the hotel. The Nigerians, most notably King Sunny Adé and Fela Kuti, went to their respective homes.

Ghana was slated to have been the next stop. We were due to depart from Lagos to Accra. We were scheduled to head to Abidjan the capital of The Ivory Coast from Ghana. Based on the developments, it was evident that Benin would be the last leg of the tour.

Many persons had been left holding the bag including the drivers of the truck which were ferrying the equipment. Luckily, the promoters had taken care of the hotel accommodation before we arrived. We already had our plane tickets to fly from Lagos to New York. In the original itinerary we would have finished our tour in Abidjan and then returned to New York through Lagos. Since the tour was aborted, we would simply use the Lagos to New York leg of the ticket which we already had. The only challenge we faced would be to reschedule the flights since we would be leaving Africa earlier than expected due to the abrupt end to the tour.

All kinds of rumours were swirling regarding the location of the promoter. Some said that he had gone back to Liberia. The truck drivers came to my room and swore that they were not moving until they got the balance owed to them.

The buses were ready to leave Benin for Lagos. Sugar Bear had all the keys to the buses and the drivers were under constant monitoring. We had even bought clothes for the drivers. We were all set to leave when Mr T and his thugs turned up at our hotel and told us that nobody could leave until he got paid. Mr T had been stiffed by the promoter and he was holding us hostage. The sweet irony was that it was Mr T who had forced us to play without being paid who was holding us hostage because the promoter had not compensated him.

Later in the afternoon, I was sitting in the lobby when I saw a bunch of soldiers and security men driving into the hotel compound. I went to find out what was happening. Our MC Tommy Cowan was in a military vehicle surrounded by soldiers pointing guns at him. "Tommy what are you doing in the soldiers' vehicle?" I asked. I cannot recall his response.

Tommy later told me that he thought about his little son Nathan back in Jamaica and he remembered his mother always telling him that "You should always try to save yourself when the ship is sinking". He said that when he saw the imminent danger, he tried to save himself by sneaking out of the hotel and hiring a car to take him back to Lagos where he could get a flight to New York. On his way back to Lagos, Tommy ran into a police roadblock. Tommy had been part of an advance team that had gone to Benin along with Keith Wilson to recruit people to work in various capacities on the show. Policemen and soldiers were hired to provide security and they had not been paid. Tommy knew that if the police and soldiers caught him, he would be in trouble. That was exactly what happened.

One of the soldiers had looked behind the front seats of the taxi, saw Tommy lying on the floor and exclaimed, "Ah, look what we've got here, it is Mr Yes Indeed himself. We have not been paid. We need to be paid now".

Tommy said he was scared stiff as he thought they were going to beat or kill him. He explained to them that he was not the promoter and that he was one of the acts from Jamaica who had just been assisting the organizers and he had not been paid either. They told him that he could not leave until they were paid so they brought him back to the hotel. I said to Tommy, "I cannot believe we are all here in the same boat and you tried to get away without letting us know". Tommy started laughing and began singing the Freddy McGregor song with the refrain "we are all in the same boat".

We needed to get back to Lagos but had to face the reality that Mr T was using us as pawns in his efforts to get paid. He and his thugs were hanging out at the entrance to the hotel with the hope of spotting the promoter while keeping close tabs on our movements.

As the evening turned into night, I came up with an exit strategy. I asked all the members of our entourage to take their belongings quietly through the back door of the hotel and load them on to the buses. I told them to mill around in the lobby to act as a distraction to Mr T so he would not suspect our intentions.

The plan was for us to board the bus one by one, slipping out of the hotel through the back door. When we were all on board, we would push the buses down the hill and would not switch on the engines until we were at the bottom of the incline. It was a very risky proposition. We would have paid a heavy price had Mr T caught on to our scheme.

The production manager, Zola Burse, could not be a part of our escape plans. Zola had to remain, unwillingly, in Benin to protect the expensive equipment which were on the trucks. Zola had rented the equipment from Studio Instrument Rental (SIR) in the United States. It was his responsibility to return them in good condition.

At about 3:00 am the buses slipped away from the hotel. When we reached the foot of the hill, we started the engines and headed off to Lagos. However, our hearts were in Benin because we had left Zola behind. How would Mr T react when he realised we had slipped away right under his nose?

We eventually reached Lagos and out of harm's way. I didn't know where the promoter was, but I had a gut feeling that he would not have been far away from our hotel. I called a few hotels and asked for "a Keith Wilson". I called the Sheraton and got connected to his room. We spoke. He promised he would come over to my hotel to see me. He kept his word. He came to my room very late. While we were there talking one of the musicians came up to my room to fetch some condoms. He saw the promoter and went back to inform other members of our entourage.

Within a few minutes those to whom the promoter owed money were in my room. Suddenly, Flash came flying through my door shouting at the promoter,

"I want my fucking money now or I am going to kill you". The promoter travelled with two bodyguards, one of them was a retired army general and the other an officer in the Nigerian Police Force. Flash dashed outside my room and returned with a large flowerpot. He began chasing the promoter.

The two security men tried to protect the promoter from Flash who hit one of the bodyguards over the head with the flowerpot. The man fell, bleeding from his face. Hearing the commotion, hotel guests were running in their pyjamas and nightgowns screaming in fear.

Sugar Bear attempted to restrain Flash who was still trying to get at the promoter. The other member of the promoter's security detail took up the metal stand from which Flash had taken the flowerpot and held it aloft. He was about to behead Flash who was being held on the ground by Sugar Bear.

I grabbed the metal stand from behind the promoter's bodyguard preventing him from killing Flash. The promoter was so scared that he seemed to have wanted to jump through the window. I had to remind him that we were on the tenth floor. He managed to leave the hotel unharmed.

We still had the issue of Zola and the equipment in Benin to be resolved. Mr T and his men were beating Zola. It broke my heart hearing Zola cry on the phone. I felt helpless but not hopeless. One of my Nigerian friends, John, who had more than a passing acquaintance with Mr T came to visit me at the hotel. I explained the challenge I was facing. He volunteered to go to Benin to get Mr T to release Zola and the equipment.

Although I knew where Keith had been staying, I did not share that information with anyone as I did not want any further incidents. If Flash had a whiff of where Keith was booked, I am sure he would have gone there and created a scene. Flash wanted his money and was prepared to die in Africa for it.

The next day John came over to see me on his way to Benin. I gave him US$50 to take care of food and transportation. I didn't know how he would secure the release of Zola and the equipment and I didn't ask.

We were worried that Mr T would have accompanied John to Lagos as a way of guaranteeing that he would eventually be paid. I called Zola and gave him the news that a friend, John, was on his way to sort out the problems. The artistes began making their arrangements to leave Nigeria. I had to stay. There was no way I was going about to abandon Zola. Judy Mowatt, U-Roy, Tommy Cowan, Kotch and Chalice remained at the hotel with me.

Late one evening, I heard a big commotion downstairs. I looked through my window and saw trucks loaded with equipment entering the hotel parking lot. My friend

John had delivered on his promise. Zola and the equipment had been released.

John came upstairs to my room with Zola and the drivers. The scent of unwashed bodies was unbearable. Yet, we had more pressing problems. The drivers said they were not releasing the equipment until they got paid.

Zola came up with an idea. He said he was going to his room to make a call to Mr Johnson the CEO of SIR (Studio Instrument Rental) in NY and ask him to wire some money to take care of the amount owing to the drivers. While Zola had gone to make the call, I asked John how he had managed to get Mr T to release the trucks. He said he told Mr T that he had confiscated all our passports so none of us could leave the country until we paid him and the truckers. Mr T took him at his word.

The "Burning Brass" all-female horn section L-R Pam Fleming, Nilda Richards, Jenny Hill backing Burning Spear on the **Reggae Sunsplash** African tour, 1988. (Enid Farber Photos)

Zola returned to my room and told me that Mr Johnson was as mad as hell but had agreed to wire some money to help with the payments to the drivers. Covering the truckers' fees (even though it was not his responsibility) was a small price for Mr Johnson to pay for the return of his equipment. The drivers would not be swayed by the argument that Mr Johnson had not hired them and that he too had not been paid for the use of his equipment. They were using his equipment as their bargaining chip.

The funds arrived from Mr Johnson the following day. When the money was converted into naira, it was insufficient to pay the drivers in full. The truckers had not only charged for the trip but for the time they had spent on our assignment. I called Fela Kuti and told him that I was coming to see him as I needed his help. I related the quandary I faced and told him that I wanted him as a mediator in settling the impasse. Fela agreed.

I wanted Fela to give the impression that he had given us a loan to pay the drivers but that there was a shortfall in the amount he was able to provide. Fela, himself, had not been paid so such a claim would seem plausible. If the drivers knew that the money to pay them had come from the United States, they would have demanded the full amount.

Chalice, one of the acts billed on the African **Reggae Sunplash** tour, 1988. (Chalice Music)

Fela turned up at the hotel with an entourage of about 25 people. I called all the truck drivers to a meeting in my room with Fela. The drivers knelt in deference to Fela. Luckily, my suite was large enough to accommodate the throng.

Fela explained that he himself had not been paid. He told them that he had some money which could not cover all that was owed to them but it would be better than nothing. Fela had spoken. The drivers looked at one another and asked for a few minutes to confer among themselves. They retreated to my bathroom for a huddle.

After reaching their decision they all came out of the bathroom and bowed before Fela. They agreed to take the money Fela had offered them. Fela had one request. "Before I give you any money, I want you to take the trucks to the airport and offload the equipment onto pallets and then come back to the hotel and I will pay you". They all bowed in agreement. The truckers drove to the airport and offloaded the equipment onto the pallets which were placed in the containers and taken aboard the plane.

On completing their assignment the drivers came back to the hotel. Fela gave them the money as he had promised and told them to share it equally among themselves. I thanked Fela for his handling of the delicate negotiations. He invited me to come to his shrine later in the evening as he would be performing there. I took Fela up on his invitation. He gave a great performance at the shrine. Some of his wives were dancers and were part of his act. I thoroughly enjoyed myself.

The next day I called the Sheraton and realized that Keith, the promoter, was still there. I decided to pay him a visit. I went over to the Sheraton along with Judy Mowatt and U Roy. They both wanted to speak to Keith. They told him that they needed the balance he owed them. Keith paid them. He also gave me the remainder of my fees.

He then turned to me and said, "This guy Flash thinks he can just come into Africa, hurt people and get away with it? He is going to rot in jail". Keith confided that he had some police friends waiting at the airport to arrest Flash. I pleaded with him to call them off. He refused my request pointing out that his bodyguard was in hospital on account of Flash. He repeated his threat that Flash would "rot in jail". Going to jail in Lagos is not a fate I would wish on my worst enemy.

U-Roy "Mr Chikka Bow Wow Wow" was a huge hit on the **Reggae Sunsplash** tour of Africa in 1988. (Beckford Music)

I left Keith and went back to my hotel. I called the airport and spoke to a representative of the airline on which Flash was booked. I asked if a Greg Gordon (Flash) had already checked in. They told me he was standing at the counter. I requested to speak with him. I asked Flash if he had encountered any problems at the airport. He told me that some soldiers and police had come and taken him away saying they were going to arrest him on a number of charges. Flash said he gave them US$50, and they told him he could go. When I heard that I ended the conversation as I wanted him to get on the plane as quickly as possible. He boarded the plane. It took off. He was out in a flash.

I didn't hear anything more from Keith while I was in Nigeria. I left for the airport the following day to take my flight to New York City.

When I got into New York, I checked in at the Howard Johnson Hotel. I had to remain in New York to replace my stolen green card. I saw Robbie Shakespeare at the hotel. His first visit to Africa was not what he had expected. He confided that as a result of his experiences in Africa he was going to cut his locks. He said he was traumatized.

I saw Robbie a few weeks later in Jamaica. He said he wanted to get the balance of his money for the African tour. He went to look for Bunny Francis who was a Jamaican associate of the promoter (Keith Wilson). Francis had a thriving fishing business in Kingston.

Robbie went to Bunny Francis' office. He saw Bunny's wife and asked her to tell her husband that he needed the balance of the amount due to him from the recently concluded African tour. Mrs Francis, who was perhaps unfamiliar with the workings of the music industry and the strange mannerisms of its personalities, called her husband in panic.

Bunny Francis contacted Jim Brown (one of the most feared personalities in Jamaica) to rein in Robbie. Bunny did not know that Jim Brown and Robbie Shakespeare got along quite well. Jim Brown called Robbie and told him what Bunny Francis had reported to him. They both had a good laugh.

Bunny Francis told me that he was in possession of a US$50,000 cheque. He promised that he was going to Atlanta to cash the cheque which was originally made out to Third World who had decided not to do the tour. He promised he would pay the outstanding balances when he negotiated the cheque. Bunny went to the USA; however, he never delivered the payment.

CHAPTER 17
WORLD A REGGAE

In 1989, after spending many years on the road with numerous artistes and groups, I decided that it was time to organize my own tour – *Reggae Superfest*. I selected Dennis Brown, Freddie McGregor and Lieutenant Stitchie backed by Lloyd Parks and We The People Band for the inaugural tour. Along the way we added the Nigerian Fela Kuti and Africa 80. We also had some special guests in attendance including the Marley family and world welter and lightweight champion Simon Brown.

All went well until we reached Salt Lake City in Utah where our booking agent, Paul La Monica, informed our team that two legs of the tour had been cancelled. This meant that US$30,000 had suddenly disappeared from our budget. I was in Miami when the news broke. I called my brother Patrick (the tour manager) to ask him if all the members of the entourage had been paid up to date. He said that they had been. I suggested that we call off the tour and send everybody home.

Patrick called me about a half an hour later and said he had met with the artistes and musicians, and they all had decided that they would prefer to stay on the tour rather than go home. I told Patrick of the risks associated with such a decision but conceded that if they all were willing to roll with the punches it would be fine with me.

A promoter in Florida, popularly known as Peppers (sister of the late great Jamaican promoter "Jack Ruby"), called me about a date for a show which she wanted to stage in Miami. I was reluctant to give her a commitment due to our mounting financial challenges. I was not sure I would have been able to keep the show on the road long enough to accommodate her timeline. I finally decided to take the gig and

Scenes from the Reggae Superfest, 1989. Copeland flanked by promoter "Pepper" and Marcia Griffiths; John Holt and Marcia Griffiths; promotional T-shirt. (Copeland Forbes Archives)

use her deposit to prolong the tour. I flew to Arizona and met the entourage. They were performing at the Celebrity Theatre in Phoenix. We then went west where we were booked to perform at the Celebrity Theatre in Anaheim, about 45 minutes from Los Angeles where we were staying.

The band and Dennis Brown left on the tour bus for the venue about 90 minutes before the scheduled show time. Freddie McGregor, Lieutenant Stitchie, Dave Rodney (Lieutenant Stitchie's manager) and I would leave later by taxi. When we got to the venue, the promoter told us that they had seen neither Dennis nor the bus. Dennis was slated to close the show. Stitchie and Freddie were at the venue but there was nothing we could do. The entire band and Dennis were missing on the bus. We had to wait.

Around 9:30 pm the manager of the theatre told me that we would have to cancel the show and refund the patrons. We followed his instructions. This meant that we had now lost US$20,000 in revenues in addition to the $30,000 hit we had suffered previously. The bus with Dennis and the band finally arrived just after we had refunded the patrons. We asked the driver what had happened, He said he had taken the route towards San Diego instead of Anaheim. There was a gaping $50,000 hole in the budget. I thought it didn't make sense to go any further with the tour. I decided that I was going to send everyone home.

While I was making travel arrangements for our return to Jamaica, somebody called the promoter in Florida and told her that the tour had ended prematurely. She was very upset. However, she was most accommodating. She told me that she would be willing to foot the additional charges (food and lodging) for an extra week in order to ensure the staging of her event. She went to the airport in Miami and took the artistes and crew off a Kingston bound flight. She booked them at the Holiday Inn on University Drive.

We were ready to head to the venue on the afternoon of the show (which was scheduled to start at 1:00 pm) when Lloyd Parks came and told me that some of his band members said they were not moving until they got paid. Pepper (the promoter) heard about the standoff and decided to go to the hotel to settle the matter. She gave Freddie– who was representing the artistes and musicians- US$10,000. Freddie told everyone that he had received the money from the promoter and that he would share it after the show. Lt Stichie said he needed some cash to pay some bills and asked for a thousand dollars. We gave it to him. He promised that he and his friends would drive behind our tour bus to the venue. Stitchie said he needed to pick up something along the way. He was scheduled to open the show. When we reached the venue, he was nowhere to be found. Stitchie had taken the money and headed straight to the airport. Everyone was disappointed in him. During the tour he had been having a sore throat and had missed a few dates. Although we had to take a reduction on the guaranteed fees at some of the venues (where he did not perform), we still paid him his full weekly salary. The promoter had booked John Holt and Marcia Griffiths, so Stichie wasn't really missed. Reggae Superfest 1989 ended on a sour note.

Reggae Superfest 1990 - Europe

I was not much in favour of staging a 1990 **Superfest** tour, given what had happened the previous year. However, we finally decided to put a package together for Europe. The contingent included Dennis Brown, Freddie McGregor and Marcia Griffiths all backed by Lloyd Parks and We The People Band. The driver of our tour bus kept complaining that the vehicle was transporting more people than it was legally allowed to carry. When we reached Italy, the driver insisted that we would have to find another means of transportation for some members of our entourage as he would not continue to exceed the stated carrying capacity of the bus.

Freddie had a good talk with the driver. However contrary to what Freddy believed, the issue had not been settled. When we were ready to leave Italy, the driver insisted that he would not be taking more passengers than the vehicle was licensed to carry. Freddie was incensed, delivering some choice Jamaican curse words while giving chase to the intransigent driver who ran into the hotel lobby shouting, "If

Freddie McGregor, Marcia Griffiths, and Dennis Brown (partially hidden) on the **Reggae Superfest** 1990 tour of Europe. (Helen King Photos)

you're going to kill or hurt me then do it where people can see what happened." We eventually had to ask some members of our entourage to take the train to our next stop, Holland. We immediately made arrangements with the bus company to replace the uncooperative driver.

A highlight of the tour was acquiring pieces of the Berlin Wall which had just been torn down. On our way to West Berlin, in Germany, we had to drive through the communist East and decided that we should each get a piece of the historic wall. Our driver stopped. We all got out and borrowed sledgehammers from the other folks who were also trying to get a piece of the historic wall.

A piece of the Berlin Wall which had divided East and West Germany. (Copeland Forbes Archives)

Reggae Superfest 1991

In 1991, Rita Marley approached me to coordinate a tour to commemorate the 10th anniversary of her husband's passing. I told her about **Reggae Superfest**. She said the tour would be a good vehicle to celebrate the important milestone. **Reggae Superfest 1991** would be headlined by: The I-Three featuring Rita Marley, Judy Mowatt and Marcia Griffiths with special guest the "809 Band". The tour commenced in Europe during the summer.

The 1991 **Reggae Superfest** tour had quite a few highlights including a leg at the Lorelei Festival in Germany which saw a scintillating performance from Ziggy Marley and the Melody Makers. We had a grand reunion concert in Italy with Julian Marley, The I-Three, Ziggy Marley and the Melody Makers, The Wailers Band, Mrs Cedella Booker (mother of Bob Marley) and Gilberto Gil from Brazil.

The tour went on to Scandinavia where we had a series of shows scheduled for Sweden and Denmark. In Stockholm, Sweden we were slated to be part of a huge festival. The promoter, was not able to pay the balance owed to the I-Three who decided that they would not be performing unless they received the remainder of their fees. The venue was teeming with fans eager to witness the Jamaican trio appear. However

Judy Mowatt, Rita Marley, Marcia Griffiths (The I-Three) headlined the Reggae Superfest package in Italy to mark the 10th anniversary of Bob Marley's transition, 1991. (Copeland Forbes Archives)

if the artistes had wanted to perform, there would have been no sound. The promoter also had a balance owing to the company which provided the public address system. The technical crew had gone on strike.

We were all sitting backstage when a gentleman, whom we did not know, came up to us saying that he had driven miles to see the I-Three perform and he would be very disappointed if they did not take the stage. He asked the reason for the delay. I told him we could not find the promoter to pay the balance owed to the artistes. He asked how much money was owed to us. I told him US$15,000. He assured me that he would cover the balance. He wanted to see the I-Three perform.

He spoke to the sound engineers. Suddenly, I could hear the speakers being energised. The fan who had given the assurance to pay the I-Three had also agreed to pay the operators of the public address system. A representative from the company providing the sound reinforcement system told me that the gentleman who had made the undertaking was well connected and was an associate of Arne Naess (the husband of Diana Ross).

The I-Three gave a beautiful performance and the gentleman whose pledge had underwritten their appearance was thrilled. He told me that he had a nightclub in the city and that he wanted us to come and hang with him later in the evening. We all agreed. Later that evening he sent a huge Rolls Royce to take us to his club where we received royal treatment. We felt reassured that we would be paid. We thoroughly enjoyed ourselves and went back to our hotel in the wee hours of the morning.

At about 8:00 am, my phone rang. It was the owner of the club. He said he was downstairs in the restaurant waiting to have breakfast with us. We all got dressed and went down to meet him. He gave me one of his business cards and told me I

I-Three perform on Reggae Superfest at "Paradiso" in Amsterdam Holland, 1991. (Helen King Photos)

should keep in touch. He then handed me a brown paper bag filled with US$100 bills. I didn't bother to count the money. I trusted him.

We were scheduled to leave Sweden for France later in the evening. I got word, however, that the hotel was looking for the promoter who had not paid for the rooms which he had booked for the artistes and their entourages. We decided to slip out of the hotel way before the checkout time. When I reached the airport, I called the hotel to speak to some of the artistes and the members of their teams whom we had left behind. They reported that they were not able to leave as the hotel had held on to their luggage for the unpaid bill. We flew down to Paris and continued the tour which ended successfully in the UK.

Reggae Superfest 1992

In late 1991, my European booking agent Dave Betteridge came to Jamaica and met with Freddie McGregor and me. We decided to put the package together for the **Reggae Superfest 1992** tour. Dennis Brown, Freddie McGregor and Andrew Tosh along with the 809 Band were billed for this tour which was scheduled to kick off in January of 1992. A few weeks after the meeting, Freddie and Dennis came to me and requested that I put Beres Hammond on the bill. Beres was not yet popular in Europe, however, I sent their request to the promoters who said we had to take Hammond at our own expense. Freddie and Dennis had forged a close relationship with Beres and they wanted him on the tour. Beres had been to Europe previously but only on small tours with Zappow. He had not yet developed a real presence in Europe as a solo act.

The finale with Freddie McGregor, Andrew Tosh, Beres Hammond and Dennis Brown with backing vocalist Christine McNab at the Paradiso in Amsterdam, Holland at Reggae Superfest, 1992. (Helen King Photos)

Dennis and Freddie said they would combine their fees and split it equally among the three of them. I told the promoters to put Beres on the bill. They readily consented. After all, they were getting an additional act without having to pay more in fees. All the artistes were given equal billing. They were all allowed the same amount of time on stage. Beres took his assistant, Mervis Walsh, with him on the tour. Mervis had worked with Beres' sister who was a show promoter in Florida. Beres asked me to teach Mervis the ropes. She learned quickly and seemed to enjoy the business.

On one of the legs on the tour Beres got sick. I believe he had caught the flu. He told me that he wouldn't be able to perform that night in Austria. I asked him if he could just do two or three songs and then I would be able to explain to the audience that he was not well. He came to the venue and did the three songs as we had agreed. The response was so good he returned for an encore and ended up doing six songs instead. I explained to the audience that he was sick and had done the annotated performance as a goodwill gesture. The crowd truly appreciated it.

The tour was going smoothly but Mervis seemed to have had a concern and took the posters from the various shows and pointed out to Beres that he was not being billed equally with the other stars. The tour contract rider stipulated that all the acts would get equal billing and each artiste would be given the same amount of time on stage to perform. The promoters were not abiding by this provision of the agreement. Realistically, Dennis was the biggest act on the tour followed by Freddie McGregor and then Andrew Tosh. Beres was the least known of the acts in Europe, despite the fact that he was quite popular in Britain. Many of the promoters on the tour were billing the artistes based on their relative drawing power at the time.

When we reached Germany, Mervis again got the poster for the show and took it to Beres. He summoned me to his room and started to complain about the billing. I showed him the contract. I told him that I didn't know why the promoters were not abiding by the terms of the agreement.

Klaus Maack, the promoter, was coming over to pay the outstanding balance due to the artistes so I instructed the front desk, to send him up to Mr Hammond's room when he arrived. Klaus arrived about ten minutes later and came up to the room. Freddie McGregor, Nambo Robinson, Mervis Walsh and Beresford Hammond were present. I told Klaus that Beres was complaining about the billing. Klaus did not realise Beres was even in the room and shouted, "Copeland I told you that this guy means nothing here, he has no value to us. I told you not to bring him and you did." Klaus was really angry. "I have to put the artiste who has the greatest pulling power at the top of my billing", he continued. Everyone listened but no one raised any objection. Klaus then handed me the balance of the fee and left the room.

We did the rest of the shows in Europe and then we crossed over to the UK. Beres was a big hit in Britain. He was able to get the level of billing consistent with the terms of his contract in the UK. Everything was going well until we got to the last show which was at the Brixton Academy in London. A large number of fans wanted to see Dennis Brown.

While we were upstairs during the show somebody came and said there were about 10 cops downstairs asking for Dennis Brown. I sent someone to find out why they were looking for Dennis.

Dennis Brown - Wanted

We were scheduled to play at four major concerts between the United States and Canada (one at the famed Studio 54) after we left the UK. I went down to meet the cops. When I confirmed that the cops had a warrant for Dennis, I went back upstairs. I decided that we could not allow Dennis to go through the back door as the cops would have nabbed him. Dennis left through another exit and was able to elude the cops.

We were originally scheduled to leave Britain almost immediately after the show. I changed to a later flight, departing at 2:00 pm, to give everyone a little time to rest before we departed.

Brown had decided to stay back with his wife to work out some personal matters. He had planned to travel to the US the following day. I had Dennis' passport. His son, Daniel, came to pick it up at the airport. While we were checking in, we noticed there were several strange-looking men, all dressed in suits, milling around the counter. Each time a member of our group handed in his passport at the counter, one of the officers would peek at the name on the ticket. I turned to Dennis Brown's son, and I said, "Tell your dad what is going on here. These cops are looking for him."

Guitarist, Dalton Browne, checked in his documents. His ticket had D. Browne printed on it. A police officer looked over, saw his name and held on to him. I walked up to the counter to ask what was the problem. They said they had a warrant "for this guy", referring to Dalton. A uniformed policeman who was standing away from the rest of the men pulled out some papers. It was a warrant with a picture of Dennis Brown. He looked at the picture then at Dalton. He realized they were not the same person. They had the wrong man. I said to the other cops, "This is not Dennis Brown. We are going home; the tour is finished. Dennis lives in England."

The cops stood there and watched everybody check in until the counter closed. Freddie and I had stopped at a foreign exchange window to change some pounds into US dollars. After completing our transactions, we were walking towards the gate when we heard someone shout "Freddie, Freddie! Where's Dennis Brown?" Freddie replied "Dennis is at home. He lives in England."

When we boarded the plane, we saw the same cops walking down the aisle. I guess they didn't believe that Dennis Brown was not on the flight. Suddenly, they came over to Gibby, our guitarist. They told him to take all his stuff and follow them. They wanted to speak to him outside. Gibby took down his bags. They searched him and found nothing. The flight attendant told me that the lady who had been sitting beside Gibby had seen him mixing some white powder. He was finicky about his food and was always making strange concoctions. The powder was part of his diet. The lady thought it was drugs and reported it to the pilot.

I was really worried about what to do about Dennis. I came up with the idea that I would let a friend take him over on the ferry to Holland in a car trunk and then fly him to New York. I quickly dismissed the thought. It was too risky, and it was illegal.

Beres Hammond, Andrew Tosh, Dennis Brown and Freddie McGregor share a light moment during a leg of the European tour 1992. (Helen King Photos)

We arrived in New York. The promoter took us to the Howard Johnson in Manhattan where we would stay a few days before driving to Toronto for the first show on the tour. Beres Hammond, Freddie McGregor, Andrew Tosh and the 809 band were meeting the press in New York. Suddenly, somebody asked where was Dennis Brown. Beres said Dennis was in England and added that there were some issues but, "You have to go speak to Copeland".

I was up in my room trying to get some sleep when I heard a knock on my door. I got up and peeped. Six people were outside my door. I realized it was the promoter Barney and his team. They had come to find out what kind of problems Dennis was having in Britain. I told them exactly what had happened. I decided to call a friend of mine who was a lawyer in London. He advised me to let Dennis turn himself in to the police. He promised to accompany Dennis to the hearing and that he would ask for time to allow Brown to finish the tour. The lawyer tried to reach Dennis who wasn't answering his phone. Dennis was in hiding. I had to call his brother's phone to get a message to him.

The lawyer in London advised me that he needed to put up a cash bond in order to get permission for Dennis to leave Britain. The courts wanted a £10,000 pound cash

Leroy Clarke (Brown's brother) Freddie, Dennis, Beres and guitarist Dalton Browne celebrate Dennis' birthday during the **Reggae Superfest** tour of Europe, 1992. (Copeland Forbes Archives)

bond. I didn't know where to find that amount of money at such short notice. At that time, this was the equivalent of US$15,000. My only option was to go to the booking agency to see if I could get an advance of US$15,000. I called Paul La Monica to see if he could help. He said, "Copeland you will have to come in and speak to the boss himself." I went to Associated Booking Corporation and I met with the boss, Oscar Cohen. I explained the situation to him. He agreed to lend me the money which was to be paid back within the first four days of the tour. I asked Cohen to wire the money to our lawyer in the UK.

Dennis' court hearing was on the same day of the show in Toronto. He would have to fly from the UK straight to Toronto for the show. The hearing would be at 10:00 am GMT and the paperwork would take no more than half an hour. The attorney assured me it could be done. Dennis would be on the flight scheduled to leave at 2:00 pm GMT.

I told Dennis and his brother, Leroy, who was traveling with him, to take their suitcases with them to court and go straight to the airport as soon as the case was heard. At about 2:30 pm GMT, I called the UK just to make sure that everything was going as planned. I called Leroy's house and was shocked when I heard him answer the phone. I shouted, "Leroy I don't understand how you answering the phone when you should be on your way to Toronto?" Leroy said that after they left the court, Dennis went to take care of some personal business and he hadn't seen or heard from him since then.

I called the Toronto promoter, Denise Jones. I informed her that Dennis had missed his flight. We started discussing the alternatives to get Dennis Brown to Toronto. We checked on other flights. The last one from the UK would arrive in New York at 9:00 pm. The last flight from New York to Toronto would leave at 9:45 pm EST from LA Guardia Airport. Dennis would be arriving at JFK. He wouldn't be able to make the connection. The only alternative was to charter a flight to take Dennis from New York to Toronto. Our booking agent gave us some contacts for a chartered service. I called the company. They said yes. The charter to take Dennis to Canada was US$15,000. It was US$7,500 each way but the plane would have to fly back to New York, with or without him.

Nobody asked me about payments. I thought the promoter was going to pay for the chartered flight. I assumed everything was fine until I got a call from my booking agent in New York. La Monica told me that I needed to get in touch with the charter service. I called them. They told me they had to get the money for the charter in advance. We then realized that the idea of Dennis' reaching Toronto was not going to fly.

La Monica told me that I should put a notice at the door stating that "Dennis Brown will not be appearing tonight due to circumstances beyond our control". He added that somebody should make an announcement 40 minutes before the show so that those who needed a refund could get it. La Monica said chances were, most people would not want a refund. The promoter agreed. Later in the evening I was at the hotel doing my accounts when I got a call from one of the band members saying that I should come down to the venue as soon as possible as my son Colin (the road manager) had been arrested.

When I arrived at the venue, hundreds of people were outside. The police were pushing people away from the door. I noticed that the sign that we all had agreed on had not been posted. One of the cops took me to the promoter. I turned to the promoter and said "Denise, where is the sign that we agreed to put up at the door so people would know that Dennis Brown would not be appearing?" She confessed that she had changed her mind.

I tried to get inside the venue. It was packed like sardines. Patrons were saying that they had bought their tickets months ago and could not get into the venue. The promoter had presold 2,500 tickets. The capacity of the venue was 3,000. This meant the promoter should only have sold five hundred tickets at the gate. She paid no attention to this reality. She just kept selling tickets.

When the folks outside heard that they would not be able to use their tickets (bought months in advance), they were mad. The cops said they didn't care about what anyone had to say. They were interested in saving lives and would not be letting any more patrons inside. The promoter started to cry, saying she was going to lose a lot of money. The cop said he didn't care if she lost weight or money. He was standing by his position.

I went to the dressing room to find out why they had arrested Colin. I soon learnt that someone, whom Colin had not recognised, came into the dressing room and started to remove a large quantity of food and drink. Colin tried to stop him. Colin and the interloper got into a shoving match. He pushed Colin to the ground. Colin picked up a bottle of Guinness Stout and hit the man over the head. The man was taken to hospital. The cops arrived and arrested Colin.

After the show we decided that some of us should go to the precinct to check on Colin.

We got there about 3:30 am. The police seemed to have been asleep and weren't too pleased when we woke them up. I introduced myself and told the officer on duty why we were there. He was angry. Colin had injured a cop, who had been moonlighting as a bouncer. The cop at the station recommended that we go to the court where the hearing would be taking place.

The hearing was scheduled for 10:00 am. We left the hotel at about 8:30 am and drove to the courthouse. While we were sitting inside the courtroom, we saw four well-dressed men of African descent looking at us. They came over and started talking to us. We explained to them that one of our team members had been arrested and charged for injuring a cop. I pointed out that it wasn't Colin's fault as he was attacked. One of the well-dressed men looked at me and said "Listen brother let me tell you something. This is Canada. Once you injure a cop, no matter who is at fault, you're going to be the one to take the rap". "Who's your lawyer?" he asked. I told him we didn't have one. He advised me that Colin would have a hard time getting bail as he was not a Canadian citizen or a resident. He agreed to represent Colin who was brought into the court in handcuffs.

The lawyer spoke strongly on Colin's behalf. The fact that Colin didn't live in Canada meant that he would have to put up a cash bond of CAN$3,000. I paid the bond. We left the court and drove to the next venue which just across the border in Albany, USA. When we arrived in Albany, Dennis Brown and his brother had already checked into the hotel.

The next show was in Brooklyn and the masses turned out. The final show at Studio 54 in Manhattan was also well attended. The next day the band was heading to the Cayman Islands with Freddie McGregor. We got up early to finalize our financial arrangements. We agreed to meet in Beres Hammond's room. We called Dennis Brown's room but didn't get him. Present at the meeting were Dean Fraser, Freddie McGregor, Andrew Tosh, Nambo Robinson,

Soon we heard a knocking on the door. It was Dennis. We let him in. He wanted to know why we hadn't called him. We told him we had tried but could not find him. We allotted the amount for each artiste. Dennis wondered why his share was smaller than Beres and Freddie's. I reminded him that we spent US$15,000 to pay his bond in the UK. He asked why he had to pay that cost by himself. I asked him who should pay. He said the tour. Freddie jumped in and said, "It's your problem not ours. We should not be paying it for you".

Dennis turned to Beres Hammond, whom he called "Michelangelo" and said, "Do you think it is right that I alone should pay this?" Beres didn't give a straight answer. He just kept laughing. Beres had already told me that he was not going to use any of his money to pay for the bail bond. Freddie got up and said he had a flight to catch. He took up his portion of the money and gave Nambo Robinson his share for the 809 band. He handed Andrew Tosh his balance then presented Dennis with what was due to him. Freddie then left the room. As soon as Freddie walked out Dennis looked at Beres and said, "Michelangelo, you know dem call him di High Priest but is not the High Priest it's the High Teef".

I suppose one might find it strange that Dennis would have expected the tour to underwrite the costs of his legal obligations in Britain. Yet, upon reflection, it might not have been as unreasonable as it might appear at first blush. It should be recalled Dennis had been willing to join forces with Freddie McGregor to give up a sizable portion of his income to accommodate Beres Hammond on the tour. Did Dennis believe that his taking a cut in earnings to have Hammond on the tour should have been reciprocated? On the other hand, would it have been too much to ask Freddie to subsidize Brown's legal costs? After all, McGregor had already taken a significant cut in order to have Beres on the tour.

Beres Hammond delivered a string of hits, despite having the flu, at Reggae Superfest, 1992. (Helen King Photos)

Reggae Superfest 1993

The lineup for **Reggae Superfest 1993** tour of Europe included: Frankie Paul, Beres Hammond (who had asked to return), Dennis Brown, Half Pint and the 809 Band. The bus company decided to make a concession to us. They would provide an additional bus for the same price we had paid for a van. Previously we had a bus and a van.

The tour started in Scandinavia. We went all over mainland Europe. When we got to France, we stopped at the border to do the regular check before entering the UK. I was upstairs sleeping in my bunk. I woke up and suddenly realized that the bus had stopped and that someone was opening the curtain of my bunk. A man in uniform appeared. He asked me if I was the chief. He told me to step out of the bunk. He asked me to follow him. I walked with him downstairs. Guitarist Bopee was sitting by the door of the bus. He spoke to me out of the side of his mouth saying that they had found hard drugs on Rads, Dennis Brown's cousin.

Rads had been selling merchandise on the tour and was found to be in possession of drugs. The police were going to search the bus. The immigration officer said he wanted me to accompany him while he searched the bus. The entire entourage was outside the bus.

The names of the occupants were on their bunks. The officer searched the bunks, sorted the items (based on where they were found) and recorded his findings. Each time he found something, he considered noteworthy, he pointed it out to me. He looked in Brown's bunk and picked up an Anacin bottle containing two marijuana spliffs.

I was stepping over piles of stuff which the officer had emptied on the floor, and noticed that the vent atop the bus was open. I was curious that the vent was not closed since the vehicle had just gone through the power wash at the gas station. I climbed up and looked through the vent. There I found a plastic bag full of marijuana sitting atop the bus. Somebody had pushed it through the vent and left it there. They, apparently, didn't realize that people could see the top of the bus from the buildings. I grabbed the bag of marijuana and quickly pushed it in my underwear.

I continued to accompany the officer while he searched each bunk. He turned to me and said he wanted me to find out from the guys where they had hidden the drugs. He promised that if they were honest, he would not make an arrest but would just record the findings.

The police in France had a three-strike rule. The officer explained that if he found more drugs and nobody claimed it, he would pin it on me. He told me that the dogs would be arriving in half an hour. I realized fifteen minutes had already gone.

I thought, "If these dogs come on the bus the first place they are going to jump would be between my legs". I said to the officer, "Let me go out and speak to the rest of the group to find out where the drugs are." The artistes and members of the entourage had, by now, been placed in a room. I walked in and asked, "Who put the bag of marijuana on top of the bus?" No one answered. I asked three times. I got no response. I told them that I had taken it down from the top of the bus and it was in my underwear. I added "I'm going to give it to one of you to go and flush it in the toilet." Nobody took it from me. I decided to go to the toilet and get rid of it myself.

I returned to the immigration officer and told him that I needed to go to the bathroom. The restroom door was broken. It could not be locked. I had to put one of my feet behind the door to brace it. I pulled out the plastic bag of marijuana and threw its contents in the toilet. I pushed out one of the tiles in the roof and placed the empty bag in the ceiling. I flushed the toilet but most of the marijuana was still floating. I waited for the tank to refill. I flushed again. The weed was still floating. If the police saw the weed in the toilet, I would be in trouble.

I started to worry. I saw a piece of wood in a corner and decided that when the tank was full, I would use it to push the weed down. I soon heard a knocking on the door. "Who is it?", I asked. I partially opened the door with my pants at my knees to give the impression that I was using the toilet. It was the immigration officer. He turned his head the other way and said, "Okay hurry up. Please hurry".

I prayed. I took up the piece of wood and used it to make a push. I flushed again. I used the piece of wood to make another push and repeated the cycle. Everything had disappeared. I gave a sigh of relief.

Half Pint, Frankie Paul, Dennis Brown and Beres Hammond singing the finale "Ragamuffin" at Reggae Superfest, 1993. (Helen King Photos)

Half Pint bringing "Greetings from Jah" on the 1993 staging of **Reggae Superfest** in Europe. (Helen King Photos)

We returned to the bus and the police kept searching. He found a big clump of substance which I could not identify. He showed it to me. He said, "Why don't you go and ask all the guys where are the drugs on the bus?" I addressed the group, "Listen. They found something on the bus, and it looks like ash. The gentleman said all you have to do is claim it and he will record it. He will not arrest anyone.

We figured the best person to take ownership of the drug should be someone with a British passport. Frankie Paul's cousin Adrian decided that he would make the claim. He had a British passport. The officer took Adrian to his office and asked him who owned the strange substance found in the bus.

I had gone back to the bus, when I saw Adrian running towards me saying he was not going to take ownership of the contraband. I convinced him that it was ash. He finally agreed to take the rap. The paperwork was done. They said we could leave, but without Dennis' cousin Rads who was being held in a room. Rads was found with what was described by the officers after testing "as illegal drugs", which didn't fall under the "three-strike rule" so Rads would be facing possible criminal charges.

We had missed the ferry for which we had been booked. I spoke to the captain of the craft that was next in line to leave. He said he would do his best to accommodate us and asked the drivers of some of the trucks and lorries to move closer to make way for our bus. We found space. I told everyone to board the bus quickly. We saw Rads running towards us, as the ferry was pulling up the steps. He jumped onto the craft as it was pulling away. We sailed across to Dover. I was worried that when the immigration officers in France realized that Rads was missing they would call Dover to hold on to him.

When we arrived in Dover the customs officer was shocked to see the state of the bus. He asked why the bus was so messy. We told him that the officers in France had searched the bus for nearly six hours. He told us to get our passports and go through immigration. I told everyone to hurry up. I was still concerned about Rads. We would all be in trouble if they found him in our entourage. The promoters from Birmingham were waiting for us at the dock. The UK leg of the tour went on for about ten days where it ended without any further incidents.

Reggae Superfest 1994 #1

In 1994, we planned two back-to-back tours. The first featured Sugar Minot, Junior Reid, Mutabaruka and the 809 band. The itinerary included four dates in the former East Germany. This was the first time Jamaican acts would be performing in this region since the fall of the Berlin Wall. A German band, Messer Banzani, was the opening act on the tour. Going to the former East Germany was like entering a time warp. It was like going back 50 years in the past. Goods and gears were cheap. A pair of sneakers which would go for £60 in Britain went for £20 there. We all went shopping.

The sound equipment was outdated yet, despite these obstacles, we managed to give some great performances. The only real problem we had on the entire tour was with the man who called himself "The Headliner". All the artistes had equal billing. Before we left Jamaica, Junior Reid came to me and said he wanted to close the shows on the tour. I agreed.

Dancehall pioneer Sugar Minott on the **Reggae Superfest** 1994 tour of Europe. (Copeland Forbes Archives)

In Jamaica, the artistes are accustomed to the practice of "wheeling". Reid was pulling up and wheeling. Fans were leaving after Reid performed three or four songs. It can be annoying to the uninitiated. I heard some fans asking "Why is this guy stopping the song? Doesn't he remember his own song?" The audience was annoyed with the "pulling up". Junior was blaming the band for the negative response. He said the band was tired. I told him that was not the case. The band had backed 25 acts on many shows. There were only three acts on this tour.

Junior also wanted us to cut Mutabaruka's time on stage. I refused his request. He went to one of the musician's rooms and punched him in the eye. The rest of the band members were

Mutabaruka embraces Winnie Mandela. (Allan Hope Photos)

upset and decided that they would not provide backing for Reid. We had one week left on the tour. I asked Dean Fraser and Nambo Robinson to reconsider their decision. They discussed it among themselves and agreed to continue to back Reid for the rest of the tour.

Reggae Superfest 1994 #2

The second 1994 tour consisted of the Mighty Diamonds, Lieutenant Stitchie, Frankie Paul and the 809 Band. I left my son, Colin, in charge as I had to fly to New York to meet with Maxine Stowe at Sony Records. After the meeting I went to Jamaica. I called Colin and told him I would not be returning to the tour. I was physically spent. I had to rely on Colin to take the tour to its conclusion.

Reggae Superfest 1995

In the latter part of 1994 I received a call from some Sri Lankans living in Canada. They explained that the National Hockey League (NHL) was on strike and, as a result, large venues had become available for the staging of concerts. The Sri Lankans wanted me to put together a big concert at the Maple Leaf Gardens in Toronto for 21

January 1995. I told them about my *Reggae Superfest* series. They agreed to stage the concert under the *Reggae Superfest* banner.

The first artiste we signed for the event was Buju Banton. We contacted Garnett Silk who was one of the hottest young acts at the time. He had never been to Canada. They asked me to check on Shabba Ranks. I spoke to Shabba's manager, Specialist, who promised to give me a good deal. "Normally we would charge US$50,000 and up, but I want to give it to you for a reasonable fee" Specialist declared. I called the promoters in Toronto. They agreed. Shabba Ranks' agent, Erskine, was handling the bookings from his office in New York. I signed Lady Saw then Third World.

Garnet Silk – A Tragic Loss

I was ready to book Garnet Silk. I had his deposit. Garnet should have met with me to sign the contract and collect his advance at 2:00 pm at the 809 rehearsal room on Grove Road on the Friday afternoon. He called me at about 11:45 am and said he had to go down to Manchester because he was building a house for his

Mutabaruka performing at **Reggae Superfest** 1994 European tour. (Copeland Forbes Archives)

mother and intruders were stealing the construction material. I begged him to sign the contract and take the money. I didn't want to be driving around Kingston with US$7,500 in cash.

He asked me to keep the funds and suggested we meet at noon the following day (Saturday) at the same location. Later that Friday night he perished in a fire. A gas tank exploded in the house which he was building for his mother. He had managed to get out safely but went back inside the burning house to rescue his mom. They both perished in the flames. My brother, Junior, managed artistes in the Tristate area. He had a young act who called himself Junior Jazz. The promoters agreed to have Jazz do a tribute to Silk. Jazz would be backed by Garnett's band, Jahpostles.

While I was still in Jamaica making arrangements for the show in Canada, DJ Cobra had a performance at the Mirage Nightclub, located in the Sovereign Plaza, Liguanea. I went to the show and ran into Donovan Germain, Buju Banton's manager, who said, "Glad I see you because I was going to call you later tonight. Why you treat Buju like that?" He said that Specialist had told him how much money Shabba Ranks was getting, which he claimed was way more than what he had originally requested and to which I agreed. Germain said that Buju would ask for more money once Shabba was on the bill.

Poster for Toronto leg of **Reggae Superfest**, 1995. (Copeland Forbes Archives)

It was the first time that both artistes would be performing on the same bill. I called the promoter in Canada and told them about Buju's request. They agreed. The next day I got a call from Germain. He said Buju wanted to speak to me. Buju was mad as hell. He said that he wanted nothing to do with "Shenco" and his people. I asked, "Who is "Shenco?" Buju pointed out that when the gay and lesbian community had come down on both of them, he had asked Shabba (Shenco) Ranks to let them do some positive songs together to show that they didn't hate anyone. Shabba had rebuffed his request. Buju's song "Boom Bye Bye" had created a ruckus. Buju claimed that it was Specialist who produced that song and to date he had not received a dime in royalties from the song which almost ruined his career. He declared that he was not going to do the show and hung up the phone.

At 11:00 pm that night my phone rang. It was Buju. He stated, "Mr Forbes, I have great respect for you. I don't like when my name is advertised for an event, and I don't show up. Irrespective of what the problem is they always blame the artiste." Then he said to me, "I am going to do the show and it's just because of you". I was elated. I started the application for the Canadian work permits.

A few days later, I got a call from a member of Shabba's management team asking for twice the amount we had agreed to for the show. I told the caller we already had an agreement and that Shabba's 50 per cent deposit was already with his booking agent. The caller told me that any show with Shabba and Buju would be a big money maker. I informed the caller that it was better to drop Shabba from the bill rather than to pay him more money. The caller asked that I speak with Specialist immediately. I did. I informed Specialist of what the caller had said. He pointed out that he was travelling and would be in Jamaica soon and we could work things out . When we met, Specialist told me that Shabba said that after all expenses were deducted, he would like to net a certain amount for himself. I told him that it was impossible to get more than we had already agreed. He kept saying "Don't worry, we will work it out, we will work it out."

We had a huge travelling party of 72. This event was going to be the biggest reggae concert in the Maple Leaf Gardens since Bob Marley & the Wailers played there in 1979. Maple Leaf was the Canadian equivalent of Madison Square Garden in NYC. A huge press conference had been arranged in Toronto for Thursday, the day after we were scheduled to arrive in Canada. We were all due to travel on Wednesday. The concert was slated for Saturday.

On the day of our departure from Jamaica, I received a call from (Spec Shang) Shabba's office in Kingston asking that I should come over to see them., I told them I couldn't as I was dropping off all the passports for those who were travelling. They insisted that I should stop by the office. My phone rang again. It was the same person who had called earlier. He said Specialist needed to speak with me. I stopped by their office.

Shabba's entourage had about 15 people. Ten members of his crew travelled economy and five in first class. The first-class passengers were flying from New York. Epic Records had planned a birthday party for Shabba who was already in New York. Specialist wanted me to release a certain amount of money from Shabba's deposit in New York. I told him no. The contract had not been signed. They called the booking agent, Erskine, about releasing the funds to Shabba. Erskine told them that there was no way he could touch the money. He pointed out that only Copeland Forbes or the investors in Canada could authorize such a transaction. Specialist asked me, again, about the increase in guarantee. I categorically told him "No". Specialist shouted to Delroy Thompson who worked with him, "call the bus and tell them to return to the office".

Delroy got on the two-way radio and told the bus with the musicians, technicians and the dancers to return to base. The bus pulled into the Spec Shang compound. Band leader, Nigel Staff, came out asking what the problem was. "I don't know, go ask your boss I told him." I immediately called Canada and told my partners what was happening. They instructed me to drop Shabba from the line-up and they would get a big-name act to take his place.

I drove out of Specialist's office and went to pick up my luggage and head to the airport. By the time I got to the airport, I saw the Ruff Cut Band, the Spec Shang Crew and the dancers at the check in counter. I asked them what had happened. They said Specialist told them they should just go to the airport and get on the flight. We all flew to Canada together.

When we arrived at the airport in Canada, we saw a woman carrying a baby. She had a big bag. The baby almost fell from her hand. Buju Banton, (who was standing close to the woman), caught the baby before he hit the ground. The customs officer thought their behaviour was suspicious. They searched the lady. Apparently, she had been carrying drugs on her person. They thought Buju knew her. He didn't. He was simply trying to protect the baby. They searched Buju but found nothing.

The next day there was a huge press conference with a large number of journalists and media personnel in attendance. We apologized for Shabba's absence. Specialist was still calling from New York trying to secure an increase in the guarantee for his artiste. He also wanted me to release funds to him immediately from the deposits which were being held by his booking agent. I told him, "I can design a way for you to get the extra funds you have wanted". I added, "Let us draft an addendum to the contract in which you are guaranteed the fee to which we originally agreed, win lose or draw. The promoter would have to recoup his expenses before you would be entitled to the additional amount you requested. Once you were paid the extra amount you are seeking then the promoter would be entitled to the remaining surplus". Specialist asked me to repeat. I did. He said he liked the idea and said he would go with it.

I was, however, somewhat concerned that with the huge expenses incurred by the promoters to stage the event (rental of the Maple Leaf Garden was over

$200,000, and our traveling party had 72 people), it would be difficult for Specialist to get anything more than what he had been originally guaranteed. We would need 17,500 people inside the Maple Leaf Gardens for us to be able give Specialist anything beyond the original guarantee. It was a tall order. I told Specialist that as soon as they arrived in Canada, I would call New York and instruct their agent, Erskine, to release the funds to whomever he designated.

They finally reached Canada. I had told them that they should head straight to my room as soon as they arrived. I informed them that the limousine was downstairs waiting for them to go to Much Music TV and that they had to leave immediately. They kept saying I should call NY and give the order to release the funds to their representative. I told them I would. Once I confirmed that they had reached Much Music, I called New York and told Erskine that he could release the funds to Specialist's representative.

It was stipulated in the contracts with the artistes that on Saturday (the day of the show) all outstanding payments and matters had to be settled by 6:00 pm. The show was slated to start at 8:00 pm sharp. The investors came and settled with Donovan Germain, manager for Buju, then with Third World and with Specialist for Shabba Ranks at the original guaranteed amount. We had to await the numbers from the box office at the Maple Leaf Garden and from Ticketron outlets to finalise any additional payments to Specialist. When they checked, they had only sold 7,000 tickets. That was less than half the capacity of the Maple Leaf Garden. It was evident that the profit-sharing condition in the agreement with Specialist would not be met.

Lady Saw, The Jahpostles Band and the entire technical crew had not been paid. The investors decided that these artistes should wait until after the show to receive their balance. I knew that waiting until the end of a show to settle outstanding financial matters was a risky proposition. I told the promoters that I wanted to settle all financial matters before the show started at 8:00 pm.

When I got down to the Maple Leaf Garden, Junior Jazz, Lady Saw and the Jahpostle Band had finished performing. I didn't have the balance for them in my possession. I could not find the promoter. A balance was also due to my company, Comar Productions. Third World had performed and Buju Banton was about to hit the stage. I was concerned about the outstanding payments. I would not wait any longer.

I took out my contracts and went to the ticket office. I spoke to the guy in charge of the box office. I told him I was going to stop the show as I should have had the final payments from the promoters before showtime as was stipulated in our contract. The man at the box office said, "I cannot allow the show to be stopped as this could lead to serious repercussions. I know how West Indians are, when things like these happen." He told me that the final attendance figure was 7,500 patrons. He confided that he was holding cash in the box office for the promoters. I gave him the contract and he saw all the conditions. He made copies of the contract for himself and gave me the outstanding balance.

I told the artistes to go ahead as everything was fine. The investors didn't know what was going on until Shabba Ranks was on stage. A Jamaican man who worked with the promoters came and asked me who had given me permission to go to the box office and ask for money. I said, "I didn't go to the box office to get money. I went to tell them that I was going to stop the show as I hadn't been paid the balance of the fee owing to me".

Reggae Superfest was a huge learning experience for me. The tour taught me that there was a vast difference between working for others and running your own business. Knowing that someone else is ultimately responsible can be a source of comfort. Realising that the buck stops with you can be a most daunting prospect. In the words of Shakespeare, "Uneasy is the head that wears the crown".

CHAPTER 18
LORD GIVE ME STRENGTH

I was heading to Jamaica to sign a contract and pay a deposit to Luciano's manager, Phillip "Fattis" Burrell for a show in Florida, to secure the services of the artiste for a show in Florida. Luck was on my side that day as I succeeded in getting Air Jamaica as a sponsor for the show through a chance meeting with Butch Stewart on a flight from Miami to Kingston. I had travelled on an Air Jamaica sponsored ticket to the Reggae/Soca Awards in Florida. I had stayed for nearly two weeks after the show, not knowing that the return leg of the ticket was valid only for the weekend of the event.

Butch Stewart, the then chairman of Air Jamaica, was standing close to the check in counter and overheard the clerk telling me that my ticket was invalid and that I would have to purchase a new one. He went and spoke to the lady at the counter. Shortly afterwards she called me back and said Mr Stewart had instructed her to put me in first class on the flight. I went over and shook his hand and thanked him. He said, "You may not know me, but I know who you are, and I see what you've been doing for reggae music". When I boarded the flight, I realized that my seat was next to his.

During the flight we struck up a conversation. I informed him about the award show that I had recently attended in Florida. He told me that his mission in Florida was to finalize arrangements for Air Jamaica to start flying a new route to Ft Lauderdale. I used the opportunity to introduce the idea of securing sponsorship for the upcoming Luciano concert in Ft Lauderdale. I told him sponsorship would entitle

Early Luciano. (Copeland Forbes Archives)

the airline to use the tagline "Luciano flies courtesy of Air Jamaica". Butch Stewart smiled and said he loved the idea. He told me that he and his family loved Luciano's songs especially "Lord Give Me Strength" and "It's Me Again Jah".

He wrote a note addressed to Betty Jo Desnoes at ATL (Halfway Tree Road) and gave it to me. The next day on my way to meet with Luciano's manager, I stopped by the ATL office and met with Betty Jo. She was a very nice lady. We did the paperwork for the sponsorship. She asked me to send her the names of Luciano's entourage and the dates of travel. I left her office in a good mood and went to meet with Fattis to sign the contract and pay him the 50 per cent deposit, in cash. I told Fattis about the Air Jamaica sponsorship deal and showed him the agreement. Fattis and I signed the contract to book Luciano. I took out the 50 per cent deposit to pay Fattis. He told me that he would prefer if I kept it.

I was a bit surprised when Fattis gave me 18 names for the entourage. He told me he had other artistes in his roster apart from Luciano who served as opening acts for the Exterminator Crew. Among them were: Mikey General, Sizzla Kalonji, Ragnumpiser, Jesse Gendah, and Shadow Man. Fattis explained that he wanted to give these young acts the chance to perform and make a name for themselves.

I started the application process to secure work permits for the entourage. As we got closer to the date, we arranged radio interviews, but, somehow, the artistes did not turn up for the engagements.

In the week of our planned departure, I saw an article in the *Gleaner* (a Jamaican newspaper) about an upcoming Luciano performance in St Mary, scheduled for the same Saturday he was due to appear in Ft Lauderdale. The visas were already processed. The entourage was slated to leave Jamaica for Florida on Friday, the day before the show. On the proposed date of our departure, Fattis and I went to the US Embassy to pick up the last set of passports so the entourage could leave on the scheduled 6:00 pm flight that evening. Fattis asked me the time of the flight. I told him. He said, "Okay". He kept the passports for all his artistes. I took control of the passports for the 809 band and Frankie Paul who was a special guest on the show.

Poster promoting Luciano's first concert in the USA. (Copeland Forbes Archives)

I went to the airport with the 809 Band and Frankie Paul and waited for the Exterminator Crew. The departure time came and went but there was no sign of Fattis or his entourage. I called the Exterminator home/office and Fattis' lady told me he had left for the airport a long time ago. Luckily, I had told the agent to offload my luggage just before the flight closed.

I told those who had already checked in to head to Fort Lauderdale. I decided to go to Fattis' place in Hope Pastures to find out what was happening. When I arrived, I saw Luciano at the gate about to leave. I asked him why he was not at the airport. He stuttered a little and said I should speak to "Fada" (Fattis). After we spoke, Luciano was attempting to leave. I told him, "No, come back with me". We went into Fattis' house together.

As I entered the house, I noticed that everyone appeared relaxed. Luciano and I went into the office. Fattis did not even know I was in the house. I asked Luciano, again, why they were not at the airport. He told me that Father (Fattis) had informed him that he hadn't received a deposit for the show. I was shocked. I immediately took out the money from my bag and I showed it to Luciano. I said, "Here is the deposit, Fattis told me to keep it". I informed Luciano that I attempted to give the money to Fattis a month before, and I also showed him the contract that Fattis had signed. Luciano looked at it. He seemed shocked. He shouted to the manager, "Yo Father, Mr Forbes is here". There was no answer. We waited about 30 minutes before Fattis finally came out to speak to us. Fattis asked, "How much money are you going to lose?" I said, "No that's not the important thing, why was nobody at the airport?" He gave some vague response.

1. Luciano and Copeland Forbes in Accra, Ghana, West Africa.
2. Former Jamaican Prime Minister P.J. Patterson greets Luciano at Margaritaville, Island Village, Ocho Rios, Jamaica.
3. Chris Blackwell welcomes Luciano to Island Village, Ocho Rios, Jamaica.
4. Luciano, Copeland Forbes and Jewish Orthodox reggae artiste Matisyahu. (Copeland Forbes Archives)

Legendary Phillip "Fattis" Burrell. (Exterminator Music)

While speaking with Fattis, I recalled the advertisement in the local paper about Luciano appearing on a show in Saint Mary. A woman from the US Embassy had called and told me that she was surprised and confused as she had seen a show being advertised in Jamaica with Luciano for the same time that he was scheduled to be in Florida. She was the one who had assisted us in expediting the processing of the visas. I told her I was not aware of the Jamaican show but would find out from Luciano's manager. I later informed her that I had met with Luciano's manager, and he had assured me that I had nothing to worry about. I became curious, however, when Dean Fraser asked me to change his travel date to the Saturday morning. However, even if Dean had left on the Saturday morning, he would still have been able get to Florida way ahead of showtime which was at midnight.

I could not get any answers to my questions. Fattis kept asking, "How much money are you going to lose?" I said to him, "You're asking me stupid questions". Finally, Fattis said that they would go the following morning. I stayed at Fattis' house until midnight and called everyone in Florida to tell them what was happening.

The news that Luciano was not in Florida on the Friday spread like wildfire. He was scheduled to do interviews on several radio stations.

I returned to Fattis' house later in the morning to find out what time they would be leaving. I began hearing talk about "going to Saint Mary to do a show". I quickly realized that they were talking about the event that had been advertised in the paper. I could not believe what I was hearing. I thought about the backup singers who were almost at the airport on Friday when Fattis called and instructed them to turn back. They were shocked and disappointed. Their first trip to the United States had been aborted.

I stayed at Fattis' house and made some more calls to Florida. I spoke to some of the DJs at the Caribbean radio station, W.A.V.S. I remember speaking to radio jock, John T, who had a show (The Morning Ride) on the station. John T spoke directly to

Fattis and told him of the importance of showing up for the event which had been heavily promoted. Despite all the entreaties Fattis and the entourage performed at the event in St Mary instead of going to Fort Lauderdale. I went with them to the show in St Mary because I wanted to see what could have caused Fattis to make such a decision. The show was held in someone's backyard. I later found out that the promoter of the event was a journalist who worked at one of the local newspapers.

We rescheduled the show in Florida for the following weekend. Fattis decided that his entourage would go to Florida on the Monday following the show in St Mary. The flights were scheduled for the Monday at 6:00 pm. This would give him enough time to do interviews for damage control. On Monday, I checked and was informed that the group had left on a flight in the morning for New York. I decided to go to the US Embassy and cancel all the visas. when I heard that they had gone to New York on the work permits I had secured for them.

While waiting to speak with an officer at the embassy, I got a message that Fattis was on the phone and wanted to speak to me. Apparently, Donna had found out that I was at the US Embassy and called Fattis in NY telling him that I was about to cancel the visas. I refused to take his call. A while later a security guard came to me and said it was important that I take a phone call. The guard must have spoken to Fattis who persuaded him to come and get me. Finally, I took the phone call.

Fattis convinced me not to cancel the visas. He had hoodwinked me into thinking that they were going to Florida from NY. We soon discovered that Fattis and his team were going to Senegal from New York. I had no choice but to cancel the entire show. I immediately brought the band, crew and Frankie Paul back to Jamaica and waited until Fattis and his team returned from Africa so we could decide on another date.

Fattis and I had several arguments when he returned to Jamaica. I was even more disturbed and embarrassed to face Air Jamaica. We rescheduled the show for a few months later. Fattis and the crew finally went to Florida and the show was well attended. Luciano gave an excellent performance. I became a part of their team after that show. I believe Fattis realized that I had the experience and patience to help his team. I liked Luciano and his enthusiasm. We developed a great rapport. He showed so much promise.

Despite my best efforts there would be many more missteps. Luciano was invited to appear on "Good Morning America" on NBC in New York. His publicist at Island Records had secured his appearance. Everything was planned for Luciano to go to New York to appear on the show. Days later I saw an article in a Jamaican newspaper, (X-News) by New York-based journalist, Vinette Pryce. The article spoke about Jamaican artistes having "this nasty habit of not showing up for TV or radio interviews".

Luciano was mentioned in the piece. I was confused. "How could this be?", I asked. We were preparing to leave for our first US tour. An appearance on the "Good Morning America" show would have been a great boost for Luciano's career and the tour.

Later that day I ran into Luciano at rehearsal. I asked him why he had not gone to the interview in New York. He looked surprised. He did not seem to know what I was talking about. I told him I was referring to the "Good Morning America" show. He said he knew nothing about this appointment, adding that nobody had told him anything about appearing on GMA. I had to communicate with Neil Robertson at Island Records on a daily basis, so I asked him about the aborted interview with Luciano on NBC. I told him what the artiste had told me. "Really, that's what the artiste told you?" Neil asked. "That was not what the manager had told me," he continued. Something was not adding up. Neil and I ended our conversation.

Neil called Fattis after we spoke and told him what he had heard. Fattis called me and demanded to know who had authorized me to contact Island Records asking questions. He was in a rage. He didn't give me a chance to explain. I thought he was being disrespectful and hung up the phone. He called back several times, but I refused to pick up the phone. Fattis knew my mother's number in the US. Both our mothers had known each other since their childhood.

Fattis called my mother and told her that he had been trying to get a hold of me and that he was worried because I was not answering my phone. He feigned fear that something might have happened to me. He asked her to do a three-way call with me. My mom called me. I did not pick up until I heard her voice leaving me a message. I answered the phone saying, "Hi mom, how are you? I was in the country all day and I just got in". Then I heard Fattis saying, "Oh that's why I couldn't find you. You were out". He then said to my mother, "Okay mom, thank you". He ended the call.

Fattis immediately called me back. I had no choice but to answer his call. He told me he was going to tell me the truth about what happened with the interview. He apologized for his response to me earlier in the day. He said that he had not let the artiste know anything about the TV interview because there was no money involved. I asked, "What do you mean no money?" He said Luciano would not have been paid and that was why he had not shown any interest. I explained to him that the artiste could not have expected to be paid for his own publicity. I informed Fattis that an appearance on the "Good Morning America" show would have given a significant boost to the tour and artiste's career.

My brother Junior Forbes (who was also in the music business) gave me a call from a studio in New Jersey. He said he was with someone who wanted to speak with me. I asked who it was. He told me to wait. He put the person on the phone.

I said, "Hello". It was Eddie Murphy on the line. I asked, "the real Eddie Murphy?" He responded in the affirmative. My brother was at Eddie Murphy's studio working on a project. Eddie found out that he was Jamaican and asked him about the new artiste, Luciano. Eddie told me that he liked Luciano's voice and wanted to do a song with him. I felt so excited. Eddie had written a song and wanted to perform it with Luciano. He promised to send a cassette with the song to Jamaica so that Luciano could listen to it.

At the end of my conversation with Eddie, I immediately called Fattis. I told him that he should expect a package coming from Eddie Murphy with a cassette. I stressed that it was a great opportunity for Luciano. I waited for one week before I called Fattis to ask if the package had arrived. He said no. Two weeks passed. I thought that it was strange that there was no package. I called Eddie Murphy's office and they told me that the package had been sent two weeks before, and that they were waiting for a response from Luciano's management They tracked the package and contacted me the following day. They informed me that FedEx had confirmed that the package had been delivered to the recipient and signed for at the listed address. I decided to go to the Fattis' home to see what had happened. Donna informed me that Fattis had gone to the country. I asked her if a FedEx package had been delivered to the house. She said, "Yes a package came about three weeks ago. Fattis took it but he did not even open it. He threw it under the computer desk".

I found the package. It was covered in dust. I confirmed that it was, indeed, the one from Eddie Murphy. A few days later I confronted Fattis about the package. I asked, "How could you do this?" He replied, "Yu caan mek dem bwoy tink yu a run dem dung." I told him that we had not called Eddie Murphy. It was Murphy who had shown interest in working with Luciano. I soon received a call from my brother telling me that Eddie Murphy's team had decided to abandon the project because they had not heard from us. When I told Fattis, he did not seem the least bit perturbed.

One afternoon I was at Fattis' house. We were watching basketball. Fattis fell asleep. The phone rang, I answered it. The caller, who identified himself as Jimmy Jam, asked if he had reached Exterminator Records. He was one half of the famed Jimmy Jam and Terry Lewis production team. He wanted to speak with Fattis. "Jimmy Jam, where's Terry Lewis?", I jokingly asked. He told me Terry was on the road with Toni Braxton. He said he was calling because he and Terry were scoring a movie, *How Stella Got Her Groove Back*. They needed five songs from Luciano to use on the soundtrack.

I immediately roused Fattis from his slumber and told him who was on the line. His response was, "Who dem?" I tried to explain to him that Jimmy had been the producer of Janet Jackson's In Control album. Fattis was not impressed. He got up from his seat and went to the bathroom. He then went to the kitchen to make himself a glass of Milo (a Jamaican chocolate drink similar to Ovaltine). I was on the phone making excuses and keeping Jimmy distracted. I placed the call on hold and told Fattis to hurry. "Mek de bwoy wait", he replied. He finally took the phone. He listened to Jimmy. He did not ask any questions. After approximately 10 minutes, Fattis told Jimmy Jam to give the information to Donna. Fattis handed the phone to her.

Jimmy had inadvertently told Fattis that he had received a track from Beenie Man. Fattis' response was "Who?" Jimmy Jam said "Beenie Man". Jimmy told Fattis that he and Terry would use the Bennie Man track at the beginning and end of the movie. Fattis said, "Okay" and hung up the phone. Fattis then told me that he was not going to be involved in any project with "Beenie Bwoy". He did not send the tracks nor communicate with Jimmy Jam. Shaggy, Maxi Priest and Beenie Man were included in the project.

The actor Malik Yoba was a huge fan of Luciano. Malik had always wanted to cover the song "Lord Give Me Strength". He loved the song. Malik was shooting a movie and wanted Luciano to play a role in it. The negotiations were not properly handled and what seemed to be a promising prospect ended in another missed opportunity.

I remember that the first time we played at The Cameo Theatre in Miami Beach in 1997, Chris Blackwell was in town. Neither the artiste nor his manager had met Blackwell before. I told Chris that Luciano was playing at the Cameo Theatre. I went to the hotel, and I told Fattis and Luciano that the head of Island Records was at a nearby studio and he wanted to meet the artiste. Fattis and Luciano gladly decided to go. I introduced them to Chris. Blackwell liked Luciano's aura and music. Chris suggested that Luciano should do a video for a single which appeared on the *Where There Is Life* album.

Luciano flew to London and did some shooting. He then went to The Bahamas and finally to Cuba with the great Ernie Ranglin. The video was superb. Fattis called me to the house to discuss the finished product. I told him that I thought it was impressive. He turned to me and said, "I don't like it". I asked him why. He said the video had the Union Jack in it. It was one of the best videos I had seen for a reggae song. Fattis said he had already told Chris Blackwell not to release the video. Fattis said it was defending the queen. The video was never released. This video cost over

US$100,000. The money to produce the video was charged against Luciano's royalties. Luciano did another video in Jamaica for the song. It was nothing compared to the original.

In 1998 we were scheduled to do the **Reggae Japansplash** tour. I heard that robbers had stolen the deposits for Reggae Sumfest and Japansplash from Fattis' house. A few weeks later we all went to Japan. The tour had just ended, and we were in Osaka getting ready to leave for the airport when Fattis gave me some envelopes to disburse. I did not know how much money was in them. The tour included Mikey General, Luciano, Sizzla Kalonji, Dean Fraser, Frankie Paul, Nadine Sutherland and the Firehouse Crew. I handed out the envelopes while we were still at the airport in Osaka. A few minutes later, the artistes returned the envelopes to me with the money inside. Everyone, except the bass player, claimed the money was short. I decided to wait until we got to Tokyo to raise the matter with Fattis. Luciano, Sizzla and Fattis were all sitting in first class. When I got off the plane, I started looking for Fattis. The members of the entourage were irate. They felt short changed. One band member Winston "Bopee" Bowen was in tears saying he needed his money for his kids to go back to school.

When it was time to board, I saw Fattis coming towards the shuttle which would take us from the terminal building to the plane. I caught up with him and told him that members of the entourage had returned their envelopes in disgust. I showed him the envelopes. He asked, "How much is the total shortage?" My response was, "It's easy, everybody's envelope is short by US$1,100". I told him that Danny, the bass player was the only person who had not returned his envelope. Most people went home upset.

The team was booked for two shows in The Bahamas, I had booked those shows. Luciano was also slated to appear in Guyana, which would be before the Bahamas shows. I didn't go to Guyana but went to the Bahamas, after which I left for Canada with Dean Fraser, John Holt and Marcia Griffiths to do two shows for promoter Iley Dread. While we were in Canada, I heard that Luciano had called an emergency meeting is Jamaica.

When I got back, I heard that things were falling apart. Luciano decided to leave Exterminator Records and go on his own. Luciano brought in a new manager. We had another meeting at my house where the new manager was introduced. His name was Paul , son of Don Banks, the former president of National Commercial Bank (NCB). Fattis was now left with Sizzla as the only artiste under his management.

We went on the first tour under new management, the team quickly concluded that Paul was not bankable. They wanted a change.

I took over Luciano's management in 1999. His relationship with Island Records was by then coming to an end. The artiste embarked on a recording spree. He entered into a number of record deals which I knew nothing about. He signed a worldwide deal with VP Records out of New York. He did an album (New Day) for VP Records which Dean Fraser produced. New Day was nominated in the Reggae category for the 2002 Grammy Awards. Damian Marley won that year with the *Welcome to Jam Rock album.*

Luciano told me that he had a one album deal with VP. That was inaccurate. He also had another worldwide project with Jet Star Records in the UK appropriately titled *Great Controversy*. We toured the US promoting both albums. After the US tour we returned to Jamaica for a short break before embarking on the **Great Controversy** tour in Europe.

It was the first time, as far as I am aware, that Jet Star Records had been so involved in an artiste's tour. The CEO of Jet Star, Mr Carl Palmer, and his daughter were very supportive of Luciano. We were able to secure tour support to the value of nearly £40,000. Luciano and I were scheduled to leave Jamaica for Britain two days before the rest of the entourage. The PR Department at Jet Star had arranged several press interviews and promotional activities for Luciano in London.

I was at home packing to depart for London with Luciano later in the day when I received a very disturbing phone call from Jah Messenjah's Complex on Washington Boulevard. This was Luciano's base, the headquarters of his operations. The secretary told me that a fight was about to break out in the rehearsal room between Luciano and a certain band member. I requested to speak to the band leader Dean Fraser, but he had already packed up and left in disgust. I tried speaking with Luciano, who was still on the compound. He came to the phone. Luciano stated firmly that he would not be going on tour with certain members of the band. I was at a loss for words. Luciano wasn't even supposed to be at the rehearsal which was just for the band members and backup singers. He hung up the phone. When I called back the secretary, Sonia, told me that he had left. She stated that the last thing she heard him say was that he was not going on the tour with some of the members of his band. I continued to pack.

The tour was scheduled to last six weeks. I kept calling Luciano but couldn't find him. I had to reschedule our flights. I called the band members to arrange a meeting at Dean Fraser's house. Everyone turned up except Luciano. The tour bus, which had come all the way from Holland, had been sitting at Heathrow Airport in London for three days, waiting to pick up the entourage which was still in Jamaica. We couldn't do anything until we located Luciano. We couldn't find him. I cancelled the tour. All the publicity for the tour went out the window. The bus company demanded payment for the entire tour.

The road manager, Teddy Laidley, my assistant Patrick Forbes, and I decided to fly to the UK to meet with Jet Star. We spent over a week in London trying to see how we could clean up the mess. We tried reaching Luciano on the phone to no avail. We had to go back to the drawing board. Some of the promoters, especially those in the UK, had made deposits which we had used to cover some of our preparatory costs. Later in the year, after a replacement of some band members, we did some make up dates for the promoters in Britain.

A friend of mine, Stephan Schulmeister, who was the manager of German reggae artiste, Gentleman, was instrumental in securing a deal for Luciano with EMI Records. EMI released some of the recording funds to Luciano. I soon got a call from Joel Chin at VP Records saying that he had heard that we had secured a deal with EMI. He asked how we could have done that when we had a deal with VP to complete three albums and had only finished one album. Luciano had told me that he had a one-album deal with VP. Joel sent me the contract. It was, indeed, a three-album deal. I checked the date to see when the contract was signed. I clearly remembered that Luciano and Mikey General had left Jamaica around the time stated on the agreement, purportedly, to do some dubplates at Don One Studio in Brooklyn. They had really gone to sign a contract with VP behind my back. The VP deal was legally binding.

EMI, however, was not willing to cede any ground. EMI had distribution rights for the entire world. VP also had global rights. Chris Chin, CEO of VP, told me that he was willing to give EMI the rights to the rest of the world but he did not want to give up their rights in the US. This was a major concession from VP. Chris even offered for VP to distribute on behalf of EMI in the US. EMI would not budge. The lawyer from VP went over to EMI and demanded to see the contract for Luciano. The people at EMI were very upset and decided to terminate their agreement with Luciano. VP decided to continue with him. One would have thought that this development would finally have brought an end to the chaos. However, there was more to come. Much more.

Luciano brought back saxophonist, Dean Fraser, as band leader with responsibilities for recordings and productions. I soon received a call from VP that a producer, Jack Scorpio, had turned up at their office with an album entitled *Serve Jah* from

Luciano. VP Records decided to take the master from Jack Scorpio and make it into the second album under their deal with Luciano.

VP decided to invest a substantial amount of money to produce the third album under their deal with Luciano. They suggested that we utilize the state-of-the-art facilities at the Geejam Recording Studio in Portland, Jamaica. The recording sessions had some top-flight musicians. Luciano wrote some beautiful songs for the project. A release date was set for the album *Serious Times*. The Agency Group was commissioned to book the tour to support the album.

Almost on cue I got a call from our booking agent in NY telling me that a record company in New Jersey had called asking for the itinerary for Luciano's upcoming tour. The caller wanted to use the tour to promote a new Luciano album. Peter Schwartz, our booking agent, found the request rather strange. As far as he was aware, the tour was geared to support the VP album.

Peter asked the representative from the record company in New Jersey, how he came to be handling Luciano's new album. The caller told Peter the album was from a Jamaican producer, Bulby York, on the Fat Eyes imprint and that Luciano had received a huge deposit. Peter checked out the caller's claim. It was true. There was a signed deal with a company in New Jersey, Shanachie Records, for the release of the album *Lessons of Life*. I called Shanachie and begged them not to put out the album until VP had released theirs. At first the representative at Shanachie Records agreed to wait. A few hours later he called back and said he had changed his mind and was going to put out the album to coincide with the tour. About a month later Joel Chin from VP Records called me saying he saw another album by Luciano on a German label named Hair. Joel was right.

Luciano serenades Lillian Forbes, mother of the author at Reggae Sunfest in West Palm Beach, Florida. (Copeland Forbes Archives)

On tour, the artiste performed some of the tracks from the VP, the Jet Star and the Shanachie albums. There was yet more to come. We discovered another album entitled *Jah Words*. This one was from Sanctuary Records in New York. When the tour got into NY, I went down to Sanctuary to meet with the CEO. I wondered whether Luciano thought that collecting record labels was a pastime, similar to saving baseball cards. These deals were all supposed to be exclusive. If a record deal were a marriage Luciano would have been a rabid polygamist. Luciano must have misrepresented himself to a number of these entities.

He was not finished. Soon, there was an album from Murray who was the producer and manager for reggae/dancehall artiste Mr Vegas. The album was entitled *Child of a King*. Murray took the album to VP Records for distribution. Whenever Luciano did albums for Jamaican producers, they would take them to VP for distribution. VP was in a catch 22 situation. If it did not take the albums from the producers, the company would lose control of the release schedule. VP eventually reached a point, however, where it just wanted to be done with Luciano.

Luciano and Sean Paul, with promoter backstage at Reggae Fest in St. Maarten. (Copeland Forbes Archives)

I soon learned (through the grapevine) that Luciano had signed a new management contract. The agreement was entered into with a man who had promised to get the artiste a huge deal with Sony Records. I confronted Luciano about the allegations. He flatly denied them.

Luciano and the team went to New York to do a show dubbed "Coalition to Save Reggae Music" promoted by Sharon Gordon and Carlyle McKitty. It was then that I decided it was perhaps best for me to step away from the chaos. I could not trust someone who was doing things behind my back and whose assurances meant nothing.

I called a meeting in my room. I told the group how I felt and that I was going to leave. Luciano was in the room. He was looking at the ceiling while I was speaking. Luciano asked us to give him five minutes and promised that he would be right back. He left the room. Everyone remained waiting for his return. Soon there was a knock on the door. It was Luciano. A man accompanied him. Luciano introduced him as his new manager. We then found out that the new manager had been staying in the same hotel as the rest of us. After the introduction, the new manager made a five-minute speech. It was filled with promises. "Next year this time you guys will be touring with the Rolling Stones, and Mariah Carey". When some of the musicians heard this, they fell to the floor with laughter. Soljie Hamilton rolled like a log.

The "new manager" told me that he would like me to stay on to run the tours as he had no knowledge of that side of the business. He claimed that he ran a multi-million-dollar corporation in the US and was not familiar with certain aspects of the music business. I listened to what he had to say. I took the opportunity to ask him about the proposed deal I had heard he was negotiating for Luciano with Sony Records. He looked at a poster of the album *Child of a King* which I had in my hand and said, "That's the album which caused us to lose the deal with Sony". He explained, "Sony Records found out that Luciano had quite a few albums out with different people". I strongly doubt that there was ever a deal with Sony. However, I agreed to stay on with them to do bookings and tours.

The new manager had booked a gig for UCLA and another in Atlanta, Georgia. I stayed home for both shows. The band and the artistes did the shows and returned home. Nobody received payment. The manager told the artistes and musicians that he needed to change a cheque from the promoter in order to pay them. The entourage returned to Jamaica empty handed. Everyone was now uneasy. While he had been denying the existence of the new manager Luciano had booked some dates with a Japanese promoter.

Poster for the Northern Ghana Flood Relief benefit with Luciano and John Legend in Accra, Ghana. (Copeland Forbes Archives)

The bandleader, Dean Fraser, took a stand and said he was not going anywhere until he received at least a 50 per cent deposit. He said he was simply tired of excuses and hard luck stories. The Japanese promoter had transferred the 50 per cent deposit for the tour six months before to Luciano's account. However, the band had not been made aware of this fact.

Dean later decided that he and the band members would not be leaving for Japan until they received full payment. After some back and forth (involving the Japanese promoter) Dean finally received full payment. The promoter had no alternative. The band would not have left Jamaica if Dean had not received payment. Dean Fraser quit the group while he was in Japan. The rest of the band members, with the exception of the bassist, Maurice Duncan, aka Jah Lloyd, followed suit.

Luciano found out that his "new manager" was not only mishandling his affairs but damaging his reputation. He came to the painful conclusion that he had no alternative but to fire his "new manager". However, the "new manager" would have the last laugh. Luciano had gone to New York to do a show with Capleton at Amazura. When they arrived in New York the immigration officer looked in his computer and saw that Luciano's work permit had been cancelled. Luciano not knowing his work permit had been cancelled had told immigration he was going to do a show. 'The new manager' had simply cancelled Luciano's work permit without notifying the artiste. Immigration revoked Luciano's B1/B2 visa claiming he would be entering the US to work illegally.

We were subsequently scheduled to do some shows in Australia and were due to travel from Kingston to Miami, then to LA, and finally to Melbourne. Three days before we were supposed to leave, Luciano came to my house advising me that the US Embassy had turned down his application for a B/1/B2 visa. He said that when he asked the reason for the decision, they told him he should get an attorney.

We had a large contingent heading to Australia. Ernie Ranglin, Warrior King and Toots and the Maytals were the other acts billed for the event. I called the promoter, Peter Noble, at the last minute and told him about the situation. He ended up spending an additional US$5,000 to fly Luciano from Kingston to London. Luciano then flew from London to China, and on to Singapore, then to Sydney and finally to Byron Bay for the Blues Festival.

This is a cautionary tale for aspiring artistes. Here was an artiste with enormous potential who through the series of bad decisions did not optimize his great potential. Fattis was an extraordinary producer but failed, in my estimation, as a manager. Luciano seemed oblivious of the consequences of his own actions and the effects of Fattis' miscalculation and paid dearly for them.

Fattis was a large and reassuring figure. We always felt safe in his company. We knew that once he was around only the most daring or stupid would seek to pose any danger to us. Disrespectful promoters would keep their distance from our crew or suffer the consequences, once Fattis got wind of their transgressions. Yet, Fattis was kind and shy. He preferred to work in the shadows. Whenever he made a trip abroad, he would return with barrels of shoes and clothing which he would give away to his many friends and acquaintances. It was, however, a grave error to take his kindness for weakness.

"I called Chris Blackwell and gave him the news. He was shocked. I told him that Duckie had found a replacement and that his name was Junior Reid. Chris paused and then said to me, 'Copeland if it's not Michael Rose, Puma Jones and Duckie Simpson I am not interested'."

▸ Pg 151. Chapter 9

CHAPTER 19
ONE LOVE US TOUR

The year 2002 marked the 40th anniversary of my involvement in the music business. I decided to stage a tour entitled *One Love* to celebrate this significant milestone. I selected artistes from the different eras, including Toots & The Maytals, Israel Vibration, Tony Rebel, Queen Ifrica, Luciano, Tanto Metro & Devonte, Dean Fraser, Morgan Heritage, Chaka Demus & Pliers and Stone Love, with Rory at the controls, rounding out the billing.

Prospective sponsors were sought to support the tour. Among those we approached were the Jamaica Tourist Board (JTB), GraceKennedy (their latest product at the time was Tropical Rhythms); Air Jamaica (they flew to 11 of the 13 cities in which the tour would be playing); and JAMPRO, a Jamaican Government investment outfit for which I had spearheaded a tour back in the nineties at the Midem Expo in France. We sent all four entities letters outlining the rationale and objectives of the tour. The BBC had voted "One Love", as "The Song of the Century" and the JTB used the song to promote the island as a popular destination.

After several months of waiting, we got a reply from the then tourism minister through her representative, Francis Yeo, who told us that the JTB was out of funds. The Air Jamaica representative also had me waiting for quite a while. I decided to call him. My booking agent in NY felt time was running out. The well-known Air Jamaica officer responded angrily, telling me that if I couldn't wait, I should go and deal with another carrier. He hung up the phone. I went to GraceKennedy and met with the gentleman in charge of product promotion. I tried to show him that the tour would be a great promotional vehicle for his newly-introduced Grace Tropical Rhythms. He gave me the run around. I left empty handed.

I approached a US-based carrier for sponsorship. The US airline noted that while it was unable to provide us with a sponsorship deal, it would reduce the cost of the tickets for the entourage by 30 per cent. A number of US-based service providers offered to supply transportation and other related support at reduced cost. We got sponsorship from a beverage company which supplied us with refreshments throughout the tour. The month-long tour was booked by Comar Productions which I headed and The Agency Group Ltd which Peter Schwartz helmed. We had a total of 57 people including a crack technical crew led by production manager Robert "Chuckles" Stewart assisted by Mark "Brigga" Brown.

The tour started in San Francisco and worked its way across the US playing in many of the major cities at prominent venues including the House of Blues, Manhattan Centre in NYC, the Greek Theatre in Los Angeles, San Diego State University Amphitheatre, Tower Theatre in Philadelphia and the James Knight Center in Miami, Florida. The popular television show "On Stage TV" (with host Winford Williams), travelled with the tour for about a week. We performed to a packed house in Denver, Colorado.

I was in the office checking off the ticket sales with the promoter when Chuckles came to me and said they needed me urgently by the stage. Toots had walked

Dancehall Queen Carlene and Copeland Forbes at the New York leg of the **One Love** tour, in the US,2002. (Copeland Forbes Archives)

Israel Vibration, one of the headliners on the Copeland Forbes 40th Anniversary **One Love** tour, USA, 2002. (Reggaeville Photograph)

Toots and the Maytals performing on the **One Love** tour, USA, 2002. (Copeland Forbes Archives)

off in the middle of his performance. I ran outside and saw Toots' band members and the road manager standing in a corner. I tried to find out what had happened. Everyone looked relaxed. I approached Toots to find out what was the matter. I held on to him and he shoved me aside. Luciano, who claimed he was close to Toots, said he knew what could calm him down. He approached Toots but had to make a hasty retreat.

The audience was in a frenzy but the members of Toots' team had resigned themselves to his behaviour. In fact, they were expecting it. They realized that he had been without his "tranquilizer" for four days. Toots had walked off the compound. I followed him. He was cursing like crazy. He told me to tell the engineer Soljie not to "f*ck with him". Toots finally returned to the venue after I promised to get him his "pacifier".

Toots went back on stage to an ecstatic audience. He teased the audience asking his fans to say his name. The fans answered with: "Toots", "Pardie", "Frederick" and "5446". He simply responded "No, my name is Nyah and if you f*ck with Nyah I'll give you fire". The Reggae icon picked up where he had left off and delivered a high energy set. Everyone was in great spirits. Toots came to me after his performance. I gave him his "pacifier". He was back to his jovial self. The next morning when we got up, Toots went around to the rooms of the team members and apologized to everyone

Former Minister of Tourism and Jamaican High Commissioner to the UK Aloun Ndombet Assamba with Luciano on the California leg of the **One Love** tour. (Copeland Forbes Archives)

Actor Steven Seagal and Copeland Forbes. (Copeland Forbes Archives)

Former World Heavyweight Boxing Champion Evander Holyfield and Copeland Forbes. (Copeland Forbes Archives)

Tony Rebel and Queen Ifrica joined forces on the **One Love** tour of the US. (Copeland Forbes Archives)

for his behaviour. He promised it would never happen again. The tour ended in Atlanta, Georgia with Toots performing to a jampacked crowd.

The Air Jamaica representative whom we had approached for sponsorship lost his job after the airline changed ownership. He now works for one of the leading distributors of reggae in the US. This reminded me of the famous line from one of Marley's songs: "The stone that the builder refused will one day become the head corner stone". It is alleged that the JTB which did not support our tour later spent US$135,000 to bring a travel agent from the US, who promised to promote Jamaica by staging a seminar to attract more visitors to the island. The effort came to nought. I later found out that JAMPRO had spent US$90,000 to support a privately-owned Jamaican food chain which had expanded overseas. The venture folded within two years. The guy at GraceKennedy was eventually fired.

"My friend went to the house disguised as a delivery man. He rang the doorbell. A man opened the door. It was Dennis Brown."

▸ Pg 161, Chapter 10

CHAPTER 20
SPECIAL BANDS

There were two special bands that I had the privilege of managing which are certainly worth mentioning: Live Wyya and Girlztown. These groups did not achieve great success as recording artistes but left a lasting impression as backing and show bands.

Girlztown

I met the members of what would later become the Girlztown Band on my return from the Ugandan tour with Chaka Demus and Pliers in 1996. I was staying at the Sea Castles Hotel in Montego Bay where I had accompanied some of the acts which I was managing for their appearance at Reggae Sumfest. I was having dinner outdoors and noticed an all-female band on the stand comprising ten young women and featuring a four-woman horn section. I was blown away.

I started thinking about having these young musicians backing the female acts which I represented. I hurried to the lobby and called Marcia Griffiths, who had just checked in. I asked her to accompany me to watch the girls in the dining area. They performed renditions of some of Marcia's hits. She was impressed.

When they took a break, we decided to approach them. I congratulated them on their performance and expressed an interest in working with them. The saxophonist, Deneka Tracy, thanked me for the compliments but was a bit sceptical noting that many persons had expressed similar sentiments, but their promises amounted to

Girlztown Band and Copeland Forbes (far right) at the Avery Fisher Hall, Lincoln Center in New York City. (Roland Hyde)

nothing. I told her that things would be different with me. We exchanged numbers and promised to stay in touch.

When I returned after a few months to see the band members in Montego Bay, they told me that they had done their due diligence and were ready to take me up on my offer to manage them. I relocated them to Kingston where they did three months of rehearsals with some of the leading lights in Jamaican music including: Sly and Robbie, Dean Fraser, Lloyd Parks, The Firehouse Crew, Bowie, Chico and Myrna Hague to name but a few.

We changed the name of the band from New Wave to Girlztown.

The first engagement for the newly branded band was in Negril where they shared the stage with Luciano and the Firehouse Crew along with Buju Banton and his Shiloh Band. They then appeared at the Penthouse Family Fun Day at Crystal Springs in Buff Bay, Portland where they delivered another rousing performance. Girlztown was soon a hot commodity. The band booked appearances at Rebel Salute,

All Reggae Woman Concert and the Bob Marley Anniversary Celebration. They became the backing band for Marcia Griffiths and also for the I Three.

They had their first overseas gig in New York at the Avery Fisher Hall in the Lincoln Centre where they provided backing for Griffiths at an event which featured some giants of Caribbean music including the Mighty Sparrow. Girlztown would eventually be included in the lineup for *Reggae Japansplash* promoted by Tachyon Records and Minoura Hatanaka. On that tour, the girls had a solo slot but still provided accompaniment for Marcia Griffiths, Thrilla U, Worl A Girls and Caterpillar, among others. On their return from Japan, Girlztown did their first recording – a cover of "It Must Have Been Love". The single was produced by Sly and Robbie. The girls were more than holding their own.

Promotional poster for Girlztown on Japansplash, 1997. (Copeland Forbes Archives)

However, a band is a most unstable entity and breakups seem almost inevitable. Girlztown was no exception. Despite reassurances from the members that their love of the music would keep them together there were stronger forces at play including migration, marriage and maternity. I will always have a high regard for the Girlztown aggregation which included: Samantha Waite (bass); Charmaine Hayles (drums) Andrea Stennett (keyboard), Shawnett Haywood(guitar), Deneka Tracy (saxophone), Susan Stephenson (trumpet), Nadine Stewart (trombone), and Angeline Gayle (trumpet). Michelle Smith and Marsha Scott were the vocalists with the band. It is important that I also recognize the part time members of the band: Charmaine Bowman, Antoinette, 'Roots Dawtah' Hall, Joy Fairclough, Sharon Dunn and, yes, a man had to find his way in there somehow. His name was Edward 'Chinney' Campbell.

Live Wyya

Live Wyya was a six-member musical aggregation hailing from the tourist resort of Ocho Rios. The lead singer Errol Bonnick approached me with a request to manage the band. After several meetings, I finally agreed to work with them. They entered 'The Battle of the Bands' and won the local leg of the competition. They were selected to represent Jamaica at the finals in London which was a star-studded event. Bono of U2 was one of the judges. Live Wyya finished among the top five bands in the contest.

Live Wyya would go on to back Gregory Isaacs on his 2006 world tour which started in Hawaii. The band was definitely in demand and caught the attention of then incarcerated artiste, Jah Cure who requested that Live Wyya be his backing band upon his release. After Gregory's passing the band decided that it did not wish to continue backing artistes but, instead, wanted to record its own music and become a self-contained unit. I believe that this decision might have been premature.

Live Wyya, 2004. (Copeland Forbes Archives)

Live Wyya would go the way of all bands. It began disintegrating. Lead singer Errol Bonnick migrated to the United States. He was replaced by American-born Elijah Dixon who chose to emigrate from his native land. After a while Dixon returned to the United States to live. Delroy "Katt" Burton took his place but was later replaced by Jerome "Jay Wyya" Smikle. Keyboardist Triston Richards took a job on a cruise liner and jumped ship. Chad Munroe filled Richard's spot. Bassist, Carl Edwards, drummer Orlando Bolt and guitarist Michael "Colgate" Downer are the three original members who have remained with the group. Keyboardist Kirk Gayle who was a part of the group under my management has left the band and has been replaced by Kadeem Martin, while guitarist Shadrick Downer (son of Michael "Colgate") also joined the present lineup.

"Maxi agreed that he would refund Keithy his deposit for his no show. He did not, however, give any indication, as to how he would make amends for sleeping with Keithy's woman."

▸ Pg 192. Chapter 13

CHAPTER 21
BACK TO THE BEGINNING: JONES TOWN VIOLATION

In 1994, I had the pleasure of being on the road with some members of the Shocking Vibes crew on the annual *Reggae Japansplash* tour. The touring party was divided into two groups. One went south and the other headed north. Both groups came together for the last two shows in Osaka and Tokyo

The Shocking Vibes acts included: Tanto Metro, Little Kirk, Snagga Puss and Beenie Man. I developed a great relationship with all four acts. Shocking Vibes originated in Jones Town, where I was born.

In December of the same year, I received a call from the management of Shocking Vibes inviting me to be one of the guest speakers at the press launch of their annual *Ghetto Splash* concert. They thought it was fitting for me to speak at the launch given the fact that I was born in Jones Town where the event would be held. I accepted the invitation. I was very happy for the opportunity to revisit my birthplace and to be associated with Ghetto Splash which saw top Jamaican artistes performing free of charge as a gift to the community.

I was scheduled to leave Jamaica the day after the concert for a series of shows in the UK with Frankie Paul and Cutty Ranks. On the day of the concert, I was very busy running all over the city finalizing all the arrangements pertaining to the UK tour. I got home very late and was exhausted. I decided not to attend the concert and to spend most of the time packing my bags and getting some well-deserved rest ahead of my long flight.

At about 12:40 am, on the morning of my departure, I received a call on my cell phone from a member of the Shocking Vibes crew. The concert was still going on. He asked my whereabouts. I told him that I had been out all day running all over the city. I explained to him that I was exhausted so I would not be able to attend the concert and that I needed to get some rest before my long flight later that day.

He was very disappointed to hear that I would not turn up for the concert which was by then in full swing. He begged me to come even for a cameo or as he put it "to show yuh face". He pointed out that quite a few of my friends, whom I hadn't seen since our adolescence, were waiting to greet me. He was quite persuasive. I left my house about 1:00 am and arrived at a spot at the corner of Benbow and Baker Streets, just a few yards down from the Admiral Town Police Station where a parking space had been reserved for me.

Thousands jammed the access ways to the stage. I was taken through many back alleys and short cuts to get near the open lot at the top of Livingstone Street where the stage was located. I ended up at the home of one of my former Boy

Shocking Vibes artist Beenie Man, one of the fixtures of Ghetto Splash, and Copeland Forbes. (Copeland Forbes Archives)

Scouts colleagues, Teddy Phipps. He was so happy to see me after so many years. Teddy introduced me to the rest of his family including his father who had moved out of the area and was living in Portmore. The concert, which began around 10:00 pm, went on until sometime after 4:00 am. I had totally forgotten that I had originally intended to spend only 10-15 minutes at the concert and that I had not finished packing for my trip. Teddy asked me to give his dad a ride home even though the elder Phipps lived miles away from Mona where I resided. I, however, agreed to take Father Phipps to his home.

Four members of the Phipps family (including Tyrone and his dad) accompanied me to my car. No sooner had I reached my vehicle when I heard a voice saying "don't move a bumbo claat, dis is a robbery. Hands in di air." Tyrone Phipps shouted, "Mine weh unnu a do, a my ole man dat", pointing to his dad. Everyone who had been accompanying me (including Father Phipps) took off faster than Usain Bolt.

I was left alone to face the thugs with their high-powered weapons pointing at me. They went through my pockets. They took everything they found on my person including my Motorola Dyna Tac cell phone. They searched my car and removed anything of value they could find. I had hidden US$300 in my socks before I left my house. They asked me if I had any more money. I denied having any more. I worried about what would happen if they found the hidden dollars in my socks. After giving me another search, they ran down a dark alley.

I was shaking like a leaf, frantically looking for my car keys and not realizing that the gun-toting thugs had taken them too. Suddenly, one of the gunmen appeared from the darkness of Benbow Street wanting to know why I had not yet left the area and whether I was waiting for the cops to arrive. I told him that someone in his group had taken my car keys. He shouted into the darkness, "Who have di man car keys? Bring it come". A teenager, with what looked like a high-powered weapon, emerged from the darkness, and handed me my car keys. I was shaking badly. I attempted to open my car door but kept missing the keyhole. After what seemed like an eternity, I was able to open my car and jump into the driver's seat. I reversed all the way to the police station where I saw three policemen looking over the wall. The gate to the station was chained and padlocked.

I related my ordeal to the lawmen. They didn't move an inch. I was surprised when one of the lawmen shouted to me, "Pardie weh yu a do dung deh, yu no si seh we naah gu dung deh". I told him that I grew up in the area and had been invited to be a special guest at the concert. He said "Yu mussi mad, a pure gunman deh dung deh so". The cops stayed behind the wall while I stood beside my car on the road, talking to them. A young man came up to me and advised that I leave the area, warning that the gunmen could return and open fire on us. I jumped into my car and started to make my exit. Three vehicles loaded with lawmen suddenly appeared on the scene. One of cops in the vehicle shouted my name.

When he came out of his vehicle, I realized that it was someone I knew very well. He was attached to the Cross Roads Police Station. I recounted my story to him. He went on his radio and called for backup which arrived quickly. They took all my details and went in search of the gunmen. I drove to the intersection of Torrington Bridge and Slipe Pen Road. I was shocked to see members of the Phipps family. I asked why they had abandoned me. I got no answer.

I left the scene and went home with the intention of returning to the station. After spending about an hour at home I returned to the Admiral Town Police Station. It was teeming with people in a fiery mood. The lawmen had rounded up some of their relatives. The cops asked me to identify anyone who resembled the robbers. It was a very hard task as the robbery took place in the dark. The lawmen began beating some of the men suspected of the robbery with batons and sticks. This angered the crowd. The relatives of the suspects started threatening me. I decided to make my escape through the back door. I scaled a wall. My car was parked a little distance from the police station. I ran up the road, jumped into my car and headed home. I flew to Britain later that day.

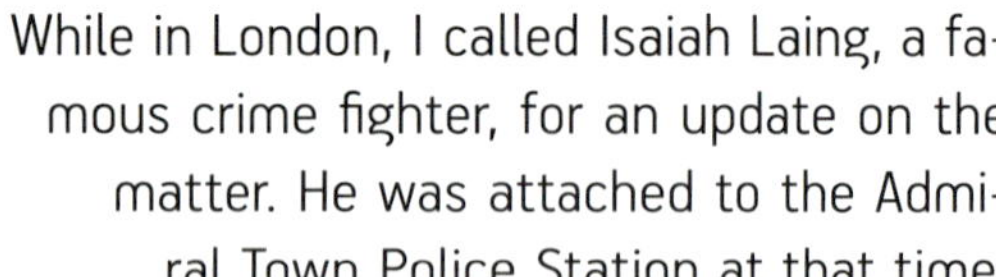

While in London, I called Isaiah Laing, a famous crime fighter, for an update on the matter. He was attached to the Admiral Town Police Station at that time. Laing told me they had received tips on who the culprits were. He took my contact information and said he would keep me informed. A year later there was a shoot-out in the Waltham Park area

One of the many posters advertising **Reggae Japansplash,** 1994. (Copeland Forbes Archives)

Tony Rebel and Garnett Silk were regular performers on the annual Ghetto Splash concert in Craig Town, Kingston. (G.Smith/P.Barrett /Flames Records).

between gunmen and lawmen. Several gunmen were killed. It was reported that the mastermind of my ordeal was killed in that shootout. I have not been back to Jones Town since that ordeal of December 1994, and I am not sure that I will ever return.

“I could not help thinking that Freddie could have gone to Zion in an effort to protect his Psion.”

▸ Pg 194. Chapter 13

CHAPTER 22
REFLECTIONS

I now spend most of my days between Florida and Jamaica relaxing and reminiscing with my wife Juanita, except when I am called upon to appear on the lecture circuit or am required to give my advice on some planned tour. While I enjoy the fact that I am no longer forced to be away from home for long stretches, I have no regrets about the time I spent on the road. I would not have traded the world for the privilege I have had of being paid to do what I love. Yes, there were hairy moments when I thought my life might have been on the line but there were so many times of incredible joy.

Favourite Spots

I have been asked (given my extensive travels) which spots on our planet has left the most lasting impression on me. Uganda and Thailand would be at the top of my list.

I visited Uganda for the first and only time in my career. I was accompanying Chaka Demus and Pliers who were then regular fixtures on the international record charts especially in the United Kingdom. It was also the first trip for the dynamic duo to the landlocked East African nation.

We received a royal reception in Kampala, the Ugandan capital. I had heard about the Ugandan leader, Idi Amin Dada, who was represented in the western media as a despicable despot who ruled his country with an iron fist. I saw Uganda as a peaceful African nation whose citizens loved reggae and adored Chaka Demus and Pliers.

We were booked to stay at the Nile Hotel in Kampala where Chaka Demus and Pliers gave their first performance in Uganda for government officials and dignitaries. Sisters of Blackness, who provided backing support for the duo, opened the show. They gave an excellent performance. Spanner Banner (younger brother of Pliers) followed and thrilled the audience prompting fears that he might upstage the headline act. His single "Michelle" had been a huge hit in Uganda. It was pandemonium however when the featured act Chaka Demus and Pliers hit the stage. They dug

"Sisters of Blackness" providing harmonies for Chaka Demus and Pliers, Uganda, 1996. (Winston "T'Shaka" Mayanja)

Dancehall Queen "Carlene" was a big hit in Uganda, through her videos shown in night clubs. (Copeland Forbes Archives)

Dancehall Queen Carlene and her dancers appeared in the "Murder She Wrote" video. (Copeland Forbes Archives)

into their huge catalogue of hits which included "Tease Me" and "Murder She Wrote". Their performance was met with thunderous applause.

Hit makers Chaka Demus and Pliers. (Chaka and Pliers Photos)

Their next performance was for the public and was held in the National Stadium which was packed with screaming fans who were excited to witness the Jamaican hit-making duo on Ugandan soil. Chaka Demus and Pliers reeled off hit after hit and the appreciative audience lapped up every note of the memorable performance. The final show was in Entebbe which was the scene of a daring Israeli mission to free passengers on a hijacked flight which had been diverted to the African nation. The hijackers were killed in a dramatic firefight and the hostages were freed. The amazing rescue effort became the stuff of legend inspiring several films including *Victory at Entebbe* and *Operation Entebbe*.

The fans at Entebbe were held as willing hostages to the mesmerizing performance of Chaka Demus and Pliers. The duo had their own victory at Entebbe and those fortunate to witness that show will long remember that day.

My journey to Thailand was at the invitation of my friend Steve Creighton an enterprising businessman who, with his associate Larry Riggs, had left what was a thriving business (the Reggae Cafe) in Florida and had gone to the land formerly known as Siam to set up shop.

I arrived in Bangkok – the Thai capital – after a six-and-a-half-hour flight from Nagoya, Japan where I had just finished a major tour with Marcia Griffiths, Bushman, Sanchez, Chuck Fender, the Live Wyya Band and the Immortal Stone Love among others.

I spent most of my time in Thailand on the island of Koh Samui where Steve had his Bikini Beach Restaurant.A grand welcome party was held in my honour. The place was bedecked in the Jamaican and Rasta colours and the guests were thrilled to know that they were in the company of a man from the land of Bob Marley.

Steve introduced me to a Mr Khun Lersak owner of the Reggae Pub who didn't know a word of English but was deeply immersed in Jamaican culture. The Reggae Pub could accommodate 4,000 patrons for an event. The venue hosted the famed Bob Marley Day celebrations which was held annually in February. I had a lively conversation with Mr Lersak who also owned several outlets where he sold reggae merchandise and souvenirs depicting Rastafarian and Jamaican themes. I struck a deal with Mr LerSak to bring Jamaican selectors to Thailand.

Sasha, Igor and Forbes en route to the Full Moon Party, Haad Rin Beach. (Copeland Forbes Archives)

Copeland Forbes and Russian businessman Nikolai Leukin discuss plans for Jamaican acts to perform in Moscow, Russia. (Copeland Forbes Archives)

During my visit I was able to savour some of the amazing culinary offerings of Thailand while enjoying some of the most breath taking vistas I had ever beheld. We sailed out to the Gulf of Thailand near Viet Nam. I visited the famed locales of Phuket and Chang Mai. I had the great fortune to attend a huge party on the remote island of Koh Pah Ngan where a full moon party was taking place on a beach called Haad Rin. There were some 20,000 patrons in attendance dancing to the music of 90 selectors (spaced across the island) playing almost every form of music imaginable. The patrons used various forms of seagoing vessels – ranging from sturdy canoes to luxury yachts – to reach Haad Rin. It was a truly all-inclusive party. No one was excluded.

Steve also introduced me to Nikolai Leukin, a Russian businessman who invited me to spend some time at his beautiful resort called Naissance where I met Sasha, a fabulous Russian model, who helped to make my ten-day stay in Thailand a most memorable experience.

Igor, Nikolai, Copeland and Steve at the section of the Bikini Restaurant named in honour of Forbes. (Copeland Forbes Archives)

Steve Creighton and Copeland Forbes in Koh Samui Thailand, 2007. (Copeland Forbes Archives)

Entrance to the famous 4,000 capacity Reggae Pub night club. (Copeland Forbes Archives)

Copeland Forbes with Khun Lersak operator of the Reggae Pub night club in Koh Samui Thailand. (Copeland Forbes Archives)

ABI-Reggae Festival and Cultural Conference

I appreciated the opportunity I had in April of 2015 to be a part of the huge delegation of Jamaican entertainers that went to Abidjan on the Ivory Coast, West Africa, for the inaugural launch of the *Abi-Reggae Festival and Conference*. Olivia "Babsy" Grange, now Minister of Culture, Entertainment, Gender and Sports, led the delegation of entertainers and VIPs including: Third World , Morgan Heritage, Marcia Griffiths, Kymani Marley, Judy Mowatt, Mutabaruka, along with the magnificent 809 band. I was honoured and privileged to be the tour manager and assistant to Ms Grange. The delegation included Ms Grange's trusted adviser, Lenny Salmon, Dr Jahlani Niaah from University of the West Indies and Dr Julius Garvey, son of Jamaica's National Hero Marcus Garvey. A number of African reggae artistes and bands led by the Ivorian reggae star, Alpha Blondy, took part in the four-day celebrations.

The festival was preceded by a fantastic music seminar and conference attended by intellectuals, musicians, musicologists, historians and observers from several African countries, who discussed reggae music and its evolution across the world, especially in the African nations. The festival was conceptualized by Ms.Grange and the Abidjan Government Minister Moussa Dossa when he had visited Jamaica a few months earlier.

One of the highlights of the trip for me was the closing ceremony when the band on the stand struck up the Burning Spear classic "Slavery Days" (Do you remember the days of slavery). Ms Grange looked at me and smiled. It was her cue for us to make our way to the dancefloor. She and I opened the floor and a rousing reggae dance party followed. All the VIPs, government ministers and the celebrities in attendance broke loose and threw protocol under the bus. Winford Williams and the OnStage crew travelled with the Jamaican delegation and covered the inauguration from start to finish.

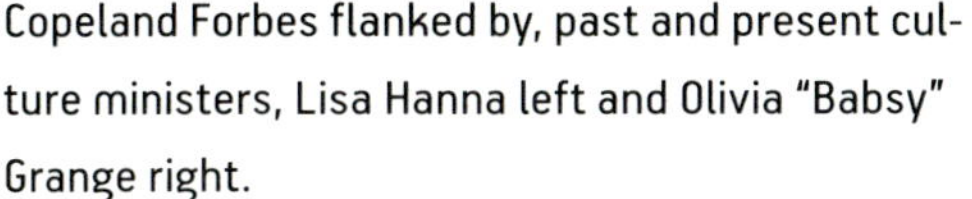

Copeland Forbes flanked by, past and present culture ministers, Lisa Hanna left and Olivia "Babsy" Grange right.

Full Moon Party in full swing at Haad Rin Beach. (Copeland Forbes Archives)

Olivia "Babsy" Grange and Copeland Forbes opened the dance floor at the Abi-Reggae Music Festival and Conference in Abidjan Ivory Coast, Africa. (Copeland Forbes Archives)

Dr Julius Garvey (son of Marcus Garvey) joined Forbes and Grange on the dance floor in Abidjan Ivory Coast, Africa. (Copeland Forbes Archives)

A Word on John Holt

John Holt was one of the legends with whom I had the privilege of working. His rich baritone was a source of endless joy to the lovers of music who flocked to see him perform. His concerts, which sometimes saw him being accompanied by sides of renowned philharmonic orchestras, were treats which fans travelled miles to savour.

John came to prominence as the lead singer of the vocal group known as the Paragons which had the legendary Bob Andy as one of its earlier members.

John scored big as a songwriter when Blondie covered 'The Tide Is High' which became a major international hit. However, he did not sufficiently capitalize on his incredible vocal prowess.

John was shy. He was afraid of flying and as a result did not travel as extensively as he should have. John was not one who could abide by the weekly payment schedule which was a feature of tours. He preferred to be paid after each show and as a result did mostly one-off gigs.

John's "Wear You to The Ball", which he recorded for producer Duke Reid featuring a version with the inimitable U Roy, is undoubtedly one of the great songs in the

Full Moon Party in Koh PahNgan, Thailand, 2007. (Copeland Forbes Archives)

history of Jamaican music. He was able to appeal to a younger generation of music lovers as he created a number of hits at the famed Channel One Studios with the legendary Sly Dunbar and the Revolutionaries during the dancehall era. Among the hits to emerge from his Channel One experience was "Police in Helicopter".

John was a gentle soul and a man of few words.

Lessons, Lessons, Lessons

While I am grateful for what I have managed to accomplish in the business, there are a number of things I would have changed were I to have been given another chance. There are so many things I would not have done with the benefit of what I know now.

Artistes should be careful of the type of people they attract on the road. Dangerous entanglements can result from casual liaisons. Certain types of companionship come freely but can be hazardous to one's health and wealth. Artistes should understand that not everyone who is a fan is a friend. Entertainers should be wary that many who hang around them only see them as meal tickets.

Entertainers should realise that they are especially privileged to have fans willing to pay to see them perform. They should never take this for granted. Fans pay to be entertained they want to see the best of the artiste. They want value for their money. Therefore, artistes should rehearse properly to ensure that their performances are of the highest possible standard.

Most importantly, artistes should always try to surround themselves with people who are willing and able to tell them the truth.

I urge the emerging artistes to extract the lessons from my experience and to avoid the errors chronicled in this book. It is important for artistes to realise that not all of them will be like Toots and Jimmy Cliff who have been able to perform in their seventies. The vast majority of artistes will have a productive life which will span a few years, if they are lucky. Consequently, artistes need to manage their resources prudently. They should always remember that, unlike civil servants and others who are regularly employed, they do not normally have the benefits of healthcare and pension and must put these provisions in place themselves. They should try to ensure that their affairs will be in good order after they are gone. It is sad to see the wrangling in the wake of the transition of our prominent artistes who did not leave their houses in order.

Peter Tosh Symposium at the UWI in 2016. The children and grandchildren of Peter Tosh surround Copeland Forbes. (Copeland Forbes Archives)

The Tosh Estate – Case in Point

Peter Tosh had a visceral reaction to the making of a will. When I raised the matter of his having one, he snapped, "Thy will be done". Peter would die intestate which would create enormous problems for his estate. He and Marlene jointly owned the house in which he was killed. The ownership of that property passed legally to Marlene. Peter's children and his mother would also be left in a lurch on the passing of the man who boldly proclaimed that "Rasta nuh go a no one burial".

It was clear that the protracted legal wrangling which came in the wake of Bob Marley's passing had very little impact on Peter's views on making the necessary preparations to dispose of his assets in the event of his death.

Attorneys Miguel Lorne and Glen Cruickshank, Alvera Coke (Peter's mother) along with the Workers' Bank, were appointed administrators of the Tosh Estate. A woman (from New York) purporting to be Peter's cousin claimed that Tosh had given her the authority to conduct business on behalf of his estate in event of his death or incapacitation.

Armed with her "power of attorney", the lady was able to conduct business on behalf of Peter's estate, including making licensing deals for Intel Diplo which controlled the artiste's catalogue. She was acting without the approval or knowledge of the administrators in Jamaica. Soon many of Peter's assets, including his musical instruments, disappeared. Many documents relating to his properties simply vanished.

Sometime in 1990, four members of Peter's family visited me. The delegation consisted of Peter's three sons Steve, Andrew and Dave. Adrian, who was Andrew's

Copeland Forbes with children of Tosh (L-R) Steve, Dave, Niambe, Jawara and Andrew) at King's House where the artiste was conferred posthumously with the Order of Merit in 2012. (Copeland Forbes Archives).

half-brother and Bunny Wailer's nephew, also attended the meeting. They had just met with attorney Miguel Lorne. They claimed that (apart from their grandmother) they were not familiar with anyone who had been appointed as administrator of their father's estate. They were seeking my assistance in unravelling the mysteries of their father's business arrangements and in establishing the Peter Tosh Foundation.

The family members also wanted to find out about a matter involving withholding taxes on money remitted from Island Records to the Tosh estate. The taxes would have been waived were Peter's heirs able to prove that he had operated a legally registered entity through which he conducted his business in the United States. I informed them of Intel Diplo.

I asked Peter's children about their seven other siblings. They told me that some of the other children were having a hard time, not being able to access funds from their father's estate.

We went down to see Miguel Lorne at his office In Downtown Kingston. We had an interesting meeting. Peter's children asked

Alvera Coke, mother of Peter Tosh, and Copeland Forbes in Belmont, Westmoreland, Jamaica, 2010. (Copeland Forbes Archives)

me to assist in securing and recovering funds belonging to the estate. I told them that I would have to be properly engaged for the task which would require a signed agreement.

I informed my attorney, Lloyd Stanbury, who placed a call to Lorne. Stanbury proposed that I should be paid a 20 per cent commission on any funds I recovered on behalf of the estate. I later learned that Lorne had informed Peter's children that I was asking for too much money. This was a shock to both me and Stanbury.

Peter's children asked me to accompany them to Dynamic Sounds which was supposedly responsible for distributing their late father's catalogue. We met with Eddie, Byron Lee's son. The children requested to see the document which had given Dynamic Sounds the right to distribute the Tosh musical catalogue. Eddie summoned Delroy Morrison who had negotiated on behalf of Dynamic Sounds with Miguel Lorne. Morrison was not able to provide evidence that the person who had negotiated with him was authorized to do so.

Morrison told Lee that he could not recall seeing any instrument authorizing Lorne to conduct such a deal on behalf of the estate. Lee placed a call to Lorne who told him that the Administrator General had not yet granted him the authorization which he was still awaiting. Lorne told Lee that he had entered into the deal because Peter's mother, Alvera Coke, was badly in need of funds. Lee was livid. The deal which encompassed a large portion of Peter's catalogue was below the value of what Tosh would normally have negotiated for a single during his lifetime. His children were incensed and threatened to take the matter to the media. Byron asked them to refrain from doing so. Eighteen months after signing the deal with Dynamic, Lorne was officially named an administrator giving him authority to act on behalf of the estate. Lorne would later be imprisoned for a charge totally unrelated to the Tosh Estate. He was removed as an administrator.

Last Words

I cannot stress the importance of sound management. This can be the difference between stardom and oblivion. Artistes should choose people they trust and who have the requisite knowledge to manage their affairs. Artistes should be careful of the advice they take from their close friends and associates unless these people have a sound knowledge of the business.

I implore artistes to take care of themselves physically, mentally and spiritually. The business takes an enormous toll on the body, mind and soul. Artistes should eat right, exercise, read, meditate, and engage in wholesome pursuits. Proper division of labour is important. Artistes should try to learn as much about the business as they can but should concentrate on the creative and performative aspects of their careers and allow others to deal with administrative issues.